Last Voyage to Wewak

Last Voyage to Wewak

A tale of the sea: West Africa to the South Pacific

Simon J Hall

Whittles Publishing

Published by
Whittles Publishing Ltd.,
Dunbeath,
Caithness, KW6 6EG,
Scotland, UK
www.whittlespublishing.com

© 2017 Simon J. Hall
ISBN 978-184995-253-8

All rights reserved.
The right of Simon J. Hall
to be identified as the author of this work
has been asserted by him in accordance with
the Copyright, Design and Patents Act 1988.
No part of this publication may be reproduced,
stored in a retrieval system, or transmitted,
in any form or by any means, electronic,
mechanical, recording or otherwise
without prior permission of the publisher.

Printed and bound by CPI Group (UK) Ltd, Croydon, CR0 4YY

Contents

Acknowledgements and thanks

The first two books of this trilogy, *Under a Yellow Sky* and *Chasing Conrad*, put a heavy drain into my swamp of memories and I felt this book might be trying to suck up information that could no longer be found. As I sketched out the framework and began to search and research the content I started to fear that it might all be a step too far. I began to devour old letters and copy logs in a way that was almost maniacal.

Curiously, though, as things progressed, it became much easier to write. It flowed, rather than having to be continuously beaten into shape. I wondered why this was. Certainly not a flowering of my literary talents; my writing remains as ragged and disjointed as ever; I leap from topic to topic like a mad man with his arse on fire. I put the flow down to … well, first, I was in my mid to late twenties when the events of this book take place, which is closer in time than my first book, which started when I was a sixteen-year-old. Second, I am writing as a mature adult, which is easier than having to try and graft the thinking of a teenager onto the pages. Third, I had a wealth of close reference material, which I need to acknowledge. Well deserved it is too. The key players:

My wife Annie: for keeping all the letters I ever wrote to you. Remember how horrified you were when I came home from the sea for our wedding and told you that I had thrown yours away. I was a shallow man in those days, still mining for depth; I am ashamed and I apologise.

My children: all of you. Thank you for giving me the perspective in life today, which I need to write of these days past.

My mother: your own memories are fading now as I write this book and now you scrabble to remember who I am. Thank you too for also keeping all my letters. I could have been a better son to you and I wish I had been. I hope your world is becoming more peaceful.

My brothers, Peter and Anthony: you are probably as bad as me in the art of gazing backward. We look too late and too little, and we forget that all we are comes from what we did. You give me focus, though, because of our shared lives, and this allows recollections to seep through, which would otherwise be forgotten.

My seagoing friends: who I see too seldom and when we meet it's never too soon or for too long. Our conversations disinter buried memories.

And you, my father: you died so long ago that I cannot remember your voice or your laugh, just your presence. You remain a force in my life and I thank you for the parts of you that you gave to me, and for which I am a better person. I wish you hadn't died so young.

And I could not have written this book without: the Canadian archives that keep ship's logs; the *Calcutta Gazette* 1806 to 1815, for a lesson of how to write as a stranger in a strange land; Tim Berners-Lee, who has made research so much easier; Herbert Spencer for his unequalled take on life; all my letters which people kept; Whittles Publishers; the Kodak 110 Instamatic camera; good beer; late nights; bad television that drove me to my desk; the patience of others.

Last, I have not mentioned the name of the shipping company that graces these pages, even though many people will recognise it instantly. This was a decent and honourable company, one of the few old British established shipping lines still trading today. It will be clear from my writing that I was unhappy with the changes that overtook the shipping world, but no criticism is made or inferred of the company itself, which coped well and treated us well; I wish them well.

Glossary of Nautical Terms for Landlubbers

AB	Able seaman
Abaft	Behind
Abeam	At right-angle to the fore and aft length of the ship
Aft	Back area of the ship, or in that direction (c/f For'ard)
Ballast	Weight put into a ship, usually water in tanks, to make her stable
Bilges	The bottom-most part of a ship, where water, usually unspeakably foul, can accumulate
Bits	The steel bollards on the poop deck and fo'c'sle head
Blues	Full jacket and tie uniform (black, actually)
Bollards	Steel posts on the dockside for securing ships' ropes
Bosun	The chief petty officer in charge of the deck crew
Bonded stores	Stores placed under seal in port; mainly cigarettes and alcohol
Bow	The front of the ship (c/f Stern)
Box	Cargo container
Bridge	The command centre and navigational centre of the ship
Bridge wings	Extensions of the bridge that hang over the sea
Bulkhead	Wall
Bulwark	Solid rail on the side of the ship above deck level
Bumboat	A small boat that ferries supplies and people to ships at anchor
Bunkers	Fuel oil for ships
Cabin	Room
Casab	Chinese petty officer; the deck storekeeper
Chartroom	Aft end of the bridge
Chief	Chief engineer officer
Chief mate	Chief officer
Choff	Chief officer
Clutter	Waves picked up by radar close to the ship
Daybed	A sofa in a cabin, which doubles as a bunk if called for
Deadweight	The way tankers are measured; it indicates everything a ship can carry, in tons
Decca navigation	System based on radio waves, used from 1940s to 1990s
Deck	Floor, as well as a particular level on a ship; e.g. the boat deck
Deck boy	Uncertificated deckhand under age 18
Deckhead	Ceiling
Derricks	Long spars used as lifting devices
DF	Direction finder; positioning device using long wave radio
Dogs	Securing lugs on hatches and watertight doors
Dodger	Curved steel plate on the bridge wing that deflects the wind
DP	Dynamic Positioning: computer engine control to retain position
Draft	The depth of the ship under the surface of the water
DR	Dead reckoning: an estimate of the ship's position.
Dunnage	Wooden planking to protect cargo from steel decks and bulkheads
ETA	Estimated time of arrival
Fathom	Six feet

Foc'sle head	The raised deck at the front of the ship
Fourth	Fourth engineer officer
Fourth mate	Fourth officer
For'ard	Forward; front of the ship, or in that direction (c/f Aft)
Gang	Team of men unloading or loading the ship's cargo
Gross tonnage	The way ships are measured, except tankers (see Deadweight)
Gunwales	The top edge of a boat
Half and halfs	Blues trousers with a tropical shirt, no jacket
Hook	Anchor
Knot	One nautical mile per hour (about 10 per cent faster than a mile per hour)
Landfall	The first sight of land (or a lighthouse) after a period at sea
Lateen	A triangular sail, as on an Arab dhow
Leci	Electrical engineer officer
LEFO	Land's End for orders
Lighter	Cargo barge
LORAN	Long range aid to navigation; similar system to Decca
Marks	The maximum load lines painted on the side of a ship
Mate	Chief officer
MacGregor hatches	Folding steel hatch covers, pulled open by winches
Monkey island	Deck above the navigating bridge
Monkey ladder	Skinny portable ladder made of hemp rope with round pegs for steps
Old Man	Captain or master
Pilot	Someone employed by the port authority to guide ships in
Point	11.25 degrees, relating to a compass bearing
Poop deck	Raised deck at the aft end of a ship
Port	Left side of the ship
Q Flag	Flown when a ship is requesting inward port clearance.
Quartermaster	Ship's helmsman
RIB	Rigid inflatable boat
Ro-ros	Roll on roll off ships; the cargo is driven in and out
Roads	Anchorage area near a port
Screw	Ship's propeller
SD14	A simple and standard design of general cargo ship
Second	Second engineer officer
Second mate	Second officer
Sparks	Radio officer
Starboard	Right side of the ship
Stays	Wire ropes that brace the masts
Stern	Back end of the ship (c/f Bow)
Stevedore	Someone who loads and unloads ships in port
Supercargo	Someone hired by the shippers to supervise cargo work in port
Taffrail	Polished wooden rail on the upper accommodation decks
Taipan company	Leading Hong Kong trading company
Talley man	Someone who counts the cargo in and out
TEU	Twenty-foot-equivalent unit – a standard-sized transport container
Third	Third engineer officer
Third mate	Third officer
Thunder box	A wooden cage containing a toilet which overhangs the water
Tween decks	Cargo storage decks under the main deck
Weigh anchor	Pull up the anchor
Wheelhouse	Forward part of the bridge
Whites	Tropical uniform: white shirts and shorts

Preliminary

By the time I was twenty-six, I had risen to the vertiginous heights of second officer in the British Merchant Navy, serving on general cargo ships that plied their trade in the Far East and South Pacific. I knew no other life, having gone to sea as an officer cadet when I was sixteen years old, wide-eyed and naïve, an innocent tossed into the maelstrom. Once I had passed the early tests, I found my feet and organised my life to travel to obscure parts of the globe, to see strange sights and to mix with people who didn't fit the common mould.

The things that were important to the majority were strange and unfathomable to me: a partner to share my life, career progression, the possessions we collect, the achievements that men measure their lives by and which signpost their passage on earth, they were all alien concepts. I would learn such wisdom in time. I would learn the importance of family, of striving for a decent home, I would learn of job security and inflation, I would learn to eat a correct diet, drink with decorum and conduct my conversations with manners and correctness so as not to offend. But at that time, when I was twenty-six, mine was the camaraderie, the adventure, the march around the edge of the abyss, the quest. I owned very little, but I was convinced I had a greater fortune.

Over the next four years my life changed. The world of ships and shipping and the life of the men who sailed in them all changed around me and I had little choice but to follow the track. My travels during this period took me back to the East, my spiritual home. I encountered many of the same characters I had grown to know since I had gone to sea, all of us aware of the dying of the light and fighting against it as best we could, while being carried along by the inexorable river of change.

I finally succumbed to late onset maturity, which made me see the world not as my playground but as a place in which we seek to improve and strive to leave our mark. I began to yearn to make myself a better person and abandon the self-serving creature I had become.

The tales that follow chart the flow. The names are altered, the events are deliberately mixed and the characters are shuffled between different ships, but this remains a true account, or as true as such an account can reasonably be. The edges are a bit blurred with time, and with the best effort in the world it's probably impossible to avoid giving offence to someone in some way when our paths may have crossed. I can only apologise to you, reader, if you are one of them, but please don't take it to heart; it's not intended.

1

The Dimming of the Sun

I was lying on a hot Pacific Island under the hot Pacific sun one afternoon, having basted myself with Coppertone suntan oil to aim for a bronzed look, watching the sea roll in, watching the girls stroll by. I was twenty-six years old, and I thought: Where has it gone? Where did all my young adult life go?

At school I had been a moderately hopeless student, lazy, disobedient, disinterested and frequently beaten for infringements. When I left to go out into the world I was awarded the poor examination grades I deserved. People always told me that when I looked back I would realise my schooldays were the best time of my life; they told me everyone's schooldays were the best times of their lives. But when I looked back, I thought: Not mine. I had disliked school and school had disliked me. I found it stifling, riven with procedures that seemed pointless, driven to expectations that held no grace or appeal, I felt closeted with nitwits. I rebelled. I was caned to the point of legality and finally expelled in disgrace for continuing bad behaviour: fighting, smoking, absconding, playing nasty pranks, failing to take my work seriously and cheeking my betters. I went to seven schools altogether, as our family moved around the country and around the world, following my father's job.

My father was a Royal Air Force officer, a pilot, a big man with a decent war pedigree and a proper moustache. After my expulsion, from the sixth school, I only had a few months to go before I took my O-levels. My parents slotted me into the seventh, where I scraped the requisite passes to allow me to apply to go to sea as a deck officer cadet. I left home at sixteen, still just a boy in shape and mind.

My father gave me a gruff talk in a deep voice on the day he drove me to the airport to fly out and join my first ship. He told me a tale about when he had been stationed near Alexandria as a bomber pilot during the war. It was late at night and he was sharing a taxi with an army lieutenant who suddenly put his hand on my father's leg. My father said to the lieutenant, sternly and loudly: "None of that!" and the lieutenant took his hand away and left him alone.

This was my father's way of warning me about the dangers of the world, illustrating true wickedness as he saw it. He didn't warn me about all the dangers and evil that I went on to encounter: a bottle whacked into my face, slashed with a knife, shot at, attacked for no reason, head-butted, robbed, beaten, menaced. He didn't warn me about the brutality of the ship's crews, about being shot at in Mindanao, shelled in Vietnam, lost and abandoned in the Philippines, chased, attacked, bullied, about being in a storm so fierce the ship could have foundered in a blink, about being ground down with work that could break a strong man and sometimes did. What was important to my father was that I didn't succumb to an advance by a homosexual, because therein lies true evil. My mother didn't give me any last-minute lectures. I heard her weeping in the kitchen the night before I left.

A life as a cadet on a British merchant ship is a speedy finishing school and an accelerated growing up, a stripping away of any last vestige of childhood and innocence. A cadetship was three and a half years. Once I had signed on the line; that was it. There was no right to argue, nobody to complain to, nowhere to hide, no forum to protest, no place to sulk, no home to run to, nowhere to go. There was just the life. From the time I stepped on board the crunching deck of a rusting tanker in Hamburg to the day I walked down the gangway in Thameshaven three and a half years later, I was made to grow up very quickly.

At sea they worked me as a beast, and I was expected to learn as I worked, from the work that I did. I painted steel decks and bulkheads, chipped rust, sanded wooden decks, cleaned out tanks, washed off accumulated filth, spliced ropes. I greased dogs and rollers and pins. I oiled wires. I worked and worked and worked. I alternated between sea and nautical college, sea and nautical college.

The nautical college was in Plymouth, and there they taught me things in such a tight regimen there was no time not to learn. When I first started, the host of subjects was so obscure and alien to me I sometimes didn't even understand the meaning of the subject word, let alone anything about the content. I was force fed schooling, I was made to absorb and translate and understand information under pain of punishment. Mathematics and meteorology, naval architecture and navigation, maritime business and law, hydrostatics, mechanics, engineering, electronics; they were all bruted into me.

I was taught to march, to sail, to survive in open water, to survive in open country, to tie complicated knots, to staunch wounds and carry out rudimentary surgery. I had to clean my quarters, wash my clothes, iron my uniform, stand inspection after inspection after inspection.

I was in a class of fourteen others, all like me very young and hopelessly naïve and trying to pretend otherwise. We made friendships too strong to be broken on the wheel of life, and I can still see those faces all these decades later as if it were yesterday.

During all my cadetship I learned to drink too much and learned what not to say and who to watch, and I learned of the violence and the cruelty and the virtues and the kindness of men.

After my three and a half years I wasn't a boy. I was a twenty-year-old man, and a wiser one than most my age. The next six years, whoosh, where did they go? They just went, they went with me crossing all the great oceans of the world, going to war, going home to watch my father die, going to the dogs, going into the gutter, going to the ends of the earth, to the ends of endurance, to the ends of the patience of all my friends. I tramped the world on old ships to old and forgotten places, ever searching for older ships and even more forgotten places, searching for a way of life that had disappeared a generation before my father was born. A quest pre-womb: an odyssey to the palace on Ithaca that never existed.

Then, all so quickly it seemed, ten years had passed, I was no longer a boy, a youth, no longer even a very young man. I was twenty-six, and the signs of maturity were upon me. My head of hair was still full although I had started to detect that it was not quite as thick as it used to be. I began to have the nightmare fear that I might lose my hair before I was ready to die, and have to walk the streets as a bald man. The thought was so horrific I drove it from my mind. My face was free of lines although there was a strong shading below the eyes, a hollowness, a pair of bags. In a bad light, in a bad reflection, I had a panda-like look. And when the morning arrived after the night before, I now took that much longer to recover. At twenty-one, I had been able to spring out of bed after three hours' sleep on the heels of an all-night party and then work all day – a bit groggy perhaps but the cobwebs gone by mid-morning. At twenty-six, I sprung nowhere and I carried the burden until lunchtime, feeling grim and miserable, snapping at people who tried to talk to me. Sometimes the real hangover would lie in wait for me, leaping on my back with a vengeance later in the day, knocking me down, punishing me for maltreating my body.

At twenty-six I had matured in my outlook and manner. I was confident at being in charge, crises didn't bother me, dangerous situations and dangerous men made me wary but not unnerved, I was more difficult to surprise. Not that these new signs of maturity had spread to my general behaviour, which remained as poor as ever and saw me continuing to cultivate the wrong type of company. A caravan of short liaisons failed to propel me forward on the personal front, although I was confident that change would heave into view sooner or later.

My friends had fled to all points of the globe. I was no longer in touch with any of them. Some were still deep sea but I didn't know where. Some were working short sea on the coast. Some had left the sea to seek new horizons, thrown off the sea, married, married and divorced, still single like me. Some would have failed, some thrived, all would eventually look back on our early life at sea as our halcyon days. But that day under the Pacific sun, I couldn't help wondering: 'My life as a young man: where did it all go, and how had it gone so quickly?'

I lay with these thoughts on Waikiki Beach, Honolulu , which wasn't a bad place to reflect on life and morals and mortality and all that leads to and from. It was late June 1980 and I had left my ship in New Zealand a few days beforehand after eighteen months away, to fly home to England. My parting gift from the New Zealand winter was a bad head cold, which had the consequence of me being removed from the plane in Honolulu on medical grounds. On taking off from Auckland I had gone partially deaf and my head felt as tight as a drum. It felt as if it was going to explode. On the descent into in Honolulu I became stone deaf and started to bleed out of one ear. My head started to vibrate painfully, as if someone was jabbing me in the ear with a blunt drill. The stewardesses became worried by the bleeding and by my general thrashing about in the seat. After we landed, they summoned the airport doctor, who shone his torch into my ears and immediately banned me from the onward flight, mouthing words to me that both eardrums were about to burst. He advised the airline staff to send me to a nearby ear, nose and throat clinic for specialist examination.

The Air New Zealand staff told me that seeing a doctor outside the airport wasn't as easy as it sounded. It would be too complicated to clear customs and immigration because I wasn't bound for the USA; I was only a stopover passenger, a refuelling passenger, not even a proper transit passenger. I was propped up on a couch in the corner of the transit lounge and given a wad of tissues to soak up the blood from my ears. Other passengers eyed me curiously. The Air New Zealand staff gathered in a huddle and held a conference to decide how best to deal with me.

US border bureaucracy was stodgy at the best of times, even if your passport was valid, your visa correct, your outward journey papers in order and your manner, manners and appearance were acceptable to the harsh-eyed guardians of the frontiers. But if your papers were not in order: woe. The strictly enforced line of US border officials was to zealously prevent anyone getting in unless they had undergone rigorous checks. If you worked in US border security at that time it was mandatory to be unpleasant and unforgiving. My papers were certainly not in order. I didn't have a visa, I didn't have permission to visit, I was not going to have an outward flight, I had nowhere to stay, I hadn't undergone checks to see if I was a vagrant, a destitute, a criminal, a drug addict, a Nazi, a communist, a carrier of disease, a rabble rouser, a general undesirable or perhaps all of those things.

The airline staff were stuck with solving my intrusion into the system, while I lay gently bleeding on the couch, watching them but aurally oblivious to what was going on. The conference got bigger, with several senior-looking people joining in. They waved their arms at each other. Some started looking angry, glaring at me, blaming me for making their life more difficult than it needed to be. They started arguing but eventually appeared to come to a decision, even though some of the group walked off shaking their heads while holding their hands aloft and vibrating them, like old-time minstrels, as if to say: 'Do what you want, it's nothing to do with me!'

The senior stewardess came over and explained the plan, squatting down and speaking close to my face, mouthing the words slowly as if I was an imbecile, so I could lip read. Her breath smelled of chocolate. The general feeling was that it would cause disproportionate grief if they started the process to clear me through the system using official channels, and this could even delay the London flight that was now refuelling. Instead, they decided it was best to smuggle me along a few corridors so I could pop out by one of the check-in desks and then slip out of the airport.

I was given a clipboard to hold and we then walked along various staff-only corridors, with me in the midst of the tight group. We weren't stopped or challenged or shouted at or shot at. The walk only took a few minutes. And presto – I was out and free in the United States of America.

The doctor at the clinic shone his torch in my ears, sucked air through his teeth, shook his head and told me I would have to wait several days before I could fly again. By making signs and mouthing the words expressively, he conveyed that my hearing should return within a few hours. He gave me a course of antibiotics and a bill for $120, told me to get plenty of rest, stay out of the sun, stay out of the sea, drink lots of water and avoid taking any alcohol. My luggage had been booked straight through to London so I only had the clothes I was wearing, my passport, money and credit cards.

I went for a walk until I started to regain my aural senses then took a taxi to Waikiki Beach and booked into the Princess Kaiulani Hotel, opposite the beachfront. I placed a call to my employer in Hong Kong to tell them the news. At that time, I was working for an old-established Hong Kong shipping company, one of the big taipans that ran a fleet of general cargo liners around the Far East and South Pacific. The personal officer clucked his tongue in sympathy and asked if I could afford the hotel. I was laden with money after eighteen months away and we agreed I would pay for everything and then submit a bill for expenses when I got back home. We then argued about the detail. The company would only pay a limit of US$50 a day for food; I tried to argue it up with limited success, only squeezing an extra $10. We then turned to squabbling about whether or not my days in Hawaii would count as further time away. He was adamant that I would not be earning more leave for loafing in Honolulu. In the end we agreed that my island sojourn would all count as travel days and my actual leave would not start until I arrived in England.

The arguing done, he wished me a speedy recovery. I thanked him, then sat on the bed and contemplated how to spend my time over the next few days. I contemplated the doctor's advice about staying out of the sun and sea and not taking any alcohol. It didn't really need much thought. I flushed the antibiotics down the toilet then went out onto the hotel veranda to sit in the Pacific sun and drink cold beer.

The Hawaiian islands in the North Pacific are the peaks of the highest mountain range in the world, a group of active volcanoes rising up from the sea bed. The group lies at 21°N and 2,400 miles off the coast of mainland USA. There are seven populated islands and a further 130 small islets and atolls. Honolulu is the capital, on the island of Oahu. The weather is balmy, warm enough for shirtsleeves most of the year: most of the year the temperature sits in the high seventies Fahrenheit, that's the mid to upper twenties centigrade in new money. Rain is frequent, although it's usually light. The predominant north-east wind rarely blows fiercely. All of these things combine to give Hawaii a good rating on the island paradise scale.

The Hawaiian islands were an independent kingdom for centuries, a monarchical society with strict succession rules and a large and complicated royal family. The Hawaiians came into dispute with neighbouring islands from time to time and settled such matters in the accepted way of warring Pacific Islanders, which was to pile into their war canoes and set off to the enemy islands, where they clubbed down the men, stole the women and enslaved the children. Overall, though, the Hawaiian archipelago was a settled place with structure and order and an established civil service; there was commerce and trade and artistic culture.

Traditionally, the Hawaiian ruling elite regarded the written word as seditious, and literature was suppressed as something evil, with people being educated by the tradition of storytelling. The islands changed when the Europeans started to show their faces in the

Pacific. Early European missionaries established schools, and this caused literacy to begin to seep into society. James Cook visited in 1778 and left to spread the word about the beautiful place he had found. He of course meant beautiful and strategic. The Russians had a go at taking control of the islands in the early part of the 19th century, and both the British and French occupied them in the 1840s, all of them trying to gain the upper hand in their board game of one-upmanship, where they used gunboats as dice and countries as counters. Throughout this period of associations and alliances and treaties and trade agreements and occasional occupation, the islands always ended up being returned to the indigenous population.

Not so when the first settlers from the United States arrived, though; they found the islands perfect for sugar plantations and set to developing them with evangelical zeal. The population frequently proved obstructive to change, and the royal family was suspicious of the long-term American motives, often blocking agricultural development and hindering progress. Finally, in exasperation, a group of six expatriate American plantation owners, aided by an Englishman and a German, concocted a rebellion against Queen Liliuokalani in 1893, during which American troops, conveniently stationed on nearby ships, were called in to save the day. The queen was forced to surrender at gunpoint to US marines.

It was an unprecedented humiliation for the Hawaiian royal family, but Queen Liliuokalani was no simple island savage; she was an educated woman, a friend of Queen Victoria, and married to a wealthy Scottish financier who had been the island governor during a brief earlier period of British domination.

An American governor was installed, but the queen pressed the case with Washington for her continued rights as serving monarch. She was eventually, and resentfully, allowed to resume her position as queen by the occupying powers. With poor judgement she immediately went back to her policy of blocking agricultural change. It proved a big mistake. The planters were outraged by the turn of events and reacted by pressurising the US government to withdraw the favoured trading status of Hawaii, which it did. This precipitated Hawaii's economic downturn. It was a high stakes gamble by the plantation owners, as they were cutting their own throats by reducing their trade terms; but they felt their future was stymied with the queen ruling, anyway. The gamble paid off: in 1898, the failing islands collapsed economically and were rescued and absorbed by the United States.

The queen was deposed for good, and her ministers and retinue were all dismissed. She was kept under arrest for a while as a troublesome character, before being allowed to live out her days peacefully on the islands, although without her royal title. American control was complete, but the appointed US governor thought it prudent to strengthen its grip still further, so he diminished the rights of indigenous Hawaiians and increased the rights of Americans and foreign commercial landowners. American carpetbaggers flooded into the new Jerusalem, and tame Hawaiians were included within the governance structure for appearance's sake. Every vote went the way of the plantation owners and developers. There was no going back, and Hawaii passed to the ownership of the USA for good. The islands were granted full statehood in 1959.

History books and government information tend to skip over the inglorious passage of the Hawaiian conquest at the end of the nineteenth century. The Hawaiian peoples don't protest

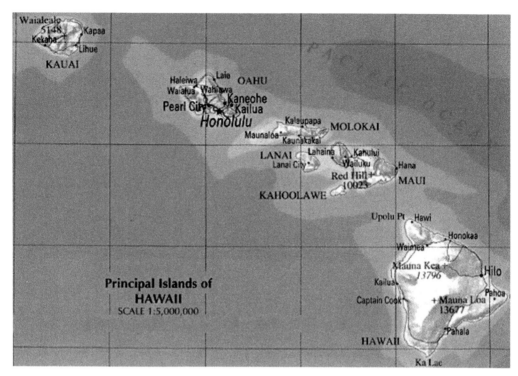

The Hawaiian Islands (Courtesy of the University of Texas Libraries)

or agitate any more, and those who do are ignored as lunatics or depicted as dangerous radicals who are a threat to the homeland. Pacific islanders make up less than 10 per cent of the population now, anyway. White Americans number 25 per cent, Asian Americans nearly 40 per cent, and the rest are mixed. From time to time someone displays anger over what happened, or a twinge of shame for the conquering of a proud people, but not often – and the feeling never takes root.

Broadly speaking, the Pacific is divided into three areas: Melanesia, Polynesia and Micronesia. Melanesia is in the western South Pacific, encompassing the islands from New Guinea to Fiji. Polynesia is the huge mass of islands from New Zealand in the south to Hawaii in the north, and right across to Easter Island. Micronesia denotes the groups of small islands that are mostly in the western part of the North Pacific.

The Pacific Ocean is huge, over twice the size of the Atlantic, with vast sweeps of islands scattered right the way across. The Portuguese and Spanish were the first Europeans to arrive in the Pacific in the 1560s, but they just established some trade links and generally passed through. It was the British and French who ran up their sovereign flags on most of the islands in the eighteenth and nineteenth centuries, for commercial and strategic gain, and because the British didn't want the French to have them and vice versa. The Germans and Americans arrived late for the island grab, although they made up for their tardiness with firm application to get whatever they could. The records show the takeover of the Pacific

Islands as being mainly bloodless, although in fact there was a wide body of resistance. As always, the reality is hijacked by the celebrity deaths. Ferdinand Magellan was hacked to death in the Philippines after crossing the Pacific. Intrepid explorer Captain Cook was clubbed to death on the beach in Hawaii. Fletcher Christian, leader of the *Bounty* mutineers, was killed on Pitcairn Island, although no one is quite sure whether it was by the locals or by one of his own men.

The Pacific Islanders have a warlike background, and if the early missionaries hadn't been successful in their wholesale conversions to Christianity, there would probably have been a lot more blood on the beaches when the Europeans started to arrive in force. A few of the earlier priests were eaten before they managed to perfect the message, although that was of small concern in the greater scheme of things.

There was resistance, however: the Mau movement in Samoa battled for the preservation of their culture; the Maori wars in New Zealand lasted three decades; the Madang revolt rattled the German administrators; the upheavals in Fiji against the British were on the scale of a full-scale civil war. The French probably had the greatest challenges, both in Tahiti and New Caledonia, although they soon mastered crowd control of this type, gunning down a large part of the Kanak population of New Caledonia and shipping out most of the remainder to work in sugar plantations in Fiji and northern Australia.

The new Pacific masters introduced modern medicine and literature, which were thought to be on the plus side, but they also brought smallpox, syphilis, alcoholism and loss of birthright. The Germans had their Pacific islands confiscated under the Treaty of Versailles as punishment for their bad behaviour in the First World War, and these were passed to the British by agreement among the victorious powers. The British gave their islands independence in the middle years of the twentieth century. The US, and France to a lesser extent, have gripped onto theirs with a firm hand.

In 1980 Honolulu was still being painted as the ultimate sophisticated getaway place for sophisticated and well-off Americans and very well-off Europeans. Hawaii had all that could possibly be desired: weather, blue seas, sandy beaches, palm trees, exotic but pliant locals who dressed the part, live volcanoes and spectacular scenery.

Sadly, along the Waikiki beachfront the place was getting progressively more ruined by block hotels thrown up with scant attempt to fit in with the environment. Of course, once the first few hotels were up, the following ones fitted in extremely well.

I was staying in one such eyesore, the Sheraton Princess Kaiulani, an ugly stack of concrete tastelessly named after Queen Liliuokani's daughter, Princess Victoria Kaiulani, who would have ruled Hawaii one day if the Americans hadn't hoofed out her mother. The Waikiki strip was further spoilt by the general awfulness of corporate franchise USA, infested with chain hotels and ghastly eating places that guaranteed early death, and bars with faux weathered exteriors and names like The Beachcomber or Surfers or The Swaying Palms. To be fair, the Waikiki area had started its decline in the early 1950s, well before my bleeding ears forced me to take refuge there for a few days.

Being marooned in Honolulu was quite convenient in that I didn't have to spend any great amount of money on clothes. I bought a pair of swimming trunks, a pair of shorts and several tee-shirts with amusing motifs, plus a couple of smarter shirts and a pair of chinos for the evening. Leaving aside the architecture, Waikiki Beach disappointed me in that it was really just another beach jammed with parents hissing viciously at their bickering children. The honeyed beauties from the films and posters were nowhere to be seen. They were all on beaches somewhere else, presumably. Still, I enjoyed myself anyway in what was a tame environment for me and where I was surrounded by people and sights that were unfamiliar. It was far removed from my usual stamping ground of shabby docks and dubious waterfront drinking dens.

I ranged around the general lower Honolulu area over the next few days, taking in the sights, cooking myself in the sun, reading, drinking cold beer and exotic cocktails, drifting in and out of conversations with strangers. The night scene was too stylised for my taste with its posers and piano bars. In the discotheques people danced competitively in front of mirrors, and nobody seemed to enjoy themselves. The loud music of the day was belted out by Teena Marie, Lipps and Roberta Flack; the after-midnight smooching took place against the background of 'Suicide is Painless' and Don Mclean's 'Crying'.

My only jaunt away from the bland was late one night when I found myself in an open-air nightclub near the beach, a rough and loud place, where I suddenly noticed that virtually all the clientele were men. Some were dancing together with alarming closeness while others were dressed in sleeveless leather shirts, as if they were auditioning for a part in a strange film. I raised this with one of the few women in the club, a meaty-looking lady with dangerous hands, and she told me with amusement that I was in a gay club. She turned to tell her congruous friends about me and they all chuckled. I scuttled away. I'm fine with homosexuals, but I didn't want to stay in a place where it looked as if the practice might be made compulsory as the night wore on. On the way out the doorman stamped my hand with a mark that showed up under fluorescent lighting. I scrubbed it off with damp sand when I got round the corner.

In the daytime, between periods of bronzing myself by the pool or on the beach, I visited the sights worth seeing. Pearl Harbor was one. In December 1942, a large part of the US Pacific Fleet had been gathered in the harbour, only to be bombed and largely sunk in a surprise attack by the Japanese Air Force. The attack caused the Americans to abandon their precarious path of neutrality and enter the Second World War, both the Pacific and European theatres. I went to the memorial for the battleship USS *Arizona* expecting quiet reflection, but the moment was spoilt by brats squealing disrespectfully, loose and out of their parents' control. I took a day to visit the wild parts of Oahu island, which were extraordinary and majestic: verdant green jungle blanketing hostile volcanoes that were biding their time.

The doctor at the clinic wanted me back for a check-up after four days. I went and feigned continuing deafness and pain and he gave me a continuance to avoid flying for another three days, together with a second bill, this time for $70. I could tell he didn't really believe my continuing discomfort, although my guilt was non-existent. I felt justified in having a week's relaxation courtesy of my employer, after a hard eighteen months away from home.

Eighteen months, a long time away, the longest trip I had ever made. The time had been split between two general cargo traders owned and operated by the taipan company, trading around the Far East and South Pacific where I had sailed as second officer. I served nine months on each. The first ship, the *Poyang,* was on a liner service between the big Far East ports of Singapore, Manila and Hong Kong, to the South Pacific islands that stretched from Papua New Guinea in the west to Tahiti in the east. The second ship, the *Kwangsi,* called at the same Far East ports, but then went further south, to call at Fiji and New Zealand.

Between these two ships I took a fortnight's break in the Philippines, a wild debauch spent in Manila and Angel City; two weeks of ferocious drinking and maltreatment of my body that at the end left me looking older than I was, my skin dry, my eyes hollow, my soul starved. I deserved my poor state, the dull thudding in my head, the queasiness, tremors, lethargy and the sour taste that squatted in my mouth. All night, night after night, in the Ermita bar district of Manila, walking erratically back to my hotel at dawn, rising at lunchtime feeling bad, wolfing codeines, eating junk, then back to the vibrant streets, back to MH del Pilar and Mabini Street, row upon row of bars, clubs, low joints, sordid shows, hot-bed hotels. Then after a few days, I took a bus to Angel City, fifty miles north of Manila. Angel City was Manila magnified. Manila looked tame compared to Angel City. Angel City was shockingly violent, *uber* decadent. It catered to mankind's every baser need. I drank myself insensible every day, I passed out several times, I ate nothing, I was robbed, I woke up bloody from a beating I didn't even remember.

When the *Kwangsi* arrived I needed rescuing, I needed to be back at sea. I had gone to Angel City for the experience, but if I had stayed any longer the experience would have killed me. I took time to repair myself in the second nine-month period.

Sometimes I reflected that it might have been better for me if I were committed to stay aboard a ship. I felt I would have fitted in well among the crew of the *Flying Dutchman,* doomed to sail the world interminably with dead men as my companions while dicing with the devil for my soul.

At sea it could be all so different. On a bright day in the South China Sea, steaming north-north-west to Hong Kong with a light breeze on the port quarter, the water was duck-egg blue and the wavelets turned over in regimen as they streamed towards the Taiwan Strait. The ship rocked gently, cleaving the pure sea, and I leant into the muted vectored flow and breathed in air that was as clean and fresh and newly minted as if it were the first gentle blow on earth by the wind god Zephyros. The sun sat on the Tropic of Cancer, ambling between clumps of cumulus, flinging my shadow onto the tar-sealed wooden deck of the bridge wing, then snatching it away again. Ships were scattered around us; nothing too close but all needing to be watched. In the middle of the South China Sea we were out of range of the close inshore fishing fleets with their miles of drift nets; those around us were all big ships, ocean-going vessels, northerly to Hong Kong and Taiwan, north-easterly to Japan and Korea, southerly to the Philippines, to Singapore, Malaysia and the Indonesian archipelago.

The ships crossed and merged and diverged, and I watched them all and took bearings, and took note of those that were destined to pass at close quarters.

When we were down in the South Pacific the life was the same only with fewer ships. Mostly no ships. The sea was bluer, there were more big wheeling birds, more dolphins and sharks and whales, more flying fish. It always seemed there was more sun in the Pacific, too; but the sun was always the same really, it just hid more in the straits of the East.

Was it that I was a debauchee when I was ashore, and a poet when back at sea? Was that it? No, of course not. Life at sea could also be hellish. I had times aboard ship when I was numbed with fatigue and cold and misery, times when I was all alone in a floating hell where I liked no one and no one liked me, and none of us cared much for anything or anybody. And sometimes when I was ashore in strange and exotic climes I had such glorious times that my soul skipped. I was just living a life of extremes in those days, and what a life it was. I was so lucky.

Before my eighteen-month trip away I had spent a year on the European coast, and before that three years with cargo liners, working for an old Scottish company sailing out of Leith for the Far East. And before that more ships, tankers, old ones, ancient ones, where I had been a cadet.

The difference between an officer and a cadet is the difference between a surgeon and the person who washes the surgery floor. Even more so in fact, as the floor washer is granted dignity in his or her job, because workers deserve basic dignity and respect no matter what their station in life and because disrespect would cause unwanted disharmony. Not so the cadet. The officers are there to manage the ship, to take responsibility for ensuring the ship runs properly and to take the blame when it doesn't. The crew are there to carry out the work planned and structured by the officers. The crew need to be given a measure of respect to ensure their effective working. And then there's the cadet. The cadets are there to do as they are told, to work as commanded. Cadets are given jobs that the crew would balk at, or do unwillingly. Ostensibly, the cadets are there to learn, to ensure that they're capable of doing every task that they would one day have to organise themselves, either to be done by their own cadets, or by the crew if there were none. The theory was that if the cadet learned to do everything and was made to do everything, no matter how foul, it would make them a better officer. That sounds fine in theory – but it paved the way for institutionalised abuse.

Not every officer became some sort of sadistic monster as soon as he had obtained his gold stripes, far from it. Quite the opposite in fact. The majority were humane and decent people. There would always be the bad apple in the barrel, although that happens in every walk of life. No, it was simply a system whereby my illusions were shattered almost immediately as I realised how I was destined to be treated over the three and a half years of my cadetship.

My first jobs on board ship were so disgusting they still make me shudder: cleaning out revolting toilets that were packed and overflowing with stinking turds, scrubbing oil off the deck with hot kerosene, getting oil and goo and filth in every pore. Of course, when I earned my stripes and escaped the furnace of cadetship, I carried on within the system. I was mindful of the sensitivities of new cadets and felt I was a caring officer, to an extent, although not so sensitive as to avoid loading them with tasks that no one else would have carried out and giving them a bollocking if they didn't do a good job. When I moved from cadet to junior officer, it was as if I had won one of the great prizes in life, which I had, I suppose.

It was all very well me tanning myself on Waikiki Beach, reflecting upon life's challenges between cooling dips in the sea. I was having a good life, even if I chose to harness myself with self-pity from time to time. But the true picture, what was it exactly? Was I was a fully functioning person, bright, educated and extremely privileged, earning a fat tax-free salary while being ferried round exotic parts of the world so that I could spend my time ordering people around? Or was I was a man trapped in a strange world, undertaking arduous and sometimes dangerous work in difficult circumstances with little or no job security, away from home and without any meaningful relationship to come back to? Looking back, I suspect it was somewhere between the two. I would dearly like to remember myself as a thinking man who had the intellectual prowess at the time to debate these two visions, but the reality was that I was thinking of neither. I was just loafing on the beach, exaggerating my earache to extend my stay in paradise, ogling the girls in their bikinis now I'd found them, and waiting for the heat to fall out of the day so I could don my chinos and go and sit in a beachside café and drink icy beer in a frosted glass. *C'était ma vie.*

I knew I was at a turning point. I had spent the past five years as a junior officer serving on old-style conventional general cargo ships, and these were disappearing from the oceans at a rapid rate. Container ships were taking over, along with ro-ros and other fast discharge vessels. Port time was expensive. Container ships got round this by having all the cargoes pre-loaded into standard-size boxes that could be loaded and unloaded quickly. Ro-ros addressed it by allowing the ship to be opened up so that the cargo could be quickly driven on and off. The port areas around these modern ships needed to be clear and clean, needed to be designed as giant open industrial parks. This couldn't be more different from the needs of conventional general cargo ships, where a mix of different cargoes was loaded directly into the holds from wharfs that had the stowage warehouses built right on them. On a general cargo ship, we would carry a wide and diverse range of goods: cases of wine, bags of grain, cars, machinery, sacks of copra, electrical goods, steel ingots, reels of cable, light manufactured goods, crates of tea and whatever else the shipping agent had managed to round up. The loading and stowage was complex, and it was necessary to keep cargoes secured and properly separated to avoid damage and taint. We were generally in port for days on end, sometimes weeks.

The maritime world was undergoing one of its periodic changes. Centuries ago, when cargoes were first carried on boats, trade was just around the coastal areas, always in sight of land, in small wooden craft propelled by strong men paddling (or, later, pulling on oars), their rafts and coracles filled with furs, vegetables, meat, iron ore, pottery, wood, cloth and whatever else they were hoping to exchange with the next village. There would have been some regularity in this, mostly seasonal although also reflecting celebratory events, pre-conflict preparation and post-conflict rebuilding.

At first, traffic was confined to river estuaries and close coastal settlements, although in time the trips became extended along further reaches. From time to time these small vessels would venture out of sight of land to cross a brief stretch of water when they knew what was on the other side, but these trips were rare. It was left to the brave to fully map out areas beforehand before the mass of coastal traffic would start to use them. Weather was the key factor in whether or not a boat left the shore; the sea needed to be calm enough to row against.

Time brought bigger boats, ships, more oarsmen. The craft became more robust and more seaworthy. A trip across a large estuary or between two close islands was now child's play; a 10-mile then a 30-mile passage could be accomplished with ease. Then one day, someone noticed that their boat was blown off course when winds were strong. On went the thinking caps and the sail was born.

Sail changed everything. Ships started to travel hundreds of miles, trade routes opened up. Three thousand years passed and sail was brought to its absolute pinnacle of development. During this period, inter-ocean charts had been produced and the voyages of great discovery made. The compass was invented. The globe was circumnavigated. Celestial navigation moved to greater precision, and finding the ship's latitude became commonplace. The first chronometer was used and a way to find longitude was exacted. Ships became bigger and bigger and ever more sophisticated. And then, right then, right when the evolution of sailing vessels was at its zenith, along came the steam ship and blew away five thousand of years of development.

Ships that were propelled by steam had their origins in Scotland in the 1790s. The first ones were coastal and short sea vessels, driven by big revolving paddles fixed onto their sides. By the 1830s, greater efficiencies arrived in the form of the screw propeller, which pushed the craft from the rear. From the 1850s onwards, the navies of the great powers and the big commercial fleets ceased ordering sailing vessels and began the change to steamships. Ships were powered by coal, which was superheated in a furnace that turned water into steam to drive turbines, which turned the crankshaft to spin the propeller that moved the ship. The beginning of the end of sail had arrived. There was a transition period where fleets were comprised of some sailing ships and some steam ships. And of course there were some owners, mistrustful of the change, who built hybrid ships that could hoist sail if the engines broke down. By the end of the nineteenth century, though, sail as the mechanics of propelling the mainstream maritime fleet was dead.

In the twentieth century, ship propulsion evolved with more efficient engines. There were better navigation systems, advancing safety standards, greater comfort for the crews that manned them. Oil started to replace coal as the primary fuel on new ships around the time of the First World War, and diesel engines slowly began to supersede steam turbines after the Second World War.

But in all these changes, from one-man coracles in a muddy inland estuary many thousands of years before Christ, to fast modern post-war liners, cargoes were loaded directly into the ship, usually in small containers such as barrels and tea chests, and manhandled individually, though after the invention of the crane, they were swayed up in cargo nets. But then, from ideas that started to flower in the 1960s, container ships arrived and changed the face of shipping and the character of docklands throughout the world for ever. Giant standard-size boxes, known as TEUs (twenty-foot equivalent units) were slid into purpose-built ships down vertical guide rails. All the boxes had been pre-loaded and so the loading operation was quick. Discharging was similarly speedy because the TEU could be unloaded at leisure after the ship had departed. Then the container itself began to be collected from and delivered to the end user. By the mid-1960s the container trade had started in earnest and all the prime routes and ports started to convert. First the Atlantic trade, then, slowly but surely, the rest of the world.

I had spent five years as a junior officer on older general cargo traders, culminating in a final eighteen-month fling to seek out the life that was disappearing fast all around me. Every time we returned to the East, though, we saw more and more change; the older ships were disappearing before our eyes, as outdated things always do.

In 1980 I was now homeward bound, albeit with my unplanned Honolulu stopover, to sit for my Master's Certificate. I had nine months' leave due and six months' study leave, and when I eventually returned to sea it would be to a different world from the one I was leaving. So I thought.

I mused over whether to take a detour on the way home from Honolulu and fly south to Brazil, which I had never visited. All my luggage, such as it was, had gone ahead to London. There was nothing in my suitcase that I needed, and it would in fact be easier in a way to fly unburdened, with just my passport and wallet and an airline shoulder bag. I could always buy what I needed when I got there.

In the event, though, I didn't go to Brazil, concluding that Copacabana beach would be much like Waikiki: full of flabby people from the US and Europe taking a break from their overpaid jobs, following where they thought the stars went, striving for reflected glamour to keep in a frame on the sideboard for when they were old. No doubt there were girls to ogle, too, on Copacabana. But on balance I decided to head for home. I had been to too many out-of-the-way places to be impressed with tourist playgrounds, and I had been away from home too long.

Leaving Honolulu was harder than arriving. Trying to fly back, I found the airline staff had changed and they looked at me blankly when I explained myself. The girl on the counter made a whispered phone call, flicking her gaze at me nervously while she spoke, probably thinking I was some sort of lunatic who was trying to stow away with the luggage. Other people came and listened while I repeated my story, and I was told to wait while they checked with those who had been on duty the day I arrived. I hung around until they came back, satisfied with my story but now dissatisfied and worried, wrestling with the problem of what to do with me. I hadn't had any inward clearance and so they couldn't decide how to clear me out.

They said they couldn't, wouldn't, just allow me to slope out through the back ways of the airport, and that that should never have happened on the way in. I shrugged and said that they had created the problem and it was up to them to solve it. I told them that I was expecting to be on the London flight later in the day, and if they couldn't get me on it then they would have to put me up in a hotel somewhere.

After an hour I'd had enough and told them that I was just going to go and give myself up to the immigration services and tell them what had happened. The thought of that rattled the airline staff. They said they were worried they might be accused of criminal abetment by bringing in an illegal alien. I said that's what they'd done.

The senior people were called in to decide how best to arrange the illegal departure of their illegal immigrant. Things got sorted out in the end, as they always do, with them agreeing some sort of deal with those minor government officials who keep the wheels turning, exchanging favours no doubt to be redeemed at a future date of the grantee's choosing.

My passport was taken and then returned to me, stamped in and out, and I was told I would be on the afternoon flight to London, stopping off in Chicago. They still didn't dare let me go through the normal departure channels, however, presumably afraid that I would spill the beans on whatever story had been concocted, so I had a repeat tour of the hidden airport corridors after all, chaperoned by two airline staff and two chunky immigration officials with guns, before being delivered into the departure lounge with passport, boarding pass and goodbyes. *Aloha* Hawaii.

★　　★　　★

Throughout most of the 1970s life at sea had been good. For someone with a Second Mate's or First Mate's Certificate of Competency, it really couldn't get any better. There was an officer shortage, and we young officers could walk into any shipping company and get a job on the spot. A young certificated officer was gold dust in the eyes of the personnel departments. Ships spent time in port; a general cargo ship was always in for days, sometimes weeks. No frantic rushing in and out with barely time to have a walk on the quay.

Tankers could be frantic of course; tankers were the hard graft ships of the merchant fleet, demanding relentless, dirty, high-pressure work. They paid better, though.

But general cargo ships, they were different. They were civilised, they were the place to be. The officer contingent was sometimes very big, perhaps a captain and five deck officers, eight engineer officers, two radio officers, two electrical officers, a catering officer, six cadets. There were also about thirty crew members, so around fifty souls in all, a big complement.

Trips could be long, six months usually. The Scottish company I had sailed with in the mid-1970s tried to keep to four months, but it was mostly six, sometimes nine. When I moved to work for the taipan company trips were eight months, usually longer. If you were content to stay they would keep you for ever, witness my own eighteen-month jaunt.

We were mostly young men in our twenties. The senior officers were older, of course, the captain and chief engineer often well into their fifties. There was a general void of people in their thirties and forties. This was due to people getting married and leaving the sea, because a life that revolves around being away from spouse and children for three-quarters of the year is not tolerated by many. The British tax rules took a turn for the better in the 1970s, and people who were on deep sea trips either paid low tax or no tax, depending upon how much time they spent away.

British ships were not run recklessly, but the suffocating blanket of the health and safety world was still over the horizon and our day-to-day working conduct would now be looked back on with a shudder. For example, reading the draft marks from the ship was always a job that left me grateful when I survived. I would fling a monkey ladder over the stern. The further down the ladder I climbed the more it would swing, right under the curve of the stern; I would grip on for my life, my arms becoming numb with lack of circulation as I wrapped them around the rope. When I was near enough to the water, I would be able to read off the draft marks. At night I had to use a torch that I hung on a lanyard around my neck. Then the slow crawling climb back to the deck, hoping my arms wouldn't give way and let me plummet into the filthy dock water.

Or in a Storm Force 10 in the South China Sea with the white water boiling over the deck and the deck cargo starting to shift, we would have to rig rope lines and wade out to make things secure. If someone was too slow, or misjudged the next wave or was just plain unlucky and the twenty-ton cargo moved into them, they could be crushed into jam.

The end result tended to be ships that were overwhelmingly manned by healthy young men who worked too hard, who were loaded with responsibilities well beyond their years and whose working environment and manner offered more than its fair share of dangers. We mostly had too much money and grasped at whatever opportunities were afforded us to seek recreation with a vengeance in whatever exotic playground came our way. It wasn't a case of over-using the old 'work hard, play hard' maxim. It was more than that. When we had time off we acted as if tomorrow was judgement day. The close confinement of men living today in a disciplined environment in extreme conditions imbued camaraderie, a close bonding. The simple truth was: we could not go home at night because we were home. I loved it.

Most of my life at sea had been spent in the tropics, mainly the Far East and South Pacific, where we wore whites. Whites was our tropical uniform: short-sleeved white shirts with epaulettes of rank, white shorts, white socks. The official footwear was white canvas shoes with leather soles, although few people wore those, preferring something casual and light. My own preference was for cut-down desert boots, which I could only find in Singapore. Others favoured daps, rope-soled deck shoes, or even sandals.

Our cold weather uniform was blues. Blues were black in fact, black trousers, black double-breasted jacket with brass buttons and gold stripes of rank on the sleeves, white shirt, black tie, black shoes. In between the two, when moving out of the tropics, or into it, we often wore half and halfs.

We rarely wore uniform hats. It seemed that a spirit of casualness had developed for the two extremities, heads and feet: hats and shoes. In the early 1970s, some officers still wore battledress jackets, and I had one myself although rarely donned it. A battledress was a short uniform jacket with patch pockets on both sides. In port in the tropics, the deck officers on general cargo ships often wore khaki uniform, because whites could get easily soiled. I didn't wear khakis myself, having spent my cadetship on old tankers where we got seriously filthy in port and had to don boiler suits. Officers in passenger ships would also wear 'number 10s', formal dress uniforms required for various functions and formalities to impress the passengers.

But I never served on a passenger ship, just on cargo passenger liners, which were more relaxed. A general cargo trader could be fitted with extra accommodation so as to carry up to twelve passengers. These ships attracted passengers who wanted a more robust experience than they would usually find on a conventional passenger liner. A cargo ship that carried twelve passengers was still considered a cargo ship. A ship that carried more than twelve was considered a passenger ship and had to have more lifeboats, more safety equipment, more watertight separating doors and a doctor, and were generally much more expensive to build and more expensive to run.

Our occasional passengers were generally older people, in their fifties and beyond. The chief officer would have the task of smarming around them. They had their own bar and dining saloon, although they occasionally ate with us in the officers' saloon. Sometimes, the more adventurous/curious/nosey types would come into our bar: they were tolerated. but nobody really wanted them there because they cluttered up the place, forcing us to de-salt our conversations and mind our Ps and Qs and. (Is that a childish abbreviation for 'pleases' and 'thank yous'? – I've never really known).

As I look back, I see there was a curious formality about our lives that I find hard to describe. We were sticklers for tradition, even the rebellious ones among us. This gave our lives structure and allowed everyone to capture and preserve their own dignity.

For example, no one would have dreamt of going into the saloon to eat without being properly dressed in uniform: that would have been as unheard of as someone going in naked. On the other hand, an off-duty officer might entertain colleagues for a few drinks in his cabin only wearing a pair of shorts. When we were together in public places, in the bar or the dining saloon or the games room, we were uniformed, and we paid deference to our seniors, to some extent. Alone in our cabins or sunbathing on the boat deck in lines or horsing around by the swimming pool on the odd occasions it was filled, we were as deliberately informal as it was possible to be.

Form of address was important. The captain called everyone by their rank, as did the chief officer. The senior officers generally called the junior officers by their Christian names and the cadets by their surnames. The junior and mid-ranking deck officers called the captain Sir or Captain, the chief officer, Chief Off or Choff, and each other by their Christian names. The cadets addressed everyone by their rank, although they might be invited by the junior officers to use their Christian names when off duty. The petty officers, the bosun and the deck storekeeper, were called by their title, "Good morning, Bosun", "Good morning, Stores", as were the quartermasters. The rest of the crew were addressed by their first names or nicknames by officers and crew alike. The crew addressed the officers by rank: "Good morning, Second Mate"; "Yes, Captain"; "OK, Chief Officer". The engineer officers had the same system in broad parallel, although they tended to be slightly more casual.

People very rarely stepped outside of these boundaries of address. When someone did they were looked at with disapproval, regarded as people who either didn't know their place, who failed to give due respect, or who were trying to curry favour. Whichever it was, the crossing of a boundary line was disliked by almost everyone on board.

The formality of our working life imbued more formality in our general life, which in turn was carried back into our work. In writing the log at the end of the watch, we were more organised in the structure of our sentences than we needed to be. It wasn't because of an obsession with clarity; it was a case of doing things in the way we thought was right for the posterity we were creating. On the older ships with the older captains who were more insistent that we carried forward traditions, we pretended to dislike them … but in truth we were pleased and took pride in them.

When we had a captain who insisted on bells being rung, the bridge officer would ensure the quartermaster of the watch came over to the bell, which hung down next to the ship's wheel, and rang the time precisely on the hour. Bells were rung in pairs throughout the four-hour watch. So, on the midnight to four watch, one o'clock would warrant two bells, rung as 'ding-ding'. Two o'clock would be four bells, rung as 'ding-ding, ding-ding'. The end of every watch was eight bells.

Bells weren't generally rung during the day; only from six in the evening until breakfast. They were always rung with solemnity, with exactness. A quartermaster who made a hash of it, failing to ring the correct 'ding-ding' sound, would be shamed and humiliated. Ringing bells badly was as embarrassing as if your trousers had fallen down in a public place.

On one old ship I was on, there was a refit of equipment on the bridge, a change of radars, a new echo sounder, an upgrade of the Decca navigator system. At the same time a brass clock was installed which actually chimed the ship's bells. We were aghast. We hated it, all of us from the lowest deckhand to the captain. On the second day after we left the refit port, I came onto the bridge for the midnight watch, arriving a few minutes before midnight. A mug of coffee was thrust into my hand and I was sipping it when the quartermaster came in from the bridge wing and rang the bells. I looked at the third mate. He shrugged. The new brass clock had disappeared. No one knew who had taken it. No one cared.

Our lives went on … the shipping world was changing around us and the light was dimming on our path, but we gripped on to what we had. We were like the old-time sailors with their tattooed boast across the knuckles of their hands, one word on each, a boast that they would never give way: 'Hold Fast'.

2

Into the Churn

When I arrived back from the Pacific in June 1980, after eighteen months away, I had to re-adjust to a life ashore, a life in Britain. The world had moved on a lot between the end of 1978 and the middle of 1980.

Labour was out and the Conservatives were in. James Callaghan was yesterday's man and Margaret Thatcher was tomorrow. The cost of a pint of beer had doubled in price, rocketing to 60 pence. Twenty Rothmans cost 70 pence and everyone seemed to be smoking. Petrol prices had doubled, from 75 pence a gallon to £1.50.

When I had left at the end of 1978 the number 1 record in the charts was the sparky dance tune *YMCA*, by the Village People; when I returned at the end of June 1980, Don McLean's *Crying* was leading the pack. This seemed a fitting anthem for a country mired in gloomy recession. The prices we now had to pay for beer, cigarettes and petrol would have made anyone cry.

The basic rate of tax had come down from 35 per cent to 30 per cent, which made it a bit easier for those in work. People seemed to dress more powerfully, with both men and women sporting shoulder-pads. The top-selling car was still the Ford Cortina.

I noticed there were momentous things happening in the world. Momentous things were of course always happening in the world, but I probably just hadn't taken much notice before. The crown colony of Rhodesia had been made officially independent as Zimbabwe, and was already creating a stir by consorting with unsavoury countries, to the rage of the British government. The United States was doing its best to arrange a boycott of the summer Olympics in Moscow, in protest against the Soviet invasion of Afghanistan. Arabs were killing Arabs, Africans were killing Africans, Irish were killing Irish, harsher health warnings were going on cigarette packets; the biggest box office film was *The Empire Strikes Back*, inflation was rising, unemployment was rising, road deaths were falling, gold was up, the pound was down.

Financially, I was in a good position. I didn't pay any UK tax because of the length of time I was out the country; I just paid Hong Kong tax, which was only 10 per cent. My coffers were full to overflowing, and I was keen to invest something before my free-spending habits started to syphon it all away.

A couple of weeks beforehand I had read an article on the wisdom of investing in rare stamps and so, easily led, I strolled down the Strand to Stanley Gibbons Stamp Merchants and Valuers, and bought a £6,000 portfolio, telling them to keep it in their safe. My brother Peter had contacted me shortly before I came home to borrow some money as a deposit to buy an apartment, which was fine by me. Better in his solid pocket than my holey one, he would pay it back into a deposit account for me over the next couple of years with interest; £4,000 went to him. My third spend was £2,000 on a Mini Cooper, a 1,275 cc model in the handsome John Player Special black and gold. That left me a few thousand pounds, which I was confident of working through during my nine months' accumulated leave and six months' study leave. I would continue to receive full salary throughout.

I had the summer off before attending one of the Schools of Maritime Studies to sit for my Master's but I hadn't decided which college to go yet. There were several around the country and I had already been to a few. As a cadet I had attended the School of Navigation in Plymouth, then I had studied for my Second Mate's in London and my First Mate's in South Shields.

For my Master's I was thinking of the nautical college in either Leith or Bristol but I didn't need to confirm it for a few weeks. The course was for six months, starting in September. I moved in with my mother, who had a house in a small village in Oxfordshire, intending to use that as a base for a few weeks until I identified my place of study, after which I would find a flat. My mother was widowed, and my younger brother Anthony was living at home. My older brother Peter was in London with his girlfriend Alex, buying their first apartment.

That summer, I sped around in my Mini Cooper, learning how to be a landlubber again. From a social standpoint, the trouble with being away at sea for long periods is that you have no circle of friends when you come home. I spent my days idling and my nights carousing with strangers. Oxfordshire and Berkshire were full of pubs, and I did my best to patronise most of them.

The nearest town was Abingdon, which was a handy-size market town. The Abingdon brewery Moreland battled with Oxford brewery Morrells for market share; I was a Moreland's man. Oxford was 7 miles away and I tended to go there twice a week, where I found enough late-night places to keep me amused. Peter was becoming more settled and Anthony was too young, so I was mostly alone, striking up companionship as it arrived, getting to know small groups in different places.

I mined contacts for anyone home from sea, but struck rock. It was either a case of nobody home or whereabouts unknown or they had just moved on. None of my friends from the early days were in evidence – all the people I had come of age with and formed my values and life's pattern with had gone. Gone somewhere of course; they were all following their own paths.

I was at the age when people married and had children and responsibilities and acquired goals in life, but my achievements in that direction were poor. I had no relationships and no responsibilities and, even less admirably, the only immediate goal I had was tending to my own vacuous desires. Still, I knuckled down to my vacuousness with intent, raising the profits of Moreland's Brewery and generally enjoying myself.

I did a ten-day tour of the south coast of Devon and Cornwall, the long stretch between Torquay and Penzance. I booked into in bed and breakfast places when I arrived at lunchtime, loafing in the afternoon, out at night in the pubs and clubs, drinking, striving to pick up girls, back late, up next day, feeling bleah, off to the next place along the coast and so on.

The south of England done, I graced the other end of the kingdom with my presence, travelling the east coast and central part of Scotland, two days here, three days there. I disliked Aberdeen, grown fat and selfish on its oil money. But I liked Inverness, and most of all I liked the smaller places where the inhabitants had time: Inverbervie, Banchory, Inverurie and Forres. I was included in the conversations in the pubs and welcome at the local hop. Some of the local lads looked at me with hard eyes, though, in case I accomplished a coup with one of the local lasses, but all in all these jaunts were enjoyable. I finished on the north coast, staying at a hotel near Dunnet Head, the northernmost tip of Scotland, where I took long walks along the beach and skimmed stones into the Pentland Firth and watched the ships steam through, creeping past the Island of Stroma, heading towards the edges of the Atlantic. One evening, I overheard locals talking about me in the bar, not knowing I was there. They viewed my solitary walks with suspicion, one was speculating that I was a spy, casing the offshore oilfields.

Bristol. It seemed the place to go. The School of Maritime Studies was a department in a college in Ashley Down Road. The grey stone building was in late Victorian Massive, and had the gloomy institutional feel that such places have. The maritime studies department was small when compared to the big colleges of London, Plymouth and South Shields, but it had a good feel.

I didn't know Bristol, having only been there once before on a boozy night out several years previously. On ships, I had called in to Avonmouth, the port at the head of the river, although we were never in for long so I rarely made it past the bar of the Royal Hotel, a run-down dive full of worn-out people just outside the main dock gate on the corner of Clayton Street.

This time, I arrived in Bristol and booked into a bed and breakfast near the college. I was fed up with my Mini Cooper by that time and had sold it and bought an electric blue Ford Consul, a huge car as seen on the Sweeney television series. I was proud of my Sweeney car, particularly the electric windows, even though they were a bolt-on afterthought, a pair of chunky boxes fixed to the inside of both front doors.

Master Mariner. Master's. This was a serious course for grown-ups. My previous college spells had been thinly disguised parties with a rush of work at the close, but this was different. For a start, everyone was older. Older, wiser, duller. Older, wiser, duller, married, serious, burdened by all the things that arrive at that stage of life, but unburdened by humour. I looked around the class in dismay; fifteen of us. At twenty-six I was one of the youngest; most were a couple of years older, there were several in their early thirties, and a sprinkling of real granddads who were over forty-five. In early conversation and observations, it became clear that most of the class were married and living in their own homes in the Bristol area, though a few lived further away and had taken lodgings for the week, going home at weekends.

Steve was English but he lived in west Wales and worked for the same Hong Kong company as me. He wasn't married but had a Japanese girlfriend in Yokohama who was threatening to come over and stay. He was a chunky man who had played rugby for England schoolboys before an accident had curtailed his potential. He replaced the endurance test on the field with the endurance test in the pub. I loved to drink, too, and we made a good pair. We found a four-person flat in the St George area, which we took for six months, hoping to get another couple of students to share the rent. That didn't take long; we were soon joined by Mike, one of the granddads, who was like a grumpy uncle, and a lad called Colin, who was taking his Second Mate's Certificate.

Our flat was above a shop that sold outboard motors for boats, and the only way into the flat was to clamber over piles of partly assembled engines to get to the back stairs. I had the biggest room, a vast bay-fronted place that was twice the size of the next room and four times as big as the windowless hovel Colin was assigned to at the end of the passageway. I paid a proportionately larger part of the rent.

Everyone in the class had their First Mate's Certificate, as it was a requirement for sitting the Master's. I thought that if I could get my Master's I would be set for life. If I then stayed at sea I would eventually sail as captain, or if I left the sea I should be able to get a decent job as a pilot, or in port management. I had taken a couple of stabs to pass both my Second Mate's and First Mate's Certificates, but it looked as if I would have less distraction when taking the Master's so I should have a better chance of passing first time.

There was a strong emphasis on ship's business and law, a good deal of theoretical ship-handling, advanced meteorology, cargo work and a heavy helping of mathematics and physics. Examination week consisted of eight three-hour examinations over four days, followed by a one-hour oral grilling by a trio of wise men. No room for laggards. I felt glum at the thought of the next six months.

The course started in earnest. The work was heavy from the word go. I hadn't been in a classroom for three years and had done no preparation, although my mind was sharpened by having been the ship's navigator for most of that time, navigation being a diet of constant mathematics. Some of the older ones started to slip after the first week, I could see them crinkling their brows as the lecturer attempted to cram complicated theory into us. Two left the course after a month, seeing it as a hopeless cause. The remaining three, Mike being one of them, struggled on bravely. They sat together at the back of the class, the back of the class in more ways than one.

A British Master Foreign-Going Certificate was internationally recognised as the best in the world. I'm quite sure the Germans and the French and the Dutch and the Americans would all claim that their own standards were just as high, if not higher. Be that as it may, the British certificate held the number 1 spot as the most meaningful maritime qualification.

In 1845, the Board of Trade had become dismayed about poor standards of officers, following a spate of maritime disasters and ruled that anyone who took command of a

British foreign-going ship should hold a Master's Certificate of Competency. To start with it was voluntary, although strongly encouraged, and it was immediately adopted by most of the big shipping lines.

Naturally, there were captains who had held command for many years who did not have any certificates and had no intention of taking the examinations. They just ignored the recommendations. In 1850 however, certification became compulsory, which was hard luck to those captains without it: it was on the beach for them, or overseas to work for a country that didn't care who manned its ships. Home trade captains would need to have a certificate by 1854, and so the system of certification was born.

Over the next few years it evolved into a series of certificates of competency for Foreign-Going ships: Master's, First Mate's and Second Mate's, together with lesser certificates for Home Trade ships: Home Trade Master's and Home Trade Mate's. A Home Trade ship was one that was restricted to trading around and near the UK coast. Over the past 150 years, these certificates have ruled and determined who can command a British ship. Joseph Conrad had one; he was probably the most famous holder of a British Master's Certificate of Competency. I intended to have one too.

The flat we inhabited in Avondale Road, St George, was pretty grim. It was the last one left on the college register, small wonder. Not just the insalubrious entrance with its obstacle course of dismembered engines. Nor the bleak street in which it sat; car-crammed, unplanned, so soulless you felt you could drop dead and people would walk over you. Nor the people who lived on the street, sad and poor and unhealthy, they walked with heads down nursing dented dreams. It was the actual place itself.

The furniture in all the rooms was old and damaged, the carpets were worn through, the windows were so filthy that curtains were barely necessary. The mattresses on the beds were lank and ancient, peppered with unpleasant looking smears and stains. Each of our four bedrooms was off an unlit corridor with a steep step halfway along, which we all fell down regularly in the gloom. There was a grubby greasy kitchen and a small dank bathroom, amateurishly constructed with mix and match fittings: chocolate brown sink, tangerine toilet, toad green bath. We had a sitting room that we didn't use much, although sometimes we clustered there late at night, sitting on the collapsed sofa to watch an ancient flickering television.

The landlord had given the rooms a cursory clean before we moved in, but it was a poor effort: the whole place needed a proper clean, a spring clean, a steam clean, a stripped-out, washed-down clean. The mouldy patches should have been scrubbed, the ingrained grime on the surfaces and walls need to be leeched out, all the carpets and furniture should have been burnt and every room washed with a strong disinfectant, painted out, re-carpeted and re-furnished. It would then have been worth the rent, barely. But we stayed, and carved up the rent on a basis we thought was fair and in proportion to the size of the rooms we occupied.

Steve and I couldn't really care less about that state of the place, and Colin wasn't in residence enough to bother; we usually heard him returning in the early hours. That just left

Mike, a family man who did bother. He fretted about the pigsty he found himself in, but at least he was only there for four nights a week; after classes on Friday he drove home for the weekend and reappeared in the flat on Monday evening, always viewing the increasing mess with dismay. Mike usually did a bit a cleaning on Monday evenings, while we cheered him on before leaving to walk down to the White Lion.

My shared flat in St George was a far cry from the cosseting at sea where stewards brought us gin and tonics and where we ate from silver service. Still, young men who are not yet settled in life quickly adapt to living like beasts, and I was no different.

We fell into a routine. In the morning, Steve and I set off for college together, being in the same class, alternating between using my Consul and his Volkswagen. Mike never wanted to come with us; Colin generally stayed in bed. We returned from college in the early evening, unless we had reason to stop off somewhere on the way back. Steve and I snarfed what food was to hand in the fridge or picked up fish and chips from the shop down the road. After we had devoured our meal we walked down to the pub for the night. We frequented the nearby White Lion or the George, or occasionally, when we felt like getting in a bit of exercise, we hoofed it 500 yards to the Fire Engine Tavern.

Steve was good company and we would sink half a dozen pints, swapping war stories, talking about this and that, before heading home to our Avondale Road lair after the last orders bell. On Saturday nights we would generally go into town and find somewhere a bit livelier, arriving back in the early hours, loud, tottering, making little sense.

Our Sunday routine saw us make a sorry attempt of domestication. One of the three of us would cook a Sunday roast for lunch, while the two others were free to make merry in the Scotchman and his Pack, a pub in town which we had designated our Sunday drinking den. At first, the cook of the day would take it seriously and stay behind to produce a decent feed, nagging and moaning if the other two came home late in a foolish state. After a couple of weekends though, the Sunday meal would just get heaved in the oven to cook while we all went out. When we returned we would eat the whole mess, burnt as it was usually, the cook making gravy to drown the meal and disguise its awfulness.

On the fifth week Mike stayed for the weekend because his wife was going away. He volunteered to cook the Sunday lunch, bought a fine leg of lamb and announced that he would be preparing roast lamb, rare, with mint sauce, roast and boiled potatoes, peas, cauliflower, carrots and gravy. The rest of us made mmmmm noises. As we left for the pub he shouted that we had better be back by 1.30 p.m. We came back at three, drunk and noisy, horsing about, lugging a case of beer we had bought from an Indian shop on the way back from the Scotchman. Mike was furious. He banged down our plates of dried and ruined food, while we sniggered and cracked open cans of beer. The next day he announced he was moving out because he could stand it no longer.

Bristol is an ancient port situated on the River Avon. Two thousand years ago, the Romans had established a place they called Portus Abonae, now known as Sea Mills, on the western edge of the city and not far from the river mouth, as a landing and distribution centre for the growing empire. There's not much there now to mark the passage of all those mail and leather cuirass-clad legionaries, arriving for a seven-year posting in the land of rain and mist; just the foundations of a villa, caged behind link fencing in the middle of a run-down housing estate. The Avon flows into the Severn estuary, the Severn having the second largest tidal range in the world. This massive movement in water causes the Avon to fill and dry, only allowing ships to move along the river at certain times of the day.

In the seventeenth century, Bristol was booming as the second busiest port in Britain after London. Although it can rightly claim to be a place of historical significance, Bristol has a chequered past as a refuge for pirates and privateers and was a world centre for slavers. The slave caves under Redland Hill still have iron rings embedded in the rock where it is believed the poor wretches were manacled while waiting for transfer to their new owners.

A lot of Bristol's wealth was founded on the slave trade. Edward Colston MP, one of Bristol's most famous sons, who endowed schools, colleges and the arts, was a merchant who made most of his money from the trade. Many of the great Regency houses in Clifton and Queen Square were homes to those directly or indirectly benefiting from the slave trade, before it was abolished in 1808. But although the slave trade was abolished, slavery itself continued. People were not permitted to have slaves in Britain (even though the conditions of much of the servant and working classes were almost as bad), but the plantations of the Caribbean colonies relied on slaves, and slavery supported the way of life in the Americas. Slavery itself was finally abolished throughout all British territory in 1839.

Bristolians tend to downplay the slavery, but are less ashamed of the city's pirate legacy from the seventeenth century, because literature and Hollywood have tended to depict pirates as loveable rogues, rather than the inhuman murdering swine that most of them were.

The most famous pirate of them all, Edward Teach, better known as Blackbeard, a real killer known for butchering his own men when he was in a bad mood, came from Bristol. The feared Woodes Rogers was also a Bristol man, although he was a privateer rather than a pirate. Essentially, a privateer was a pirate licensed by the British government to attack any ship not flying a British flag, unless they were an ally. Rogers later left privateering and turned government man to hunt down Bristol's other pirate legend, Calico Jack, the man credited with inventing the skull and crossbones flag. Calico Jack wasn't very successful as a pirate, and succumbed to Rogers without much of a fight. Rogers immediately hanged him. The last words he reputedly said to Jack before he started to swing were: 'If you had fought like a man you wouldn't be hanged like a dog'.

Calico Jack could have learned better piracy skills from Bartholomew Roberts, Black Bart, probably the most successful pirate of the era. He was a Welshman who based himself in Bristol and took nearly 500 ships in his four-year career, before being shot in the throat by a broadside of grapeshot during a battle with HMS *Swallow* off West Africa.

In Robert Louis Stephenson's *Treasure Island*, the Spyglass Inn, the setting for Long John Silver's meeting, was modelled on the Hole in the Wall Inn in Bristol. Daniel Defoe based *Robinson Crusoe* on the real life adventures of Alexander Selkirk, after meeting him in the Llandoger Trow in King Street. Selkirk had been rescued from his desert island and brought back to Bristol.

In the eighteenth century, the city fathers were concerned about Bristol losing ground to several up and coming ports, mainly Liverpool, and decided to build a complex of docks and locks and basins to trap the waters in the city centre, which would allow merchant ships to sail in and trade more efficiently. Unfortunately there was so much corruption and incompetence in the system that by the time the complex was finally completed the damage had been done and Bristol had lost its edge as a major British trading port.

In the early nineteenth century, before the ships started to move downstream to Avonmouth, Bristol had a reputation as a dangerous sailor town, particularly around the King Street and Queen Street areas. The nearby streets and alleys were crammed with taverns selling rotgut grog, the area was riven with cut-purses and footpads, crimpers and prostitutes. The tavern owners and the crooks often worked hand in hand, with the innkeeper spiking the drinks so that the sailor passed out, allowing him to be robbed at leisure. The prostitutes worked in the taverns and sometimes had a room upstairs, otherwise they used a crib within walking distance; failing that, there was always a dark alleyway.

The innkeepers, crooks and the prostitutes were all embarked on the same mission: to part the sailor from all his worldly wealth as quickly and efficiently as possible. When the job was done, the crimps appeared. Crimping or Shanghaiing was the practice of selling a drunken or drugged sailor to a shipmaster in need of crew. The crimps would buy the sailor a few drugged drinks and when he passed out they would take him down to the docks to find a short-handed shipmaster who was about to sail. The sailor would awake in the morning on a voyage to the other side of the world, broke and with his first two months' wages curtailed to pay for his acquisition costs.

Up until the early twentieth century, ocean-going vessels could be seen at the steps of the big trading houses in the city. But then the new dock complexes at Avonmouth and Portishead put paid to this, and by the early 1960s the city docks were mostly closed to commercial traffic.

So when I was there in 1980 the dock areas were mostly deserted and decaying, the buildings crumbling or in use as warehouses, the cranes were still and mute, everything awaiting eventual rescue and redevelopment.

A few of the old sailor pubs were still going, albeit functioning in a gentler manner: the Seven Stars, the Llandoger Trow, the Old Duke, the Rose of Denmark. We visited them all, Steve and me, and sometimes Colin.

The thing was, Bristol had a maritime heritage and it felt as if it had a maritime heritage; it felt like a sailor town, in parts, even if there were no ships any more because they were all downriver. I felt it right to be studying for my Master's in Bristol, it seemed … appropriate.

The classwork at the School of Maritime Studies wasn't particularly pressing. I even became irritated at the diluted pace the lecturers felt necessary to allow Mike and the other old boys to absorb information, due to their faculties having been blunted by decades out of the classroom. I didn't actually find the subject matter particularly interesting; it was just something I had to get through to move forward. The tomes of ships' business, law and insurance, and the textbooks on the physics and mathematics that underpinned hydrostatics

The Author's Master's certificate

were hardly pleasurable reading. To me, these were things to be waded through and conquered because that was what I had to do. Electronics remained a struggle, as it always had been for me. The theory of radio waves, electrostatic fields, electromagnetic propagation and the ionosphere, all the knowledge was bruted into me, painfully, until I contained sufficient to pass. For added spice, we advanced into electricity and magnetism. We spent twenty hours a week on ship-handling and cargo loading, stability, safety, ship management.

Master's was a big step up from the junior certificates, although the difference between all the professional certificates of competency and mainstream university learning remained as stark a contrast as it had always been. In the nautical colleges there was no participatory aspect, no invitation to contribute, no moulding of the mind, no group reflection, no intellectual debriefs. There was no time for related pursuits or discussions, there was no time for us to find our intellectual kernel. There was no time. We were like feed-hoppers. The lecturers pried open our minds and loaded us; information was poured in like grain into a hold. We had to absorb everything we were fed, we had to process, understand, file, recall, regurgitate.

All learning is remembering, to a greater or lesser extent, but the Master's was a matter of remembering a vast range of complex and diverse matter over a relatively short period of time. The working day at the School of Maritime Studies was eight hours, with the expectation that we would also spend a couple of hours in the evening, to test that we had properly taken the day's load on board. We were also expected to spend half a day at the weekend in study, increasing to a full day in the second half of the course. Every day was a fresh dump of knowledge, another brick in the hod.

Navigation was the mainstay subject in the junior certificates, Second Mate's and First Mate's, but was largely ignored for the Master's because we were expected to have absorbed all of that by now. Some of the more obscure supporting mathematics cropped up from time to time, and we honed up on the edges where we might have missed out. The main purpose of this seemed to be to make sure the navigator didn't put one over on the ship's master. We analysed the Marc St Hilaire intercept method of navigation, and compared it with obtaining longitude by use of the chronometer, 'long by chron' as it was playfully known. We made sure we understood the shortcomings of the ex-meridian method and of rapid sight reduction tables for star sight navigation. When it came to navigation, no junior officer was going to outwit us.

Steve was brighter than me, which was blessing and a curse. He had dropped out of Durham University because it bored him and he could absorb the morning's lectures in Bristol with his eyes shut. It was a blessing because I always had someone to lean on and call on whenever I was baffled, which was frequently; it was a curse because Steve liked to drink, and he drank more when he was bored.

We often went for a pint at lunchtime, usually to the Royal Oak on the corner of Gloucester Road. A pint could turn into two then six, and we would stumble out at three o'clock, unfit to return to college. The next day Steve would borrow someone's notes and quickly absorb the previous afternoon's work, unlike me, who would flounder for a week until I caught up. The Royal Oak was a bad place to go; it was the hangout for Bristol-based officers who were home on leave and who had plenty of time on their hands. The sessions would be prolonged, the drinking competitive. Whenever I called in and saw the crowd gathered at the end of the bar I grimaced because I knew that the rest of the college day would be written off.

I made myself pursue other things for a couple of days of the week and joined a boxing gym near the arches in Cheltenham Road, where I was racked by the owner, Grif, a merciless and mean man who thought everyone was a namby-pamby apart from him. He worked me to the point where I felt tears spring into my eyes; on one occasion I thought I was dying. I grew to hate Grif. Some days I could have killed him if he hadn't taken all my strength, sometimes I could hardly walk the following day. It didn't make me any fitter – I was already fit – but it stopped me declining, it stopped me getting fat and it kept me out of the pub, where I would otherwise have been.

We had a few class parties, wild affairs where the married men let their hair down, drank too much and acted outrageously. Steve and I didn't have to change our habits. We just acted normally, fitting in well.

We had a nasty turn with the law one evening after one such event, one I look back on in shame among the many. The lunchtime drinking session had morphed into a party at someone's house, then out to the pub again and into the night. Steve made a mistake in deciding to drive us home to our flat after it had all wound down. He ran the car up a roundabout off the Ashley Down Road, where it stuck in the grass, tyres spinning. I got out and pushed while Steve raced the wheels until the car suddenly shot backwards and across the road into a billboard. The billboard fell over onto the car, I pushed it off, jumped in and we roared away. We saw a police car spin round the roundabout to chase us. Steve drove like a demon, I shouted encouragement. We made it back to the flat ahead of the police car, leapt out and ran upstairs. We grabbed cans of beer from our stock, opened six and poured them down the sink. The policemen started beating on the door two minutes later. We leaned out the window and called down to ask what they wanted. They were angry, they wanted to come in. We asked why.

They screamed: "Let us in!"

Neighbours appeared in windows.

Holding a can of beer each, we let the police in. They were furious. They wanted to know who was driving.

Steve said: "Me. Why?"

They said: "Because you're drunk."

Steve said: "I know."

They looked confused.

"I'm drunk now. That's because I'm drinking." He held up his can of beer. "But I wasn't drunk when I was driving."

Outraged, they said he couldn't have drunk that much since he had only arrived back at the flat just before them. Steve said he was a quick drinker. They demanded to see the evidence. We showed them the empty cans in the bin. They were apoplectic, they raged and threatened, then stamped out muttering dark menace. We heard one fall over the engine parts and curse.

☆　☆　☆

Master of a ship. I wasn't sure I would ever make the grade, if I would stay at sea or even if I would live to see the possibility. But I still wanted my Master's Certificate, I wanted to know that I *could* do it. The ship's master, the captain, the Old Man, the person who stands on top of the pyramid, running a ten-man coaster or a forty-man general cargo ship or a passenger liner with two thousand souls aboard. Master is the pinnacle of achievement at sea.

I was two steps down as second mate, but soon I would be chief mate, one step down, nudging up against the top rung. When that happened, I would soon start to be imbued and tainted with the measure of the bitterness that every chief mate feels. I knew this would happen no matter how hard I tried; the bitterness where the chief mate says to the Old Man, without speaking the words, 'I'm carrying you.'

Every chief mate I had ever sailed with had the glint in his eye that said that he thought he was really doing all the work. The Old Man just glad-handed the port officials and the pilot and the company superintendent; the Old Man built his alliance with the chief engineer, the Old Man appeared on the bridge at the glory times, to take over from the officer of the watch, even from the chief mate. The chief mate ran the crew and organised the cargo and maintained the ship and kept everyone safe and kept the ship working, while the Old Man boozed and told tall tales and took the credit for everything. And the longer the chief mate stayed a chief mate, the more work he shouldered in an ever more stoic manner, while the

Old Man stole all the glory. The less credit the chief mate took, the more he smouldered, the more embittered he became, while the Old Man took the glory. I would be chief mate, soon, but would I be like that? I vowed 'Never!' but in my heart I knew I probably would.

The Old Man has no friends. The 'loneliness of command' it's called. There are plenty of people around, but it's a matter of having no friends, nor the possibility of making any. The chief engineer tends to be the Old Man's premiere drinking buddy, but most chief engineers hold a slight reservoir of bitterness themselves because the purple edge to their gold braid is testament to the fact that they can never become top dog, never command a ship, not if they stayed at sea for a hundred years.

The chief mate is fairly close to the Old Man, but he can never win an argument or over-rule a decision or set the direction of travel, except in a sly and manipulative way, because he is the direct subordinate. At times the chief mate feels like bashing the Old Man over the head, but he has to accept the situation, he has to grin and bear it; and then take out his frustration on the second mate, who takes his out on the third mate, who takes out his on the cadets. And so the world turns.

The best time for the Old Man, the very best, is when he meets another Old Man, when a sister ship is in port at the same time, or when someone organises an inter-ship party. When that happened we would all group together in our rankings: I would drink with the other second mate and third mate, the two chief engineers would get together, as would the junior engineers as would the cadets. And we would all drink too much and try and out-bullshit each other. The two Old Men would have a great time, as equals, it was as if their chains had been struck. Those occasions apart, the Old Man sits on top of the pyramid, with the point of it stuck up his arse as someone described it to me once, always alone and aloof, wanting to be there, but wanting to be somewhere else because of all the pain and loneliness. Because when it comes down to it, someone has to say the final word, which can save ship from disaster or carry it into peril, or make a successful voyage or a commercial disaster, or make life passable or a misery for everyone on board. And that man has no friends. And so I went through the course, focused on getting to the next level, focused on getting myself into a position in life so as to have the pyramid stuck up my arse.

Taking the Master's was different from the other professional examinations I had taken. The Master's was more serious work for a more serious job. I was crossing a new bridge to a new land. If I passed I could stay at sea and battle for the top, or leave the sea with a sense of pride and achievement. And that was it, I realised. After all my years at sea, all my adventures and all my dissolute ways, obtaining my 'Certificate of Competency as Master of a Foreign-Going Ship', would finally make me proud.

The first term crept into the second, and the work was loaded onto us. I knew what I would do, I knew what my technique would be, it had worked for me for the past two examinations and it would work again, I would leave the course six weeks before the end and do it alone.

Things changed in the flat in the second term, which gave me a push. Steve's Japanese girlfriend, Misaki, came to stay. Steve had been looking sheepish towards the end of the first term and after a couple of beers one evening he finally blurted out that Misaki was on her way over and would be moving in. He asked me if we could exchange rooms so he could have the big one at the front. That was fine with me, and at the end of the term I moved across into the smaller back room, on a much lower rent. Steve had to pay a double share as well as the cost of the larger space. At first, things carried on much the same.

Misaki spoke very little English and kept to herself, Steve and I still went out to the George most nights at first. As time wore on, though, I could see that Misaki had prepared his harness and was starting to pull on the reins. Steve began to stay in more. Misaki didn't particularly like me or Colin, probably thinking us a corrupting influence. I wondered what she thought of the grubby den she found herself in. The Japanese live in a much cleaner manner than the British – and, frankly, most British people live in a far cleaner manner than we did in our hovel in Avondale Road.

Steve's reining in came at the right time. It was time for me to go for gold. The Master's course was nearing the end; the last six weeks would be taken up with a few bits of tidying up and then hard revision. The dull candidates had dropped out by this time, disappearing without announcement in shame and frustration. Mike was long gone, as were the rest of his group. The class was down to nine men. My move made it eight.

I purloined the last eight years' examination papers, dozens and dozens of them for all of the subjects. I also had all the answers. My day was spent in the centre of Bristol in the big main library on College Green. I arrived when the library opened, and when I left I was usually last man out. I did four exams a day, two in the morning, two in the afternoon, every day, day after day. On Saturdays I would mark them all, note what I had done wrong, making sure I did it right when the exam came up again in the rota I'd created. When I was baffled, Steve would help me out. When I had done all the papers twice I booked my exam in London, then did all the papers again and again and again.

Saturday night was the night I relaxed, on the town with someone from the college. We followed the usual round: several pubs, a club, drinking, dancing, girls, late, late nights, overdoing it, forcing a good time, making fools of ourselves. On Sunday mornings I was wounded, torpid, hung-over, desperate to rest my overstretched brain. We still had our Sunday lunchtime outings together at the Scotchman, but now Misaki stayed behind to cook and we never dared return late.

London: my examination home. London was where I came to take my Certificate of Competency examinations, regardless of which college I was attending. The examinations took place in the Mercantile Marine Office in Ensign Street in east London, a proud Victorian edifice largely unchanged since it had been erected in 1893. It had witnessed the Zeppelin attacks in September of 1915, it had seen the rioters come streaming past as Oswald Mosley's fascists battled the coalition of Socialists, Irish, Jews, Anarchists and Communists in the big Cable Street riots in the 1930s, it seen the Luftwaffe strikes in the 1940s and watched the city burn.

The building didn't bear any scars itself from when the city was being bombed and burnt and smashed up around it. The outside was polished grey and black stone, big windows, uninviting, harsh. The inside was typical of a half-forgotten government building on which little or no money had been spent for as long as anyone could remember. The walls were cream or army green, gloss painted in the lower part and matt above. The floors were tiled in the corridors and laid with scuffed wooden parquet in the rooms themselves. Everywhere echoed. In the rooms there was a scattering of old furniture fit only for bonfires and government buildings. The atmosphere was the cloying heaviness that spoke of old people set in their ways, a sameness in their working pattern from which they would never change, of people who spent their lives looking over their shoulders at how good life had once been, never looking ahead at what was coming towards them. The only way to break the ring was to close the building, which everyone knew was the end game, but in the meantime it continued as it always had done.

I climbed the four steps and went under the faux Doric frieze and into the small smelly foyer to hand in my examination slip and obtain my place for the week, one exam in the morning, one in the afternoon, three unbroken hours for each. A wizened man who had forgotten how to smile after his boyhood had passed checked my particulars, gave me my confirmation papers.

A dozen of us were herded into the big examination hall and sat at our small desks in our hard chairs, with the big clock thudding every minute and the invigilators prowling, ever watchful for our cheating. Although the electronic calculator was becoming more and more common in the workplace it was still regarded as an instrument of the devil by the examiners, and we had to use *Norie's Nautical Tables*, a huge black volume, pages and pages of logarithmic tables, of tables on spherical trigonometry. *Norie's* was traverse tables and altitude-azimuth tables and haversine tables and ex-meridian tables, there were tables of hour angles and tables of meridional parts. Tables for everything, including the mightiest of them all: the 'logs of trig functions' tables, which no one in the world used. There was everything a deck officer could want and much more; there were tables I couldn't even understand, and I had been navigating for six years. The invigilators would randomly pick up a copy of *Norie's* from someone's desk to see if they had secreted any information.

My heart pounded when they picked up mine in case they found some scribble from years back and interpreted it as a crib sheet. When I had taken my First Mate's Certificate someone was removed from the examination for cheating. The invigilators marched the poor soul to the front of the class and lectured him in vicious whispers before tearing up his papers and pointing towards the door. I remember him trudging across the room, his face a mask of shame and abject humiliation.

The oral examination was far longer and more testing than I had been used to. Three examiners in a panel. The theatrics employed in testing the junior officers was no longer in evidence. None of the examiners adopted the persona of the bully, the bad-tempered man, the kind one; this was all business. The grilling was intense, designed to uncover real knowledge and understanding, to press for weakness, to reach a determination as to whether the candidate that sat in front of them was of sufficient calibre to command a ship on the high seas. I felt myself slipping at one stage, and thought I was in danger of folding under the pressure, but recovered, as if I were a sinking vessel righting itself. I passed my orals. They shook my hand and congratulated me, and I walked out feeling battered, feeling as if I had been to war.

Two weeks later I had the letter telling me I passed the written exams, a first time pass, my first ever. I was a Master Mariner, almost. The almost was taking the Ship Captain's Medical Course, which was procedural, I wasn't going to fail.

I went back to Bristol to celebrate and stood everyone drinks at the Royal Oak. The party went on all day and into the night. The next day I packed, said goodbye to Steve and wished him well in his exam; he was taking it the following week.

I could tell Misaki was pleased to see the back of me. Colin had already left. Misaki thought us animals, particularly after she had caught Colin urinating in the kitchen sink one evening because someone else was using the bathroom. What really disgusted her was that the sink was still full of dirty washing-up.

I drove away in my Ford Consul, my worldly possessions in the back, then took four weeks off, staying with my mother and younger brother Anthony in Oxfordshire, taking time out for jaunts.

I met a woman called Ann who was a manager of Woolworths and who owned her own house. She impressed me, as I had never met an independent professional woman like her before. Her homeowner status impressed me too – although I was easy to impress, being someone who owned absolutely nothing apart from a poor car and the items I needed to do my job: my sextant and binoculars. Ann was nice enough, but a bit grasping with a limited sense of humour. We went out in the evenings. She drove, I drank. She soon tired of my hedonistic ways, I soon tired of her seriousness. Sometimes we went back to her place but there was no spell; it was a relationship of mutual convenience.

I had a telephone call one day from Mick, the third mate I had sailed with on the *Kwangsi*, my previous ship, in the South Pacific. Mick was rounding up friends for a wild weekend in Fleetwood, where he was studying for his First Mate's Certificate. The wild weekend sounded just my cup of tea. Wild indeed: Frank was there, Frank was the ultimate wild man, another *Kwangsi* officer, the leci. Frank was confrontational. Frank could start a fight in an empty bar. We raged in Fleetwood and Manchester, oblivious to the chaos we left in our wake. We were a gang of about eight, ex-shipmates and some friends, Mick's brother, Mick's wife.

In the gang was a girl called Maggie, ex-wife of a second mate who had run off with a girl in New Zealand. Maggie and I hit it off. We drank and danced and recovered the next day, and did the same again. We vowed to keep in touch. When the weekend finished, I went back to Oxfordshire. She phoned and wrote, and phoned and wrote, she asked me to come back to Fleetwood. I thought, Hmmm, I thought, Oh-oh. I didn't know how to relate. I went back up for another weekend, it went well, we were less wild, but … it wasn't really what I wanted.

The Ship Aground pub was in Ashley Down Road, not far from the School of Maritime Studies. It was a big old scruffy pub on a hill and did a good trade in putting up college visitors. The Ship Captain's Medical Course lasted four days and was a mix of the theory and the practical.

The second officer was generally the man appointed for health and medicines. I had been serving as medical officer for several years and believed I had a good practical knowledge already. Doctors would have both scoffed and recoiled with horror at our rudimentary training. Many would have been outraged because we crammed several years of their in-depth medical knowledge into forty hours. Everyone passed the course as long as they attended, which should have been worrying in itself.

The course served its purpose though, of ensuring that a good level of understanding of emergency treatment and diagnostic ability was instilled into us. If all else failed, we always had a good book to refer to: *The Ship Captain's Medical Guide*. The week went by with the practical charade of us bandaging and strapping each other up, watching X-rated horror films of car accidents and war footage that showed mangled, burnt and detonated bodies. There was some instruction on drugs and medicines and infectious diseases. We did simulated major ops in an afternoon: drilling skulls, whipping out an appendix, applying a tourniquet to a severed leg. Great emphasis was given to the importance of carrying out operations on a solid surface, preferably the main table in the dining saloon. A table tennis table would be regarded as a poor choice because of its rickety legs.

My most memorable event during the course took place on the first evening of my stay in The Ship Aground. There were two girls serving behind the bar and I started in my usual way, showing off and acting up, getting tipsy, striving for laughs. One of the girls was unamused by my antics, one was attracted. She would become my future wife.

Annie was a calibre of person I was unused to. Most of the girls I had known were ornaments or short-term accompaniments, often tawdry, sometimes disgraceful creatures who were worse than me. It was always accepted on both sides that the relationship was fleeting. There had been exceptions, but not many and not often, and not longstanding and nothing that caused me to change my ways. Annie was different. Annie was smart and funny and attractive and decent and had morals and was unpretentious in every way. She was the sort of person I wanted to be with. And she drank and smoked and made me laugh, which was a huge bonus. She came from a good family, she had moral purpose, she was brave, she ran her own business, she worked in the pub for extra funds to keep her business afloat. I was aware of my gaping inadequacies and camouflaged them as best I could.

Whenever I reflected on relationships, which like most men was hardly ever, I theorised that my social skills in the conventional sense were stunted because of having been flung into life at sea before I had a chance to develop them. Instead of learning the procedure and protocol of meeting and greeting and courting the opposite sex, I had learned my ways in drink-fuelled encounters, with brittle laughter and stark insincerity and ambitions that rarely looked beyond the event, with any compliments only ever designed to further the immediate deed. When it came to dealing with a situation of more meaning, my wrap of insincerity was exposed. I was out of my depth, left floundering and flapping and stumbling like a minor madman.

My surface sheen earned me a first date with Annie, an evening in a pub in Clifton among civilised people, where I managed to carry myself off without incident. Whew. Then we had a second date in a country pub that didn't go so well because I disgraced myself by drinking too much and being sick. Annie gamely treated it as all good fun. It seemed to me that we were suited to each other, although I could see that she could see that I would be a poor catch unless I bucked my ideas up. I would take me another year to do this, even though she had kindled the fire that made me want the life she could give me.

⋆　⋆　⋆

I had been ashore for eleven months, the longest period ever since I was sixteen years old. I was due fifteen months' leave including my study leave. But I craved to get back to sea. I couldn't kick my heels ashore for another four months. I felt I would go mad, madder – the people ashore were driving me that way. They didn't view life the way I saw it. I found their concerns and ambitions were wretched, and if they felt the same about me I didn't notice. I didn't dislike them, I just didn't want to be with them, I didn't want to be one of them, I wanted to be at sea.

I went to London to see the personnel officer in King William Street and begged for a ship. I tried not to look desperate, although that was difficult when begging. He told me they had me pencilled in to go back in another four months; if I went now they didn't have a job as chief mate and I would have to go back as second mate, I would then get promoted either during the voyage or on the next one.

He told me what I knew already: three years previously I would have been given a chief mate's job without delay. He told me that the delay in promotion wasn't because of me; it was the downturn in British shipping. I was disappointed but felt I had no choice.

But the personnel officer said I did have a choice; I could go as chief mate in the offshore division. I told him, no thanks, I didn't fancy the idea of working in the offshore oilfields, anchor handling for oil rigs, towing rigs around, taking supplies out, hanging around as the safety vessel. I hadn't sailed on an offshore boat, but I knew plenty of people who had, who told interminable tales of the informality, the casualness, the sloppiness. I didn't want that; I want the order of a deep sea ship. To me the offshore world offered boredom and hazard, hazard and boredom, no thanks. Most of the company's offshore fleet was in the Persian Gulf, although there were a few operating in the Sunda Strait off Indonesia and off the coast of Brunei and Sarawak. The personnel officer said that if I went I would be given chief mate's position. I said that was no big deal because there was only one mate anyway, no thanks. He said the pay was higher because I would be paid as chief mate. I told him I was rich enough, I just wanted to get back to deep sea.

I accepted a deep sea second mate's position. I was so desperate to get back to deep sea that I'd have gone as the ship's dog. He told me the ship he had in mind would mean that I would be flying out to West Africa in a couple of weeks.

A couple of weeks turned out to be nearly four weeks. In the meantime I received a letter to say that my Master's Certificate had been issued and I could collect it from the Mercantile Marine Office in Ensign Street. I made the trip. My certificate looked resplendent in its gold-embossed black cover: Certificate of Competency as Master of a Foreign-Going Ship, No. 5313. The wizened man who didn't smile inked the details in my discharge book and passed it back to me with a twitch of his mouth – neither a smile nor a grimace, just a twitch.

He said: "We'll be seeing you back for Extras, then?"

I said: "Only if I'm at gunpoint."

This time he did smile.

Extra Masters was a supplementary higher certificate. It didn't confer any additional advantages in terms of being licensed to serve on ships although it allowed entry to the holy grail of membership of Trinity House, the maritime body established under Royal Charter by Henry VIII in 1514. Trinity House licenses ship's pilots and holds responsibility for lighthouses and wrecks. It also acts as a Safety at Sea body and is regarded as a forum of maritime gurus. Extra Master's was required for senior port management jobs. Extra Master's was also a must for those going down the academic path, and most maritime studies institutions liked their senior lecturers to hold one. The work involved in studying for Extras was gruelling and the standard was a far more advanced level than Master's. I had not the slightest intention of going there.

At that time, British certificates were in the process of changing. Master's Foreign-Going was going to become Deck Officer, Class 1. I was issued with a crossover certificate, Master's Foreign-Going in the front section and Deck Officer Class 1 at the back. I didn't like the Deck Officer Class 1 terminology; it sounded a poor return for eleven years slog. It didn't sound professional, it was more … industrial.

I refreshed my seagoing kit with a new blues uniform, new tropical kit. I bought chief officer epaulettes and braid in case I was promoted mid-voyage. In the meantime, as second officer with the navigation and chart work to do, I bought a new set of chart-correcting pens.

My Tamaron sextant was still working well, but my Russian binoculars had taken a knock and were continually falling out of focus. I went to the Kelvin Hughes shop in the Minories and looked at the stock. I toyed with the idea of buying a pair of Carl Zeiss, although I wasn't sold on them; they were too chunky and I wanted something a bit more robust. I cruised a few other places in London and ended up buying a pair of second-hand Francis Barker mil spec binoculars; they were so tough you could beat them with a hammer and submerge them in water without any effect.

I brought my inoculations up to date: cholera, TABT, yellow fever. West Africa was yellow fever country. The Hong Kong dollar had been sliding against the pound over the past year although I had managed to keep my financial position in check. I sent my Ford Consul to auction and achieved a disappointing price.

I twiddled my thumbs, idle and waiting, waiting at my mother's house in Oxfordshire. I waited for the post each morning, I waited for my orders. I grabbed the letters when they came each day, flung them on the table when there was nothing for me. I went round the corner to the Wheatsheaf, played dominos with the old men, played darts with the young men, talked rubbish, told tales of the sea, drank too much, tried to charm any girls that came within my orbit, then did the same the next day, and the next, while I waited for my orders.

Eventually they came: join the general cargo ship *Funing* as second officer, fly to Lagos in Nigeria in four days. Enclosed was a ticket on the British Airways flight, enclosed was a rail warrant. I whooped, I phoned the personnel department to confirm, they asked me to call in and pick up a packet of mail to take with me.

I checked all my gear, I packed. I gave my mother some money, gave my younger brother Anthony some money to go to college with, paid my bills, picked up US$500 in emergency funds, closed down my affairs, went on a couple of almighty nights out, then flew off to Lagos.

3

Dash

Murtala Muhammed airport, Lagos, eleven o'clock in the morning, the flight from London had been uneventful. The *Funing* was lying in the Bonny River in Port Harcourt, a 400-mile drive to the east, which was about fifteen hours on Nigerian roads, barring hold-ups. Or a ninety-minute flight, which the local agent was supposed to have arranged.

When I encountered my first Nigerian official, it didn't look as if I would be joining the *Funing* at all: he wouldn't let me into the country, he wouldn't let me get past the immigration desk. He took my passport and stared at it, then took my vaccination book and stared at it. He stared for a good minute then handed everything back to me, shaking his head.

"Not valid, not valid," he said.

"What do you mean, not valid?"

"I mean, not valid."

"But everything *is* valid. The passport is valid, the visa is valid, the vaccinations are valid, everything's valid. What's wrong?"

"Not valid."

"What is not valid?"

"Yellow fever."

"It is."

"It is not."

"It is."

"It is not."

"It is valid, man. I only had it done last week."

I pointed at the date. He didn't even look at it. He just stared at me with penetrating gaze.

"It is not valid. Your yellow fever is not valid. Your other vaccinations are not valid. Your passport is not valid, your visa is not valid. None of your documents are valid."

MV Funing (Courtesy of www.fotoflite.com)

We stared at each other. His eye was dark and challenging and borderline hostile. A glimmer of understanding passed across my mind.

"If your papers are not in order, you must let the next person through," he said.

I stepped aside and watched the next few people go through, which confirmed my thoughts. I got back in line. When it was my turn again I proffered my passport and vaccination book. Inside the book was a US$20 note.

The official palmed the note, stamped my passport and handed everything back to me with a short smile. "Welcome to Nigeria."

I retrieved my bag and went out into the teeming arrivals hall. There were several people waiting holding cards with names written on, but none with my name. I went to the airport bar and ordered a bottle of Star lager, watching the barman to make sure the top came off cleanly with a hiss; I didn't fancy drinking a dodgy refill.

For the next hour, I watched the airport life while waiting for the agent. The airport was crowded, chaotic and noisy, the various areas were without organisation, people pushed and shoved and shouted at each other to get what they wanted. I watched officials being bribed for little things. Heavily armed police and military occasionally wandered by, the crowd parting in front of them. The terminal had only been opened two years before but it already looked damaged, dirty, ill-treated. It looked as if it wouldn't last. The original airport had been built by the British in the Second World War as a staging post to South Africa and later became Lagos International Airport.

Nigeria was granted independence by Britain in 1960 and was gifted a completely inappropriate Westminster-style democracy, which didn't last long, tossed out in 1966 by the first of many military coups. Towards the end of the sixties there was a brutal three-year civil war when the eastern state of Biafra tried to break away. Britain, France and the Soviet Union all meddled behind the scenes, ensuring that the conflict dragged out longer than it needed to. Biafra was crushed, the people starved, and from then on Nigeria was ruled by military juntas and dictatorships, punctuated by brief stabs at civilian government which proved so corrupt and incompetent that the military soon stepped back in again.

General Murtala Muhammed was one of a string of army officers who held the reins. He was generally well thought of by the people, although not by the Biafrans, who blamed him for a number of cold-blooded killings. He was assassinated while driving to his office one day in 1976, on Friday 13th, to be succeeded by yet another army officer. Lagos Airport was renamed in his honour.

The agent eventually turned up, ambling around the hall holding a white card with my misspelt name scrawled on it: 'Simone Hale'.

The agent told me that I had missed the connecting flight to Port Harcourt, because the gate had just closed and he would now have to find me a hotel for the night. My questions as to why he was an hour late arriving to meet me just bounced off his head. We climbed into his wreck of a car and set off to town. Lagos was a mess, vehicular order was non-existent. Cars drove both on both sides of the road, the traffic lights mostly broken and those that worked ignored anyway. At junctions, no one gave way and there was an unseemly shunting for dominance. People and dogs wandered on and off the roads between the traffic, every street was jammed and we moved at walking pace. Rubbish carpeted the roads, the pavements and the grass verges: unbagged garbage, plastic waste, empty bottles, soggy heaps of paper, mud and filth and urban detritus.

We passed a man lying awkwardly on the verge not far from the airport, cars and lorries passing alarmingly close to his head. I thought he was sleeping and asked the agent why anyone would sleep there.

He shrugged and said: "Not sleeping, dead. He has been there for three days."

"How did he die?" I asked.

He shrugged. "Maybe hit by a car."

"Why hasn't the body been taken away?"

He shrugged.

In its heyday, the Ambassador Hotel would have been the place to be in: a large Edwardian building with grand porticos and large grounds. The gardens were fairly well-tended, although inside it was run down, badly. The foyer was full of loafing locals, raggedly dressed, sitting on the floor or leaning against walls, some sleeping, some smoking, some talking loudly. They stopped talking and stared at me as I stood by the reception desk while the agent bargained with the shifty-looking man on duty. I felt like an antelope on the Serengeti being eyed by the lions. The foyer smelled of vegetables and slightly of old meat. The floor was strewn with litter and the whole place looked unclean.

My room was large and the balcony looked out over a pool. I gave 5 naira to the man who carried my bag. As he was leaving he paused, then turned and said: "You must to lock your door before ten o'clock tonight and do not open it until morning."

I puzzled over this ominous warning as I had my meal in the restaurant: fish soup followed by stewed goat. Not bad.

At nine-thirty I went up to my room and obediently locked up. Not long after ten there was a tremendous racket in the corridor and a furious pounding on my door. I looked out the spy hole and saw a pair of fat women in garish clothes looking back at me, they were frightening. They beat the door and rattled the handle and shouted to let them in, promising me a good time. Other women rushed past and pounded on other doors. A couple of men strolled by, languidly. I kept the chain on and door locked. The pounding turned to kicks before eventually stopping.

I lay on the bed and read my book for a while until I heard shrieks from outside. From the balcony I could see about twenty men and girls partying in the pool, including the two heavyweights who had been trying to break down my door. Everyone was splashing and screaming at each other and having a great time. They saw me looking down and started baying like hounds. I closed and locked the balcony door and went to bed.

The morning flight to Port Harcourt was with a local airline and there was some problem with the plane. All of us passengers hung around in a group in the hot airport. No one looked irritated, just fatalistic. We eventually left at three in the afternoon; the flight was mostly full of locals, a few Europeans, some animals. It was packed and I was crushed. The smell crushed me more. When we disembarked, the Port Harcourt agent who met me said it would be dark soon and it was too late to go to the ship; we would go there in the morning.

I stayed in another hotel, outside of town, smaller and more casual than the Ambassador, built of wood with verandas running all the way round. It looked pre-war vintage, probably pre-Great War. The place was well kept although it had the feel of being on the losing side of a battle; the wood was warping, the building leaned. Even the new paint was peeling. The hotel staff told me not to leave the hotel because it was dangerous outside. I went for a short walk after dinner anyway, but there wasn't much to see, just a few roadside stalls lit by naphtha lamps and tended by people who called to me as I passed. I came to a bar that looked profoundly unsafe; idlers sat on the bench outside and watched me with flat eyes, booming music drifted from the dark within. I deliberated for a few seconds then walked on by.

Port Harcourt was one of the larger cities in Nigeria. It had been founded just before the First World War and named after Viscount Harcourt, the Secretary of State for the colonies at the time. Harcourt wasn't an admirable man. He was known as a sexual predator who was equally happy with men and women, the younger the better. He committed suicide in 1922 after being pursued in the courts for trying to bed a twelve-year-old boy. The British have founded and named cities all over Africa, although most have since had their names changed to something more African. It's ironic that a city port named after one of Britain's most notorious deviants should be one of the few to keep its founding name.

Oil has been the lifeblood of Port Harcourt since it was discovered in the Niger Delta in the late 1950s. This turned into a booming offshore industry centred on Bonny Island, at the head of the Bonny River. Port Harcourt lies about 20 miles upriver. Although it was wealthier than most other cities in Nigeria, the wealth hadn't spread to the local populace and the place was like a lot of big African cities at that time: crammed full of people, choked with traffic, filthy, corrupt and barely governable with little or no civic order. Pockets of decency were there if you looked hard enough – religious orders, striving enterprises, expatriate ventures –

but there was a sad lack of local endeavour to make things better. The name of the game was empowerment, empowerment for self and family and close kin. Everyone else could hang. I couldn't get out fast enough.

In the morning we drove down to the Bonny River. The *Funing* was upstream, and we took a small canoe with an outboard motor, I perched in the front, the agent squatted in the middle with my case. After twenty minutes we came round a bend and I could see the *Funing* a few hundred yards ahead of us, lying to anchor in the stream. At that point our engine conked out. The boatman tinkered with it for a while as we gently drifted in the quiet, then he sighed and took a paddle from the bottom of the boat. We eventually arrived at the bottom of the gangway, the boatman pushing us along the Bonny River with his paddle, me in the front of the canoe feeling like an old-time explorer. I felt as if I should have been wearing a pith helmet.

The *Funing* was an SD14 class general cargo ship. The SD14 was an unsophisticated ship of standard design which had been patented by shipbuilders Austin & Pickersgill of Sunderland. The design was well received when first launched in late 1967; some viewed its arrival as the replacement for the famed Liberty Ships that had been churned out by the thousands in the Second World War, but which were now heading for the scrapyards. Austin & Pickersgill licensed the design to other shipbuilders around the world.

A lot of seamen believe SD stands for 'Standard Design' although in fact it means 'Shelter Deck', the internal cargo deck below the main deck. SD14s started as 14,000-ton deadweight ships, but could range to over 15,000 tons. The *Funing* was one of these. It was a ship with no pretensions, nothing fancy, just a solid working vessel, four hatches forward of the accommodation and one aft. No cranes, only derricks. She could carry general cargo, bulk cargo, containers, deck cargo or a combination.

I climbed up the gangway from my canoe while one of the Chinese sailors brought up my battered globetrotter suitcase. The decks were clear; she had a full cargo of bagged cement in the holds. My cabin was a bit skimpy, no bathroom, just an uncluttered box with a single bunk, basic like everything else on the ship. The showers and toilets for the second and third mate were down the alleyway, necessitating a ten-yard stroll with a towel wrapped round me.

The second mate I was relieving had already gone, rushing off the previous day to Lagos to catch the London flight. He had left me copious handover notes, which I flicked through and then stuffed in my pocket to browse later. I went up to introduce myself to the Old Man. When I knocked on the door of his cabin the chief mate was there and they talked me through the voyage. I was signed on quickly, the Old Man offering sympathy that I wasn't getting a chief mate's berth. The chief mate speculated that I would probably be promoted and given his job when he paid off in a few months' time. I could tell the Old Man was secretly delighted that he had a second officer with a master's ticket.

The ship had loaded her cargo of cement in Rostock, to be discharged in Port Harcourt and Warri. After that there was no charter arranged, although there were rumours of

South America. The Old Man said that if nothing turned up by the time the discharge was complete then we would probably get a LEFO telegram, and we would steam to Land's End at slow revs until the owners arranged another charter. Cargo work was due to start the following day.

I went to the bridge and familiarised myself with the layout and equipment. There were two Marconi Raymark 16 radars, a Decca navigator, Sperry gyro steering system, the usual echo sounder, weather fax, direction finder. In the chartroom were all the charts of the world and all the almanacs and tables we needed. The two chronometers were there, to be wound six and a half turns every morning; the chief mate had already done them for the day. Nothing was out of the ordinary. I checked the courses that were already laid for the voyage to the Warri River and they all seemed to be in order. After the bridge I explored the rest of the ship; the main deck, foc'sle-head, the poop deck and boat decks. Then I unpacked in my cabin and went in search of the third mate, my fellow junior officer.

The people on board were generally an interesting crowd, which was always a bonus. A dull collection of fellow travellers makes for a poor voyage.

There was the Old Man, eccentric, manic, cruel, dominant. He was in his late forties, a party man, loud, boastful, intrusive, a teller of tales, a massive ego. The Old Man was either liked or loathed, not a personality to be just tolerated. As a shipmaster he was very good, one of the best I ever sailed with. He drank like a fish and this caused him authority problems from time to time. I knew him from a couple of years previously, when I had been second mate of the *Poyang*, trading in the Far East and the western part of the South Pacific. He had taken over from a quiet and nervous captain – the change was electric. The Old Man had mastered a form of mind control. After staying up drinking until the early hours of the morning, he would go to his cabin, in a slurred and terrible state, sit down on the deck, place his fingers on his temples and put himself into a meditative trance, 'deep sleep' he called it. After an hour he would snap awake, fully rested and fit for the day's work, sober as a judge.

I was deeply envious of this talent and thought how much better my boozy life would be if I too could accomplish the trick of deep sleep. I tried several times but always failed, usually falling into a drunken slumber within a few minutes, keeling over and bashing my head on the deck.

The chief mate was a couple of years younger than the Old Man and was not his greatest fan, seeing him as unprofessional, as a fool and a drinker, deep sleep trick or not. He styled and stereotyped himself in almost comic fashion as the image of the ship's mate of popular imagination. Sometimes I wondered whether his adopted persona might be in secret jest. He had grown a huge beard, smoked a pipe, drank rum and had an 'argh, Jim lad' conversational style that only encompassed tales of the sea. He was critical of those who he believed didn't give their heart and soul into the life. He was contemptuous of fools.

I moved between liking and disliking the man. I found his obsessive recounting of sea stories paralysingly dull, and his yo-ho-ho rollicking ship's mate image hard to take for any length of time. I was also repulsed and irrationally irritated by the flecks of food and tobacco that always peppered his beard. On the plus side though, the chief mate did his job to the very best of his ability and would go out of his way help others; he was fundamentally a decent man. His wife was sailing with him, a New Zealand girl, Susan, small, pretty, eager to please, much younger than him. She did her best to participate in shipboard life although she floundered from time to time. I always thought she was quite brave in the way she tolerated our harsh life and often foolish antics.

Duncan was the third mate and we became good friends. Just as well, as the second and third mate worked together a lot and needed to get on. Duncan was Scottish, from Greenock, a couple of years younger than me, tall, red-headed, quietly spoken, witty, sarcastic, interesting and always game. Some people are just good company, and Duncan was one of those. We had a lot in common: we both liked our life at sea at a time when it was fashionable to deride it, we were both single, we both drank too much and we were apt to make fools of ourselves. Later in the voyage we had adventures together ashore, and during our long stay on the West African coast we banded against the misfortunes that started to rain down on the ship.

Peter the leci was a Geordie, an older man, in his mid-thirties. He had an accent so thick we told him he needed to speak with sub-titles. Duncan and I mocked his Geordiness; we said Geordies weren't proper Brits and shouldn't be issued with British passports. We said Geordies were backward. We said that Geordies weren't properly evolved.

Peter would act like a beast, chasing the local African girls that most of us steered clear of. He drank too much and often became maudlin about home, occasionally weeping. We told him he was lucky to be leaving Geordieland behind. He took most things in his stride, gave as good as he got and was fine company.

Peter the second engineer was a small man with a large nose. Most people called him Peter the second, to distinguish him from Peter the leci, but Duncan called him Hymie because of his huge hooter. I could tell the name irritated him, even though he concealed it well. Peter the second was the size of a hobbit, but was broad and tough, as second engineers have to be.

The second engineer is the engine-room equivalent of the chief mate. In my experience, second engineers tended to be quiet and morose, probably because they were flattened on a daily basis by the intense work schedule they found themselves under, all of which was carried out in the baking, deafening inferno of the engine room. Second engineers were always dirty, always tired, always cynical, always in a bad mood. Often they were bullies. Their personality usually perked up again when promoted to chief engineer though – with relief, I would imagine, now that the worst officer job aboard ship was behind them. Peter the second was different to the more typical second engineer in that he was bright and loud and noisy, always wanting to join in. Duncan took an unreasonable dislike to Peter and mocked and goaded him continuously, although I didn't find him bad company at all.

Then there was the chief engineer, the oldest man on board, an old-style company man. He had been chief for years and most of his tales were of the 'those were the good old days' variety, which never impressed me as I was always a firm believer in that *these* were the good old days. Still, the chief was good company, if a bit petulant from time to time. He liked to socialise, liked to drink, laughed a lot and was rarely in a bad mood. He was another Scotsman, but from the Edinburgh side. The chief talked about his wife a lot, who usually accompanied him at sea; she would apparently be joining later in the voyage. Others muttered that the chief's freedom would be curtailed the moment she came on board and we would see a different character. She was known for having a large thumb under which the chief lived his life.

That was the European complement, seven of us. The rest of the officers were Hong Kong Chinese. There were no cadets. The Hong Kong officers all had adopted English names: Lee Yeung Kwai the radio officer was David, Han Chin Fong the third engineer was Malcom, the fourth engineer was Jimmy. Sparks was a regular attendee in the bar, the others were occasional. There were three fifth engineers who we rarely saw.

The crew were all Hong Kong Chinese, Cantonese. Most of them were long-serving company men. The *Funing* had been built for the company by Austin & Pickersgill three years earlier, and a lot of the crew had been on board since then, with an occasional short break whenever the ship called into Hong Kong. I had sailed mostly with British crews for my first seven years at sea but had been with Chinese ever since. From the officer's perspective, there were pros and cons for each.

British crews were mostly younger and fitter and many officers believed they could be better relied upon if there was a crisis such as a fire or collision or storm at sea that was getting the better of the vessel. On the other side of the coin, British crews tended to be harder to manage, less disciplined; they fought more, got drunk when they could and caused havoc. A lot of officers didn't like to sail with British crews because of this.

Chinese crews were usually older, better mannered and didn't cause that much trouble. On the rare occasions they did cause trouble it could manifest itself as an uncontrolled craziness, made more flamboyant with knives and hatchets and other serious weapons. Some said the Hong Kong Chinese were better seaman, although I thought the opposite in fact. The Chinese were good seaman, often appearing better than they were because they stayed on the same ship for years and so became very familiar with every working part. All in all, I was equally comfortable with both British and Chinese crews. The *Funing* crew were a sound enough bunch, and I already knew a couple of them, who had transferred in from other ships in the fleet.

The ship's complement was thirty-eight souls in total, made up of fourteen officers and twenty-four crew, which was a fairly healthy size. At that time manning levels of ships were dropping due to the squeeze in the shipping markets and to increasing technology. Not that we had much new technology on the *Funing* of course, but we knew it existed.

The next morning, grey and muggy, the discharging of the cement started. We were due to unload one-third of our cargo in Port Harcourt and the balance in Warri. Four lighters tied up alongside in the mid-morning, two on either side of the ship. The plan was to have three discharge gangs starting at eight in the morning and working until six in the evening. One gang would then come on and work into the night, finishing at two o'clock in the morning. The supercargo came aboard with them, a Swiss national who had been in West Africa for half his life.

Duncan and I decided we would do a cargo watch shift of twenty-four-hour supervision from 14:00. The person on duty would thus have six hours off to sleep, between 02:00 and

08:00. We discussed this with the chief mate, who was quite happy with the plan. On the first day we had a one-hour overlap – thirty minutes of Duncan's time and thirty minutes of mine – so he could show me the ship's working gear.

The *Funing* may have been a basic SD14 vessel with the minimum equipment, but she was relatively new and in good condition. The five hatches had modern MacGregor type steel hatch covers, unlike older ships with their wooden hatch boards. MacGregor hatch covers were pulled open by wires, with each section moving along on rollers before folding into a well. This made it easy to open and close the hatches, as we didn't have to rig cumbersome hatch tents to keep out the rain when the gangs knocked off; it was just a case of connecting a wire from the winch and pulling the covers closed. MacGregor hatches were one of the few, if the only, modern ship facilities on the *Funing*.

Everything else was pretty much the same ship design as had existed for the past few decades. There was a tween deck (a small cargo deck below the main deck) in each hold; there were four conventional derricks to each hold; there were no freezers, no side tanks for palm oil or similar, just a couple of caged areas where valuables could be locked up. If you knew general cargo ships, as I did, there wasn't much to master.

The crew had all the derricks rigged and ready for the start. The supercargo held a conference of a sort with the chief mate, although it was barely worth it as there wasn't much planning involved in taking out a homogenous cargo of bagged cement. Nets would be lowered into the hold, and the gang would sling bags into it until full, then signal to the winch man, who would heave the full net out of the hatch, swing it out over the side and lower it into the cargo lighter.

Two derricks worked in tandem over each hatch, one rigged with a wire and hook to go straight up and down, the other to pull the net across. The up and down man would lift the full net above the hatch coamings, at which point the second winch man would tighten his wire and pull the netload across the deck. When it was over the ship's rails and above the lighter, both winches would slacken off and the cargo would be lowered into the barge. This was known as a union purchase rig.

A good gang, with well-coordinated winch man, could work a union purchase rig slickly. Not so our lot in Port Harcourt. They were badly trained, probably untrained, rattling away too fast, yanking the cargo out, jerking it across the deck and letting the nets plummet downwards into the lighters below. We were forever shouting at them and complaining to the foreman that they were going to damage both the cargo and the ship's gear. The foreman nodded and promised improvement, which never materialised. The chief mate lodged a written complaint with the supercargo after a couple of days, to support any subsequent damage claim.

It wasn't an enviable job, slinging bags of cement in a ship's hold. The bad thing about working with cement is that you get cement burns. The dry cement gets onto skin that's moist with sweat, add a bit of friction and presto, an irritating rash. When I was a cadet, one of the worst jobs I ever had was cement-washing the fresh-water tanks. Apart from the stifling heat and the arm-breaking work, splodges of cement would fall all over me as I pasted it onto the tank sides with a brush, and at the end of the day I was covered in painfully itching red weals.

I hated working with cement ever since. It was oppressively hot in the holds of the *Funing* and everyone in the gang was stripped down to a pair of shorts. At the start of the shift they all had he natural ebony blackness of the West African but by the end they all had a grey-white covering of cement dust, like albinos or ghosts.

It rained in the afternoons, which called a swift halt to the work because rain and cement don't mix. We hurriedly pulled the hatch covers across and waited out the downpour. The rain started with warning splashes the size of half-crowns, followed by heavy vertical rods of water that lasted a couple of hours. On the lighters the crew pulled canvas covers over the open holds. We waited out the rain under cover, the gangs in the hatch entrance housing, me and the duty watchman on the accommodation deck under the overhang, all of us watching the rain come sheeting down. The air was heavy and mossy and humid, with a thick smell of vegetation. Once the rain passed we opened up and carried on, although sometimes the downpour was prolonged and we would only get a few hours of work done in the day.

The gangs would try and bum cigarettes, which I would usually give them, after which they would ask to go inside the accommodation to get dry, which I would refuse to allow.

They occasionally tried to intimidate me into letting them in by declaring: "We are human beings too you know, white man."

"I know, I know," I said, "but the accommodation area is private, not public. It is where we live." Thinking 'you're thieving human beings too'.

Nigeria was notorious for people who would strip a ship bare given the opportunity. Shortly before I joined, the *Funing* had suffered a raid while waiting outside the mouth of the Bonny River. A crowd of men in two fast launches tried to board but the chief mate had forewarning and organised the crew who saw them off with fire hoses, blasting the men with jets of water as they tried to climb the anchor chain, cutting the launch ropes, which had been flung over the main-deck rails with grapples.

The three day gangs diminished into two working between the rain showers. There was one night gang, working every other night. The work slowed and slowed. There was little to do, just amble around, close the hatches when the rains came, and watch the standard of work to intervene if it became so slapdash as to cause damage to the cargo or the ship's gear. I watched the tallymen counting each netload that went out. Their recording was flawed, never accounting for the fact that some slings were full and some were half-empty; they just made an assumption that every sling contained the same number of bags.

Women in canoes paddled around the ship selling sugar cane, oblivious to the rain. I bought some but found it too tough to gnaw. Some of the women were selling themselves; they were universally huge and generally repellent, although several of the crew took up the challenge.

In between the deck watches I pottered on the bridge, doing chart corrections to keep the portfolio up to date, running off courses along the African coast and up to the Canaries, but speculatively because we didn't know where we were bound next. Europe seemed a good bet, which meant that the courses to the Canaries were good, although there was a continuing rumour that we might go west to South America, which would require a completely different line. We were going to be on the African coast for at least six weeks and so would be unlikely to know about the next voyage for some time yet.

We spent our off times in the bar, as men did on ships, drinking our stock and hoping we would be able to replenish it with something reasonable. The bar on the *Funing* was of a good size, the proportion of two double cabins; it was purpose-built and well appointed. Most of the action took place at the bar end, naturally, where we gathered and drank and whiled the time away. The main body of the place had scattered chairs and tables where we played cards and games and where we lined up the chairs on film nights. There were half a dozen bar stools and a bench seat near the outer bulkhead. A couple of us were generally positioned behind the bar itself, which allowed the congregation to gather quite comfortably. Beer and gin were the drinks of the day, apart from the chief mate with his rum. The beer we were drinking, its particular quality, its comparative quality, its nationality, its cost and the speculation of what the next beer we would take on board would be, hogged a disproportionate part of shipboard discussion.

After a fortnight, we weighed anchor and sailed for the Warri River, a day's run distant along the Nigerian coast, west into the Gulf of Guinea, then north. From the European perspective, the West African coast has been christened with various names: the Slave Coast, the Gold Coast, the Fever Coast, the White Man's Grave. West Africa was never regarded as a gentle part of the world to visit. But then, from the perspective of the indigenous peoples, the last few hundred years have been anything but gentle: centuries-old warring among different tribal factions, pillaging by Arab slavers then by European and American slavers, and then exploitation by the colonial powers and, more recently, by the post-colonial rulers.

The Arabs have been taking slaves from that part of Africa for a thousand years. The Europeans were late-comers, with the Portuguese getting the credit for kick-starting the industry in the 1430s, ferrying unwilling workers to the New World, mainly Brazil. Slaving took an upturn in the 1600s when the other European powers joined in with a vengeance, with over two million souls being shipped to South America and the Caribbean between 1600 and 1700. Then it really exploded: the labour-hungry plantations of the Caribbean and newly emerging North America sucked slaves in. Nearly eight million made the transatlantic crossing in the eighteenth century.

The African slave trade peaked at the start of the nineteenth century, then went into rapid decline as the British and then the other European powers abolished slavery anywhere on their territory. The American Civil War finished it off for good in the western world, although Arab slave traders continued much as before and would do for some time, servicing the Islamic world.

In the late nineteenth century land rush, almost the whole continent of Africa was snapped up by the European powers, falling over each other in the chase for the gold-rich, mineral-rich, timber-rich continent. Britain ended up with the lion's share of eastern and southern Africa and a few chunks in the west. The French bagged the major part of the central and western parts, Belgium took the Congo and Rwanda, the Portuguese had Angola and Mozambique. The Germans were late starters although the Kaiser managed to snaffle Tanganyika, Togoland and South-West Africa, although those were later confiscated as a penance for losing the Great War. The Italians and Spanish, who apparently didn't want to stray too far from home, took ownership of a few dusty classical leftovers. Only Ethiopia and Liberia escaped permanent colonisation, but even Ethiopia (then Abyssinia) was occupied by Mussolini's Italians for a few years in the late thirties, while Liberia, founded by a private US colonisation society in the early nineteenth century, gained independence in 1847 and has somehow managed to retain its independence ever since.

Borders were drawn by the colonial powers without regard to tribal areas or indigenous historical precedence: along rivers, on an arbitrary basis along lines of latitude and longitude, along highways and byways and mountain ranges and for the convenience of the new rulers. There was a lot of land trading between the occupying powers: this plateau for that plain, this coastal stretch for that forest. And then it was done, Africa was 'owned' by Europe.

The whole continent was carved up over about twenty-five years and in the wake of the politicians and carpetbaggers came the missionaries, who thought it was time to teach the Africans to be civilised and organised and God-fearing. Many Africans didn't take too keenly to being given the civilised virtues of shoes, hats, syphilis, timetables, alcoholism, organised worship and irregular verbs. Most colonialists felt they were stupid and ungrateful. The Africans squabbled with their new masters, the masters squabbled with each other, alliances and deceptions abounded. Wars broke out, rebellions, a rage of massacres.

But there were a lot more problems in Africa than just the bickering caused and stimulated by European avarice. There was also malaria, blackwater fever, sleeping sickness, yellow fever, smallpox, typhoid, cholera, rickets, starvation, genocide, illiteracy, penurious medicine, public executions, casual cruelty, organised cruelty, subjugation, infant mortality, short life spans and historical tribal conflict. It was a challenging continent to live in, a challenging continent to visit.

The British acted badly in the Second Boer War in South Africa, interning the civilian population; the French exercised their troops by gunning down the Fon of Dahomey's army in West Africa; the Portuguese brutally subdued the Shangana to near-extinction in East Africa; the Germans used Paul Mauser's new rifle to settle the arguments wherever they went.

Until the 1930s, gold and diamonds and minerals were on the menu as the main course in West Africa, with a side helping of hardwood. Then came the dessert, oil. Across West Africa, the French were the dominant colonial power, taking sweeping ownership of most of the area – interrupted by the British, as was so often the case, who had Sierra Leone, the Gold Coast (modern-day Ghana), Gambia and the largest jewel of them all, Nigeria.

Nigeria, a huge country, the most populous in Africa, has been bestowed with enormous natural gifts: oil and gas, metal commodities, a fertile soil. It remains fashionable to stereotype the colonial powers as doing nothing but bad, although in actual fact Britain's governance of Nigeria was more enlightened than the modern-day Nigerians like to admit. In 1960, when Britain handed over the country to the first generation of African leaders, there was law and order, road and rail links, working ports, a school system, a functioning civil service and a vibrant economy.

Since that time Nigeria has endured corruption and mismanagement to such heroically high levels that by the time I was there in 1981 the economy and the standard of living had been dragged well below pre-independence levels. The government and its mouthpieces blamed Britain, blamed the west, blamed the world at large, blamed the weather and blamed anyone and everyone but themselves, while raping the country on a Brobdingnagian scale. The populace hadn't had it so bad since the Arab slave traders had arrived on the scene a thousand years before. The government officials had a below average sense of humour and an above average sensitivity to any perceived slight, and so we were under orders to tread very carefully in our dealings with all Nigerians.

The trip round to Warri was uneventful. We were on guard as we left the mouth of the Bonny River due to the occasional high-speed piracy from fast launches, but nothing occurred. We kept a good distance off the coast, which was notorious for shifting sands and uncharted rocks. The traffic was light. Occasionally we passed a coastal ferry or a small cargo ship and once a Palm Line ship, the *Ikeja Palm*, passing close down our port side. I talked to her second mate on the VHF; she was bound for Port Harcourt to pick up palm oil and timber for London and then she was being sold. We both bemoaned the decline of the British merchant fleet.

The Old Man was edgy and kept coming up to the bridge to pace around and check the position. He didn't know the waters. He was a Far East man, he was out of his comfort zone in an unfamiliar and weakly charted area. He snapped at me for sending the quartermaster up to wash down the monkey island, saying that he wanted a man on the bridge wing at all times. He also wanted the echo sounder on to take soundings, with positions on the chart every twenty minutes. There were few lighthouses on the coast and when night fell the Old Man pulled us further away to the south and west, keeping well off the land until sunrise.

The Warri River: thick, sluggish, the colour of workman's tea, cluttered with debris and detritus being washed towards the Atlantic, branches, vines, clumps of vegetation, whole trees, human refuse. We moored to two buoys, one fore and the other aft, several ropes at either end to hold us in the stream. The pilot who took us up the river was an ancient Brit with an African understudy. The pilot looked mildly drunk, and his understudy looked as if he had no earthly idea what he was doing. I prayed that on the way out we would get the Brit, drunk or not.

The estimate for our stay in port, the optimistic estimate that no one believed, was three weeks. The work started on the second day. The pace was even more sluggish than the Warri River, the gangs moving in unenthusiastic slow motion. The pattern was the same as Port Harcourt in that we had lighters moored along both sides of the ship and the cargo was discharged by the netload. Each gang consisted of fourteen men: five in the hold loading the nets, five in the lighter receiving the cargo and stacking it, two winch men, and one signaller who told the winch men to pick up, slack off and stop. That totalled thirteen; the fourteenth was the gang foreman, who didn't do much except wander between the different workers, giving unnecessary interference from time to time. We started with two day gangs that worked from eight in the morning until five in the afternoon and one early night gang that worked from five until midnight. We were promised more gangs but they never materialised.

There was a host of other people present during the day: foremen, tallymen, union officials, port management officials, shippers' representatives, receivers' representatives, customs officials, immigration officials and sundry others who had no apparent purpose. They all wanted to have a base within the ship, which we refused, so they cluttered up the deck and lay under the accommodation overhangs, chatting, smoking, sleeping. No one actually appeared to do very much.

We were concerned about pilferage, so rife on the Nigerian coast. No one was going to walk off with a bag of cement, but an open cabin would be ripe for looting. We kept the doors into the accommodation locked at all times, with the exception of one way in, which had a crew member on permanent guard. Men tried to gain entry with a persistence that was admirable, telling outrageous tales in their endeavours:

"I am from the Harbour Office and I need to see the captain."

"I am a health inspector and I need to inspect the ship for diseases."

"The chief engineer has asked to see me. It's OK, you do not need to show me the way."

"I am an old friend of the chief officer; he is expecting me."

"I am here to see the chief steward to take the order for stores."

"I am the cargo foreman and I need a cabin as an office."

And so on and so on. They were all politely turned away, which caused them to argue their case for a couple of minutes, before walking away to concoct another plan.

The Swiss supercargo had sailed with us on the *Funing* along the coast from Port Harcourt to get the work started, and announced that he would be leaving on the fourth day and his duties would be taken on by someone else based locally.

On the morning of the fourth day, the supercargo left. On the afternoon of the fourth day the ship was arrested. Two launches pulled up below the gangway and shouted for the duty officer, which was me. I looked over the side and asked what they wanted. Both launches were packed with officials, mostly in uniform, senior-looking people: they had enough gold braid between them to make a trip to the Red Sea souks worthwhile.

One shouted up: "Your ship is being arrested. I am the chief of police and I have enforcement papers."

Another: "I am the chief customs officer and I have the affixment notice." Whatever that was.

"I have the lien," said the customs officer

"I am the cargo receivers' legal representative and I have the counter lien."

They bickered.

"I am the shippers' agent and I have the papers of entitlement."

"I have the warrant of arrest," said the chief of police.

"I have the writ," said another.

"I have the notice of internment," said another.

This continued; they vied among each other as to who had the most important papers and who was the most important person. It looked serious, I told the gangway watchman to go and ask the chief officer and the captain to come to the gangway, 'quick, quick'.

The *Funing* was arrested. A copy of the writ was fixed to the mast, in time-honoured fashion. All the officials went up to the Old Man's cabin for a mighty conference. Cargo work ceased, the gangs climbed out of the holds and everyone sat around on the decks waiting for the outcome of the mighty conference. Two hours later the officials reappeared, laughing, holding bottles of scotch and cartons of cigarettes, to clamber down the gangway into their launches, making a merry racket. The foreman went to speak to the gangs and they in turn clambered down into their lighters. The ropes were cast off and then we were alone on the brown Warri River, two armed guards on the gangway to stop us fleeing.

At the time Warri, with its associated river ports, was the third busiest shipping hub in Nigeria, after Lagos and Port Harcourt. The place has an interesting and chequered history: a Portuguese missionary centre in the sixteenth century, then a slave centre for Portuguese and Dutch traders and finally the provincial capital for the British during colonial rule. Warri sits about halfway between Lagos and Port Harcourt and captures a lot of fall-off trade as a result; it's a big exporter of oil and gas, as well as the more traditional palm oil, groundnuts, cocoa, timber and rubber, Warri was making a drive towards modernisation, hence the demand for cement. The surrounding vegetation was equatorial forest and swampland, and during the weeks we were there the temperature varied from the mid-seventies Fahrenheit to the low eighties – that's 23–28°C for you metric types.

The air was heavy and humid. We were in the river for the whole of the wettest month, August, and rain it did. Duncan and I would sit under the poop deck beneath an awning and watch the rain come down in a constant heavy blanket. No wind, just rain. No pause, just rain. No slackening of intensity, no increase in velocity, just stair-rod rain, arrow-straight rain, the cloud cover unzipped and the rain fell out and into the Warri River. I liked sitting under an awning watching African rain; it gave me pleasure. The rain inhibited our work ethic because there was nothing we could do, it interfered with the practical management of the ship, it was almost hypnotic, all we could do was sit and watch the heavy rain come down and down, clattering heavily into the water, clunking on the awning, bouncing off the steel decks.

In between the bouts of rain there wasn't much that could be done either, on an arrested ship. The *Funing* had been arrested because the charterers hadn't paid the port dues or the light dues, because the shippers hadn't paid for the cargo and because the cargo receivers hadn't paid the warehouse and importation costs. All parties involved were playing the game of fending off their bills until the money arrived, but they had all come unstuck. Everyone cried unfair, everyone claimed they had paid and the fault lay elsewhere. It was a dog's breakfast, the ship couldn't move and the cargo couldn't be taken off.

The captain was called to attend a court case. A couple of us tagged along. In the Warri court, the Nigerian judge, gowned and bewigged, made a great show of looking dignified and bashing his gavel. The various lawyers squabbled in an unseemly way, like hyenas, interrupting each other, insulting each other, sometimes screeching at the judge, on occasion seeming on the verge of attack. No one appeared to know the procedure or the conduct of the court.

The ship's agent whispered: "It's going to be adjourned for a week."

The judge said: "I am going to adjourn for a week while arguments are prepared." Bang went his gavel.

Fox appeared. He was the cargo receivers' representative and also acted as a sort of supercargo, in a casual way. He was mainly a lawyer. Fox was a larger than life man, a six-foot-six-inch Texan, a broad man with long hair and a drooping moustache. He believed in all things American and all things Texan, and thought that every other country and system in the world was inherently inferior. He thought that Great Britain should apply to become the 51st State of the Union, otherwise we would crumble from being a bit player to a position of utter insignificance. We responded by calling America the colony across the pond, a place full of fat people who couldn't read and who would be overtaken in the evolutionary circle by Nigeria within two generations. Fox had little sense of humour when it came to his beloved homeland and would glower when we mocked him. He told us he was in the secret service with the Special Forces in Vietnam, operating up country on search and destroy missions. When I said that the US Special Forces must be the biggest battalion in the world because every American I had ever spoken to had been in it, he looked wounded and sulked for a while. He looked mean enough, large enough, fit enough and sharp enough to be in the Special Forces, though, however big it was.

One evening Duncan told Fox he had heard there was no such thing as a Texan until a Mexican shagged a pig, which caused him to snap. Fox chased Duncan out the bar and down the deck, roaring with rage, while the rest of us leant on the rails and hooted with laughter.

Fox camped down in the ship's hospital, preferring to stay aboard the *Funing* than in the hotel he was offered in Warri town. He took a boat ashore every morning to try and progress the mess we found ourselves in and came back in the late afternoon to give us an update report. Nothing much was happening though, the different parties were still at each other's throats. Fox spent most evenings in the ship's bar with the rest of us, where we asked ourselves the same question over and over again. How long would we be here?

We all thought that Fox was on our side, but then the Old Man went ashore with him one day and came back looking concerned. He told us to be careful when around Fox and not tell him anything he didn't know already. It had become clear to the Old Man, during a meeting with the cargo receivers, that Fox's concern, his only concern, was the cargo and how to get it off the ship. He couldn't care less about the ship herself or what happened to her. Or what happened to us. The Old Man detected that Fox might be doing a deal to allow the cargo to be offloaded and all outstanding debts and claims would fall onto the *Funing*. He hastily conferred with the Hong Kong owners of the ship, who we all worked for, and they told him they would get their lawyers more involved and in the meantime to walk carefully and not allow any cargo to be discharged under any circumstances, until he had their express instructions.

Every day, the Old Man would go ashore with Fox and they would separate on the quay, the Old Man going off with the ship's agent and Fox going off with the cargo receivers. In the evening, the Old Man would brief us, then Fox would brief us with his version. A gap opened up, the versions became ever more different. The chief mate told the Old Man that Fox was the enemy and ought to be thrown off the ship but the Old Man demurred, saying it was best to keep him close.

In the end there was an inevitable bust-up, with Fox wanting to start discharging and the Old Man refusing to open the hatches. There was a furious row. We heard the screaming in the Old Man's cabin from where we were in the bar, two decks down. Fox stormed off the ship and we didn't see him for several days. When he returned he stayed battened down in the hospital, sulking, occasionally appearing for the evening meal.

We found ways to amuse ourselves while the lawyers for the various factions argued in courts in different parts of the world. The owners were in Hong Kong, the charterers were in Piraeus, the insurers were in London, the shippers were in Rostock and the receivers in Lagos. Throw in the Nigerian Customs & Excise and the Port Authorities, both of whom had a dog in the game, and that was a lot of work for a lot of lawyers in a lot of countries. It was all well beyond us.

We started to take jaunts ashore. Warri was not a place on the tourist trail, filthy and corrupt, menacing after dark, very little to redeem it in the eyes of the casual visitor. We found a couple of bars to while away the time. The beer was vile, barely drinkable, although we heroically managed to slurp it down.

Our favourite place, or least disliked, was the German Bar, a hut, a hovel, built of wood and scrap corrugated iron with an open doorway and no windows, near the riverfront. Inside it was gloomy and smelly, there was no electricity, just kerosene lamps, the mismatched tables grimy, the dirt floor heaped in garbage. The saving grace was a huge tub of ice in which they kept the beer.

The locals tried to gyp us at every turn, gruesome local prostitutes coming into the German Bar and hustling for trade. Duncan and Peter the second and I were disgusted and ignored them, although Peter the leci was much taken with the local talent. We told him he must be mad, we told him they were ghastly and crooked and diseased. What we said made no difference, and he would stay behind and come back in the morning, grinning broadly and saying:

"Why-Aye Man, these local lasses are canny."

We would try and talk him out of going back to the German Bar but he didn't listen. He started making friends with some of the local men and they would sit together in the hovel of a bar, looking like a band of cut-throats, roaring with laughter and swigging beer from the bottles. He even talked about coming back to Warri when he was on leave.

On one occasion, we ventured into the shopping area of the nearby township, a thousand yards of small cramped grubby shops, squatting either side of a dusty tarred road. Filth clogged the edges in great heaps. Most shopkeepers kept their own frontage clear but there was no civic order, no system – the garbage was just shoved away from the shop-fronts into the road where it sat and rotted below the raised concrete walkways. Music blasted out from several shops, loud, booming, incessant, thumping, thumping, screeching and wailing.

Most of the shops sold cheap junk of unimaginable uselessness: sundry piles of household equipment badly made from bits of plastic and metal, conceived in a land beyond quality control, an array of items that all seemed so completely unfit for any purpose, so utterly worthless. There were piles of dodgy-looking children's toys that should never be allowed near a child, all sharp edges and toxic materials and looking as if they would have broken in your hand if you picked them up.

Huge trucks thundered through from time to time, stirring up storms of hot polluted dust. The side alleys were choked and ghastly, the stench was foul. We wandered into the food market and I steeled myself for greater horrors. The spice and vegetable section turned out to be surprisingly clean, though, and the thick smell of spices was a welcome diversion from the rotting odour of the streets.

But the butcher's row was a different place, with mysterious chunks of meat hanging in the sun, wreathed in flies. A clutch of nearby stalls sold dried fish. Others sold smelly fist-sized black lumps sitting on leaves, which were unrecognisable as either fish or meat and which looked downright dangerous.

There was no shortage of colour, bright and loud. The shops were painted in what was presumably the favourite colour of the owner, with little regard to the neighbour or any sort of communal appearance. There were lots of reds and yellows and blues, bright primary colours, vivid, sharp, loud. Stalls sold bolts of cloth so loud you could hear them.

People loafed everywhere. They sat on chairs, on stoops, on the ground, they leaned against walls. There were occasional pockets of activity among the torpor. I watched four workers building a wall, one was sorting bricks from a pile in a desultory manner, one sat and watched him and smoked, the other two leaned against each other in the sun, sleeping. The heat and the filth wrapped round me. Each time, I couldn't wait to get back to the ship.

One afternoon, Peter the leci and I were out with the agent, who was filling our day by giving us a guided tour of the north side of Warri, for a fee of US$20. We drove along packed dirt roads, the agent pointing out things of interest, although there wasn't much, just poorly constructed houses, patched with planks and corrugated iron and plastic. We didn't say anything as we didn't want to offend him.

The African night dropped on us quickly and we thought we had better get back, but just then the car broke down. We sat there in the quiet of the African dark, no lights, no sounds apart from insects clicking in the undergrowth. The agent raised the bonnet but couldn't see a thing. He said he knew a garage not far away and walked off into the night, leaving us alone. We locked the doors and sat quietly. After a while the agent returned with a man who wasn't a mechanic, but he had a torch. The man charged us 10 naira to let us use his torch, I paid. The agent fumbled under the bonnet and eventually started the car. We sped off down the bumpy road, leaving torch man to walk back in the dark by himself.

Corruption and bribery in Nigeria was endemic, from the highest government official to the lowly torch man, who had charged us to use his light. The term was 'dash'. Most Nigerians didn't view dashing as just being a bribe; that would be too crude an interpretation. They saw it as part bribe, part tip, part booking fee and part payment for results. Whatever the definition, to get anything done in Nigeria you had to pay dash. To get the gangs to start on time the foreman had to have dash. To arrange fresh water for the ship the chief engineer had to pay dash to the agent who would dash the port official in charge of the wharf to clear the water barge. To get inward clearance the chief steward would have to dash the immigration officer; the pilot needed dash to take the ship out. Parents needed to dash the head teacher to get their kids into school, people needed to pay dash to get a job and pay more dash to keep the job. I had to pay dash just to get into the country. Dash flowed around the whole of Nigeria; it was a whole economy and way of life built on dash. The torch man simply could not have conceived the possibility of shining his light for us as an act of kindness, and he would have thought us mad if we had suggested such a thing.

It was difficult for the chief mate's wife, Susan, in Warri. She would get leered at by the local men in a particularly disgusting manner, which would make anyone accompanying her cringe. Susan took it in her stride though, tough lady.

The local male habit was to refer to any woman as 'Maria'. So if a lady hove into view the man sighting her would allow a slow grin to crawl across the whole of his face, at the same time saying, 'Maria', in a low sonorous voice. The Maria saying had a particular pronunciation, a deep, deep pitch, sung slowly in a slightly comic style. I suppose in operatic terms the voice would be a *basso buffo*. The sound came out as 'Maa-riii-yaaa …' followed by a deep and rumbling chuckle.

We were in the agent's boat one day; the chief mate had asked me and Peter the leci to accompany Susan to the town to go sightseeing. We headed for the river's edge to disembark at the small wooden jetty that projected into the stream. In the shallows was a group of people, bathing and relaxing in the thick brown water. As we got nearer, we could hear the murmuring of 'Maria' as they spotted a white woman sitting in the boat. The sound became louder as we neared the jetty, building into a ragged hymn: 'Maaa-riii-yaaa …' – all the men baying in harmony, like a choir of hounds. I glanced at Susan. She was looking stoic, staring straight ahead.

As the shallow-bottomed boat slowed to come alongside the jetty, a massive fat man erupted out of the water a few feet away, he was naked and holding his huge member, which he waved at Susan; it looked as if he was gripping a giant black snake. He roared: "MAA-RII-AA!" She shrieked. We all leapt off the boat and hustled her down the jetty. The next couple of hours saw us walking quickly around the town. If we stopped too long a crowd of men would gather, leering away and muttering 'Maria'. If we just walked on, the men at the stalls would give us a passing 'Maria' as we went by. After a while I caught Peter's eye and we started to grin, it was all so surreal. Susan couldn't help but join in.

A settlement was finally reached and cargo work resumed. Four weeks' work stretched ahead of us. We weren't privy to the terms of the deal; we only knew that the shore gangs would be returning the following morning to resume discharging the cement. The Old Man verified this with the owners in Hong Kong and they were in agreement. Fox sued for peace and we took him back into our social fold.

The barges arrived, the gangs arrived and the work got under way. Duncan and I wandered the decks while the gangs hauled out netloads of cement. There wasn't much to do apart from keeping an eye on the ship's working gear to make sure it wasn't abused. Occasionally we would arrange for wires to be changed or a block overhauled. Sometimes we would argue with the foreman over the competence of the winch-drivers who ran the gear too fast and coordinated badly with each other; a two-inch wire that snaps under load can whip across the deck and cut a man in half. The foreman nodded, 'yeah, yeah, yeah', but didn't really care. As soon as we were out of sight they went back to their careless practices.

Two big wooden thunder boxes were built on the poop for the shore gangs. The men would climb the steps to sit on the seats so they could then crap through the holes. Stacks of newspaper were stowed next to the seats, in covered boxes to protect them from the downpours.

It was always arresting to walk on the poop and see two men side by side on the thunder boxes, chatting away as they unloaded their goods into the waiting Warri River. After wiping their backsides with newspaper, they flung the soiled paper in the river, although often missed; gouts of it lay in soggy brown piles in the scuppers. We would harangue the foreman to clear it away and from time to time someone would shovel the whole mess into the river, leaving tell-tale brown smears on the deck, vile and glistening.

In the afternoons the rains came down and this prompted the main burst of activity as the crew turned to and rapidly pulled the MacGregor hatches closed. We all stood around for a couple of hours or so in various sheltered areas, until the downpour ceased and it became dry enough to open up and resume work.

The tallyman had twenty wives. He was a gigantic man without much muscle, just rippling bouncing flesh. The flesh flowed around his frame as he moved, which wasn't often. He had four junior tallymen reporting to him, one stationed at each hatch, counting the bags as they were loaded into the net. Every two hours there was a short break, and the junior tallymen brought the individual totals to him. His job was to then add them up and enter the results in a daybook. He did this with great solemnity, furrowing his brow as he wrote, the pencil clutched in his massive sausage-like fingers.

The tallyman wanted to position himself in the ship's office, but we wouldn't let him. We did allow him to set up a rough wooden desk outside, though, under the overhang. His adding-up responsibilities apart, the head tallyman's only topic of conversation was his twenty wives.

He was a Muslim, although he seemed far from devout because he was always begging for beer. From what I could understand, the theological attraction seemed to be that he could have his twenty wives without the prissy objections that would have been made by the Christians. He boasted of his sexual prowess and affected not to know how many children he had fathered – 'perhaps fifty'. I asked him if he was bothered about cluttering up the planet by having such a huge and unrestrained family, but he looked at me as if I were weak or simple or both and said, "It's good to have lots of children", as if that was a conclusive response. He chose his wife for the night by the immediate sensual taste that was upon him at the time, a bit like choosing a chocolate from a box.

We started to run perilously short of food. The cook was a man of low talent who struggled to make what we had interesting. There was an increasing amount of stew and slow roasted meats, and less and less vegetables, a sure sign that we were delving into the back end of the freezers and store rooms. As time passed, the meals deteriorated further to resemble prison camp fare: tinned spam and discoloured boiled potatoes; chicken and carrots and rice, most of which was carrots and rice. The desserts contracted to either steamed duff or rice pudding. The charterers had squeezed costs to compensate for their legal expenses. The

Old Man complained to Hong Kong and we were given licence to buy fresh vegetables and meat, if we could find it, at the local market. The chief steward did his best – the vegetables were good, although the locals ripped us off, but the meat was too dangerous-looking to buy. He couldn't find any decent local beer although he managed to buy a few cases of Star lager, Nigeria's finest.

Fox came good, despite his unpopularity. There was an Anglo-Saxon compound outside of town, a fortified place where the British and American expatriates lived. Inside there was a club, a restaurant and a mini-market. Fox used some contacts he had with the oil business and managed to get in. He came back to the *Funing* in a hired boat laden to the gunwales with goods: crayfish, salmon, steaks, several baskets of fresh vegetables, two boxes of fresh fruit, biscuits, chocolate, nuts, cheeses, twenty cases of Heineken beer, two dozen bottles of wine. He had rice, potatoes, eggs, bacon, ham hocks, fresh chicken, shoulders of lamb, noodles. Fox must have stripped the place.

Rumours of his arrival had us lining the rails on the boat deck, and as he came closer and we saw what he had in his boat we started cheering. All the officers and the crew were there, all the Nigerian workers who were not down the holds leant over the main deck rails and joined in. Fox steered the boat abreast of number 5 hatch, which wasn't working cargo, and the bosun had a derrick swung out and lowered a net. The casab rolled a monkey ladder down, and three of the crew clambered down to load the goods. We ate and drank well that night. Fox was the subject of frequent toasts as we welcomed him back. 'If you are a host to your guest, be a host to his dog too', as they said in Assyria 3,000 years ago. I never really understood that one, but it seemed appropriate to keep the scheming Fox close to us.

The end of our stay in Warri was in sight. We were now down to the last few tiers of cement bags in number 2 and 4 hatches, which probably meant another two days of working followed by a further day for a couple of shore gangs to clean the hatches out. We decided to brighten our time with a fancy dress party to keep our spirits up. Anything that bound us together and gave us something to focus on was usually a good idea. I'm not sure whose good idea this was but we all focused with intent.

The Old Man wanted us to gather on the boat deck initially, but that was a bad idea. The party started at six in the evening, which was the same time as the West African mosquitoes started their own party. They probably couldn't believe their luck when they saw a group of pasty-faced soft-skinned Europeans standing there as willing food, and we were soon driven back inside. Not before the off-duty gangs and other locals who were lying around the decks had a good laugh, though. They slapped their thighs and rumbled their deep-throated laughs as they watched a bizarre collection of frogmen, pirates and assorted strangely dressed people scuttle back into the accommodation. I wonder what they thought. 'Why are they doing that?' I suppose. 'Why have they put on those strange clothes and then stood out on the boat deck in a group? Are they completely mad?'

The chief mate came as a pirate, predictably. He wore a smart pirate coat of turquoise cloth with gold flashes sewn across the front. It was one of his wife's cast-offs. He had a three-cornered hat made from a cereal box, an eye-patch and a fake wooden leg. The leg was a bit of a failure; it was a length of 3×3-inch timber with a wooden platform nailed on

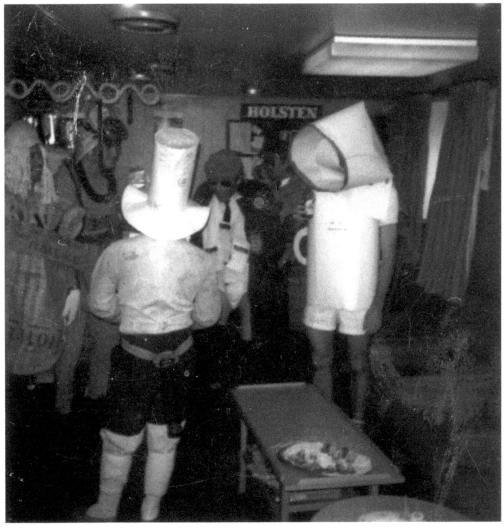

The fancy dress party.
… a bizarre collection of frogmen, pirates and assorted strangely dressed people …

the top for him to kneel on. He had then strapped his kneeling leg to the platform so that he had to stump along on the wooden one, although he kept falling over, crashing to the deck, his wooden leg and real leg waving in the air. After ten minutes he became fed up, took his wooden leg contraption off and flung it behind the bar.

The chief mate's wife came as some sort of Chinese model. At first, no one could really make out what or who she was supposed to be in her high-collared dress, slanting make-up and a pair of chopsticks in her hair. The chief mate started hissing "Suzie Wong" in a stage whisper and we all said, "Oh yes, Suzie Wong. Brilliant!" We all thought it was pretty poor, actually.

Not as poor as Peter the leci, though, who wore a pair of grubby underpants and flip-flops and a knotted handkerchief on his head, costumed as a man on an English seaside holiday.

He looked truly repulsive with his flabby freckled skin and fat white belly. We all prevailed on the Old Man and chief engineer to order him to cover up, which he eventually did, by putting on a stained vest.

Nor as poor as my effort though, or so everyone said, which I thought was unfair. I felt I had done quite well after spending the afternoon making a cowl-shaped hatch ventilator out of a few cancelled charts. The trunk of it went round my body, then curled over the back of my head to the round vent opening, in the middle of which was my face. It was probably the germ of a good idea but my standard of craftsmanship had let me down. Someone wrote 'I am a ventilator' on the trunk, because they said my effort was so bad that no one knew what I was supposed to be. Later in the evening, Duncan set fire to the back. I saw the smoke first of all and was looking around for the fire, then my arms and back were hot and I saw flames and realised I was alight. I started leaping about, tearing off the burning charts while everyone shouted, "Fire in the hold! Fire in the hold!"

The Old Man said: "Great cabaret, Second Mate."

And the Old Man. What a spectacle. He came as a flasher, and in his way was more repellent than Peter the leci. A raincoat, flat cap and Wellington boots, under which he wore underpants and vest. Elaborately strapped to his underpants, with Sellotape and elastic bands, was a long frankfurter, courtesy of Fox's recent donation of supplies. The Old Man wandered from group to group, flinging open his mac and thrusting his German sausage at them, which bounced up and down, driving everyone away, groaning and revolted. After a while his antics caused the frankfurter to break in half and flop onto the deck. That caused a problem because no one wanted to pick it up – no one wanted to touch the object that represented the Old Man's phallus. So we all walked round it carefully, all of us frightened of making contact, until someone finally stumbled and stepped on it, squashing it flat, after which the taboo was gone and the broken phallus became a frankfurter again, which was soon ground into the carpet. The Old Man walked around for the rest of the evening with the other half still strapped to his underpants, looking strangely neutered.

Duncan dressed as a frogman, wearing the ship's breathing apparatus over an orange boiler suit, together with a pair of flippers he had found somewhere. The chief was a bit upset about the use of the breathing apparatus, being safety equipment. Even though Duncan said we had a locker full of spare air bottles, the chief remained narked.

Peter the second came looking like some sort of hobbit, which caused Duncan unrelenting merriment. Peter was wearing a top hat, made from more cancelled charts, knee-length shorts and long socks and shoes with fake gold buckles. Peter the second said he was in fact a leprechaun so we called him Hymie the hobbit for the rest of the evening, which he pretended to find amusing, through gritted teeth.

The chief engineer was another pirate, a much poorer one than the chief mate, Sparks came as a rather childlike cowboy, and several of the Chinese officers turned up as themselves. Fox came as Fox, a big boastful Texan who got drunk early then became angry, then maudlin, then wept for the state of his life before retreating to his hospital lair.

It was a good night. We were fed from a buffet made from all the best things Fox had bought. Giant shrimps, lobster tails, bananas, peanuts, pineapple, cheeses, biscuits and meat paste. The stewards pushed a couple of tables together at the far end of the bar and laid everything out on white linen. As soon as they left, we fell on it without manners, as if we were starving.

Much later, about two in the morning, there was only me and the Old Man left, both tired and dull-witted by then. He had shed his mac and was sitting on a bar stool in his vest and underpants, the stumpy half-phallus still in place, I leant against the bar in shorts and scorched tee-shirt, the hair on my arms singed. All our talk was of escaping from West Africa; we were like a couple of abandoned madmen.

4

Old World

We steamed out of the Warri River six weeks after we arrived. Peter the leci was the only person with fond memories. The rest of us felt a wave of relief. Piracy was a growing problem in that part of the world at the time. There had been difficulties off the West African coast for hundreds of years, although the locally stationed warships that came with British governance had kept a lid on worst excesses. But after independence in 1960, coastal piracy had gradually increased. The worst area was around the mouths of the Niger, a 150-mile length of coast that stretched from the Bonny River round into the Bight of Benin to the Warri Delta. This was a mass of swampland that had formed around the area where the mighty Niger River approached the sea, full of islands and inlets where pirate craft could shelter undetected.

The pirates used sleek open boats, and came streaking out of the mouths of the Niger, cracking along at 40 knots, powered by a pair of big Evinrude outboard engines. They would descend on an unwary ship in the Bonny River anchorage like a wolf upon the fold, flinging grappling hooks over the rails and swarming aboard. The pirates were usually armed with Kalashnikov rifles and an assortment of brutal-looking ironmongery. Most were in and out quickly, intent on robbing the crew and taking whatever else they could find. Once on board, they would rush through the ship, blasting off a few rounds to signal their intent then carry out a swift and efficient looting of the cabins, with a bit of clubbing to hurry the slow.

They would take their time, though, with the captain and the chief steward. The chief steward would have any ship's money for shore leave plus the keys to the bonded stores, which were full of cigarettes and spirits. And pirates believed the captain always carried something, and would force him to open the safe. Most ships carried cash for emergencies, usually US dollars. The captain would generally get a beating if the safe was bare. On a straightforward robbing of the ship, the pirates would be on and off within fifteen minutes. There was an occasional kidnapping and ransom, although such cases were rare as the pirates knew that this would bring them disproportionate retaliation from the authorities.

There were of course some pirate bands with greater ambition, who ignored the pickings from the crew and went for the cargo. General cargo ships kept their valuables in lock-ups in the holds and these could be electrical goods or alcohol. Container ships were more difficult, although the more organised gangs sometimes had the container number and its location on the ship.

The big prize was oil, which meant taking the whole ship. A tanker that had just loaded in the Bonny offshore oilfields had a cargo worth tens of millions of dollars. A bold pirate attack the previous year had forced the vessel close to the coast, where explosives were planted. They threatened to blow up the ship, the crew and the cargo if a ransom wasn't paid. The oil companies always shouted that their priority was the safety of the crew although the potential loss of a cargo worth tens of millions of dollars was probably more of a persuasive argument in favour of a settlement. On other occasions, pirates had been known to try force a ship to steam to Angola, where the governance was wild and broken, so they could hold it there until payment was made, or sell the cargo. This invariably proved an ambition too far though; the ship would be stormed and the pirates killed.

Strictly speaking, the Bonny raiders weren't pirates at all, just local gangsters. Piracy is the act of taking a ship on the high seas, which are the waters more than twelve miles off the coast. But these attacks all occurred much closer to the Nigerian shore. A few of their fast launches flew skull and crossbones flags, to show what hilarious fellows they were.

West African piracy had its roots in poverty and was stoked by the endemic corruption of the oil business in that part of Nigeria, which magnified the problem by granting the riches of Croesus to the few while condemning the common herd to abject destitution. Piracy couldn't have existed in any meaningful way if corruption hadn't been a way of life. With the connivance of port officials, shippers, customs men, stevedores, police and government officials, the pirates knew which ships to hit, when they were arriving, when they were leaving, what cargoes they carried.

So once we had dropped our pilot just past Bonny Island we fled south-east for open waters. We would have been a poor catch with no cargo and depleted bonded stores – even our food was running out again – but we didn't want to take any chances. The pirates obviously agreed we weren't a worthy prize because no one came near us.

After clearing into deep water we pulled round to the west and set course to pass thirty miles south of Cape Three Points, the southern tip of Ghana. The Bight of Benin is the narrow indent at the northernmost edge of the Gulf of Guinea. It was an interesting coast to sail along. The eastern side, part of Nigeria, Benin, and Togoland, has the name Slave Coast, for obvious reasons, whereas the western side is the Gold Coast, now Ghana, having flung off the British pre-independence name.

I had been to several places on this coast a few years previously when I was a cadet on a white oil tanker. We had called into Cotonou in Dahomey, shortly before that country underwent a Marxist revolution and was renamed the People's Republic of Benin; then on to Lomé in Togoland, Tema in Ghana and Abidjan in the Ivory Coast. The tanker was crewed

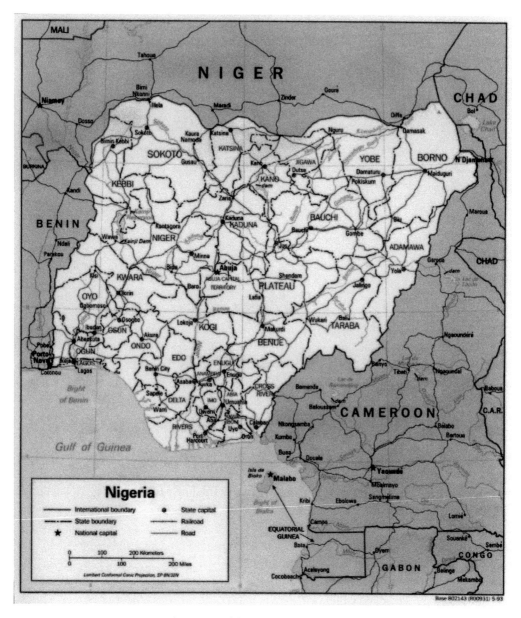

Nigeria (Courtesy of the University of Texas at Austin)

by drunks and drug addicts and I didn't enjoy my stay in that part of the world. My abiding memories were buying a West African Grey parrot, who I named Maurice, and then going down with a bout of malaria which laid me up for a week.

Before the great African land grab in late Victorian times, the whole of the coast was known as Lower Guinea, as distinct from the inland area to the north, which was Upper Guinea. In the 1960s the colonial powers cleared off back to Europe, having carved up the place into a patchwork of countries that suited their administrative convenience, without thought of historical treaties, tribal division or local sensitivities. These newly formed countries were left to go it alone and make what they could of the situation. Someone once said, a Roman notable in the fourth century I think it was: 'Empires decline because the countries they create desert them.' That may well be, to some extent – but in this case it was the empire builders that did the deserting, and the new countries that declined. Most of Africa had gone backwards since independence simply because Britain and France and other European powers had created countries that should never have been created, and then abandoned them.

Our next charter hadn't yet been agreed and we were apparently either going to swing south-east and head down to Rio de Janeiro or carry on round the coast of Africa and up towards Europe, depending upon what the owners finally decided upon. In the meantime, we had orders to steam at reduced revs to Cape Three Points and then carry on to Cape Palmas on the border between the Ivory Coast and Liberia. It was expected that before we reached Cape Palmas, the charter would be confirmed: Europe or South America. I was pretty keen to head on down to Rio, not having been there before; so was the rest of the crew. If a South American charter came off we would load in Rio and steam south to Montevideo and Buenos Aries, then round the southern tip of South America, the fabled Cape Horn, before heading north to Valparaiso and up to the west coast of America. That would be all new territory to me.

Traffic was light as we steered for Cape Three Points. We were too far off the land to be hindered by fishing canoes whereas the coastal steamers were all further inland. We passed the occasional liner bound for Nigeria, but the deep sea traffic from Europe to southern Africa would all be passing well to the west and over the horizon. There was quite a lot of detritus floating by: logs and palm fronds and forestry washed out by the big regional rivers, the Niger and the Volta. Even though shipping was scarce, we kept a good look-out for tree-size logs, which passed by occasionally, some big enough to do damage if we ploughed into them, particularly if they were dragged down the ship's side and pulled into the screw. The air was much fresher away from the coast, and the slow pace was pleasing. We had occasional rain showers although mostly the weather was balmy. The only sea life we saw was schools of flying fish.

The distance from Warri to Cape Three Points was just under 500 miles, two days steaming at our reined-back speed. There was still no charter news when we reached it, so we steamed on for Cape Palmas, another day and a half passage. To the north of us lay the Ivory Coast, although we were too far off to sight land for most of the time. The Bight of Benin, Gulf of Guinea, Slave Coast, Gold Coast, Ivory Coast, Mosquito Coast … in terms of the exotic visions created by their names, these places wiped the floor with Morecambe Bay and the Humber Estuary back in Britain.

When I came onto the bridge for the midnight to four watch, the lighthouse on Cape Palmas was on the starboard beam, fifteen miles distant. The night was clear and there was a scattering of fishing boats between us and the land, although they were all too far away to bother about. I noticed by the way the stays were rattling that the engines had been wound back up to full revs.

I said to Duncan: "Back up to full speed; we've had orders, then?"

He said: "Rotterdam."

I said: "Bugger."

✫   ✫   ✫

The charter was fixed; no South American odyssey for us. The voyage would open with three days at anchor in Rotterdam, loading electrical goods from barges at the anchorage, after which we would head for Hamburg to take on board steel girders. When we left Hamburg, it was off to Bremen, Wilhelmshaven and Tilbury, and then out through Suez to several ports in the Persian Gulf. My heart sank. The European ports would be enjoyable, but I saw the Middle East as a ghastly place, certainly not a prospect that invited me. My last outing in that part of the world had been three years previously, when we had spent weeks in the Red Sea, unloading cement in Jeddah and Yenbo.

Bagged cement in Nigeria, steel girders to the Persian Gulf: what next, a cargo of serpents for Acheron? I felt I was being punished for my life's misdeeds.

We continued our passage up the African coast, keeping at least fifteen miles out to sea. Although piracy was at its worst around the mouths of the Niger there were still incidents as far north as Sierra Leone. The navigational aids along the coast were generally unreliable, and even some of the big lights on the headlands were unlit; that part of Africa had found better things to spend the money on than maintaining its legacy colonial lighthouses. Back up to full speed, fifteen knots, we made good time. We past the Banana Islands off northern Sierra Leone then took a wide berth round the clump of rocks, shoals and small islets off the coast off Guinea Bissau, before swinging north for Cap-Vert in Senegal, the westernmost point of Africa.

The winds were fresher and the seas bluer as we passed Senegal. There was more traffic as well, now that we had joined the main north–south trade routes. The long sea passage gave the crew the chance to put the running gear in order: the ship's derricks had been in constant use for weeks, a number of wires needed to be changed and all the cargo blocks had to be stripped down, oiled and greased. The holds had been given a good clean before we left, but the bosun found a few areas that were still clogged with cement dust, which were dug out and swept out and hosed out again. The days were warm, and half the crew were set to painting, smartening the ship up a bit so the charterers could see what a bargain they were getting.

We came through the Canary Islands in the middle of the afternoon watch, passing between Grand Canary and Fuerteventura. The Spanish-owned Canaries were an impressive island group to approach, a group of volcanoes, some still active, rising out of the ocean. The highest peak reaches over 12,000 feet, and on a clear day can be seen fifty miles away. People often think the Canary Islands are named after the canary bird, understandably – but in fact it's the bird that was named after the islands. The name Canary comes from the Latin *canis*, dog; the place was named in Roman times after visiting scribes recorded that the locals were discovered to be dog worshippers. Consequently, the island was full of dogs and so named *Canaria*.

The Canary Islands have a colourful history. The Phoenicians, Greeks, Carthaginians and Romans all visited them. Ownership was taken from the indigenous people by Spain in the fifteenth century and the archipelago has remained in Spanish possession ever since. The Canaries were a victualling point for Spanish galleons bringing back treasure from the New World; they were also the tinder-box for the Spanish Civil War of the 1930s and were severely repressed after Franco's fascists claimed victory. Now, the islands are a tourist hotspot. The Canary Island group was an uplifting place to steam through: blue, blue waters and verdant green mountains either side of us, climbing into the blue, blue sky.

Our next landfall after the Canaries was to be Cape Finisterre in the north-west corner of Spain, a thousand miles on a north-north-east course. When we were two days out of the Canaries the traffic intensified as we hit latitude 34°N, the Mediterranean crossroads. Ships came out of the Mediterranean and headed either west for the Americas, north for Europe or south for Africa. Similarly, ships came down from the north, up from the south and in from the west. In the square of sea between latitudes 34°N and 37°N and longitudes 7°W and 10°W, deep sea shipping meets from all directions. We had to be on our toes. The radars were taken off standby and we kept the watchman close by in case he was needed to take the wheel.

I had a close encounter in the middle of the afternoon watch. A big freighter was three points on our starboard bow, crossing. The bearing was steady, collision course. A ship has to give way to another on her starboard side, says Rule 19 of the Collision Regulations. There is no doubt; every deck officer had Rule 19 drilled into him at an early age: 'When two power-driven vessels are crossing, so as to involve risk of collision, the vessel which has the other on her own starboard side shall keep out of the way of the other.' So it was up to me to give way, which I would have normally done at about six miles. Six miles sounds a long way off but when two ships are closing, each steaming at fifteen knots, they are less than fifteen minutes from strike. It takes half a minute for a lightly loaded ship to settle onto a new course and up to a minute for a deep-laden vessel. This brings the practical time of encounter when a crossing ship is six miles away to about ten minutes. Unless one is overtaking the other, if two big ships close to less than a mile in open waters it's either slackness or madness on the part of the bridge officers.

The crossing ship was nine miles away on a rock solid bearing. I couldn't alter to starboard to swing round her stern, though, because another ship was overtaking us on our starboard side, a Liberian tanker. If I had altered course I would have swung the *Funing* right into her. I couldn't alter to port, because another ship was crossing from that direction and she was on a collision course too and she would be altering soon to let us pass ahead, hopefully; if I went to port we would be into her. To cap it all, there was another ship coming straight towards us, just off the starboard bow, so if I altered to starboard I would be inviting a three-way prang with both her and the overtaking Liberian tanker. So, there we were: four ships all heading for the same point, from the north, south, east and west. We should have all altered course to starboard in one big ballet but I was spoiling the dance. I couldn't alter because I was blocked by a fifth ship overtaking me.

My mouth was dry, my heart hammered, creatures squirmed within me, I felt the beads of sweat break out, studding my brow. There wasn't much time, though; I couldn't just stand and sweat us into an ocean pile-up. Two choices. The first was to call the Liberian tanker on the VHF and try talk her into altering to starboard, so that I could alter in parallel. The second was to drop our speed right down to let the Liberian get ahead of us quickly, to allow me swing round her stern.

She was close enough now so that I could see her name: '*Dragon Guard*'. I didn't fancy a pidgin English conversation with whoever was on the bridge, maddeningly trying to explain to them why they had to swing to starboard, quickly. On the other hand, big ships like the *Funing* have big momentum and they can't slow in an instant, they have no brakes, they take time to lose way. I mentally anguished, three seconds. Answer: do both.

I picked up the phone to the engine room and got hold of Walter, the Chinese third engineer. "Walter, drop down to half revs quickly please. We have a situation."

"Hah?"

"Walter, reduce speed now, half speed."

"Reduce speed? Hah! Why?"

"Walter! Half ahead! Now! This is an emergency!"

"Hah! OK!"

I picked up the VHF and called on Channel 16, the open channel.

"*Dragon Guard, Dragon Guard*, this is the British ship *Funing*. Do you read? Over."

Crackle, buzz, crackle.

"*Dragon Guard, Dragon Guard*, this is the British ship *Funing*. Do you read? Over."

Buzz, crackle, buzz.

I plugged in the Aldis lamp and flashed at her bridge. The light from the Aldis is bright enough to see on a bright day.

"*Dragon Guard, Dragon Guard*. This is the British ship *Funing*. Do you read? Over."

Nothing, just buzz and crackle, and distant tinny conversation. I sweated. The stays on the monkey island ceased vibrating as the revs reduced. I thought: That'll bring the Old Man up. I put the quartermaster on the wheel. The *Dragon Guard* started to overhaul us more quickly. The crossing ship was less than five miles and starting to inch across our bow now that we had slowed, but it wasn't going to be enough.

I called the engine room again: "Dead slow ahead, Walter."

"Hah! Dead slow ahead."

I bet Walter was sweating, down below the water line, not relishing the thought of being entombed in a steel coffin. Four miles, the *Dragon Guard* was past us, but still close, too close, like a bloody tourist. I needed her to be well past before I could swing the ship. Big pile-up imminent, three miles and closing. The Old Man appeared in the chartroom door. He took it all in at a glance.

"I'm going hard over now Captain. I had to drop the revs to get round the stern of this ship."

He nodded. "It's still yours."

I said: "Hard-a-starboard!"

"Hard-a-starboard, sir!" the quartermaster yelled, and wound the wheel round.

The Sperry gyro compass started clacking loudly as we swung, the sound like an angry mahjongg game, the players on amphetamines. The ship heeled as the swing accelerated.

When the bow was in line with the stern of the *Dragon Guard*, I said, "Midships!"

"Midships!" said the quartermaster and brought the wheel to centre. The *Dragon Guard* was close; I could see tears of rust on the accommodation doors and heaps of rubbish on the poop deck.

Five seconds. "Steady now!"

"Steady, sir."

The quartermaster put the wheel to port to check the swing, then steadied the ship on a course past the stern of the *Dragon Guard*.

I called the engine room. "Thanks Walter, back up to full revs."

"Hah!"

The Old Man hung around for a while. We cleared the *Dragon Guard* and I brought us back on course.

"Good job, Second Mate," he said over his shoulder as he left the bridge. The tension leached out of me.

When we were back on course again I put the ship on autopilot for Cape Finisterre and sent the quartermaster off to carry on with his painting nearby. I lit a cigarette and leant on the taffrail, looking over the side.

The VHF squawked: "This is *Dragon Guard*, this is *Dragon Guard*. Is someone calling me? Over."

The lighthouse at Cape Finisterre has a special place in the minds of most navigators. It's one of those seminal landfall marks that heralds the next stage of the journey and shares a place with other famous lighthouses around the world. With Beachy Head lighthouse, flashing white twice every twenty seconds, the last light sighted by ships leaving the English Channel for the West Indies; with Great Point lighthouse in Nantucket, the first light seen when approaching the eastern seaboard of the United States after an Atlantic crossing; with Cape Agulhas lighthouse at the southern tip of the African continent, where two great oceans meet; with Cape Leeuwin lighthouse at the south-western tip of Australia, the first light seen after an Indian Ocean crossing.

All these landfall lights have a resonance, carved out over the decades. Before satellite navigation, before Decca, before LORAN, before radar, before DF, they shone a light to show the pathway for ships that had been long out of sight of land. They were almost sacred.

Cape Finisterre sits at the north-east corner of the Iberian peninsula in Galicia province and was our landfall light coming up from Africa. It was bright light, visible twenty-three miles out. We came abeam of the lighthouse just after midnight and I took a bearing every thirty minutes to keep track of the ship's position. The light flashed white every five seconds, without pause; that's nearly six and a half million flashes a year. I wondered how many thousands of ships over the last hundred years had sighted the light on Cape Finisterre and been saved from breaking on the needle rocks that litter the coast.

We entered the world of Decca. Decca navigation was given birth by the Royal Navy following the wartime development of a navigation system that worked by shore-based stations pulsing out low frequency radio signals. There was a master station that commanded three slave stations, known as red, green and purple, which emitted the signals from their different locations. On board the ship, there was a Decca receiver with red, green and purple dials that read the signals as they came in.

Decca charts were Admiralty charts overlaid with red, green and purple grids, onto which the signals were transposed to give position lines, one for each slave colour, which then crossed to give the ship's position. To the unpractised eye, Decca charts looked a bit way out, as the coloured lines were all parabolas, mirroring the parabolic curve of a radio pulse.

After the end of the Second World War, the system was released by the military, and the founders were allowed to set up the Decca Navigation Company and lease receivers to merchant vessels. The company was named after the record company, because the inventor, an American by the name of William O'Brien, was a good friend of the head of Decca Records, who had helped him out with funding in the early days.

Decca navigation spread around the busier shipping areas of the globe, Britain and northern Europe, Spain, Japan, parts of Australia, Canada, South Africa and the Persian Gulf. It never really took off in the USA; they had their own system, LORAN, Long Range Aid to Navigation, which was preferred by the American military, if not by most ship's navigators.

I dusted off the Decca charts we would use for our European transit after we came round Cape Finisterre. Decca coverage wasn't good in France, because the French military had shown lukewarm enthusiasm in allowing the necessary shore stations to be established. It was a useful system around the whole of the UK, though, and most of northern Europe. During sunset and sunrise the signals went a bit haywire, and at the fringes of coverage it was less reliable, although generally speaking most navigators liked Decca.

Not every captain liked Decca, though. Those who didn't tended to be prejudiced traditionalists with a narrow viewpoint. A couple of years previously I sailed with one such Old Man, who loathed Decca with a vengeance. He had a pathological hatred of the system and would rise up if we ever even talked about using it. He believed in compass bearings, celestial sights and the controlled use of radar. Decca, according to him, was both unreliable and dangerous. He used to recount a number of barely believable tales of ships that had steamed along a parabolic Decca line and gone straight onto the rocks.

Under his command, we were in the western approaches to the English Channel in heavy fog one day with only one functioning radar, which then decided to pack up. We crept along at 6 knots, sounding our foghorn. I suggested it would be a good idea to use Decca because it was all we had. I could see the Old Man hated the idea although he reluctantly gave me permission to turn it on and try to get a fix. The dials started spinning as they always did when the system was warming up and searching for a signal.

The Old Man looked over my shoulder and said: "Look at it! Look at it! It's bloody useless!"

I said: "Give it a chance, Captain, it needs to warm up."

"Give it a chance, nothing! It's rubbish!"

There was the blasting sound of a foghorn nearby and we rushed back out into the wheelhouse, to watch a big liner slid past us in the gloom, uncomfortably close.

"See?" said the Old Man, as if it was the Decca's fault.

I went back in the chartroom to try and get a position. The green dial was settling down, the red was spinning, the purple wavering back and forward. I drew a position line on the chart based on the green signal. It was hopelessly out, the system hadn't settled. I tried to rub off the position line before the Old Man looked in again, but I was too slow. He stuck his head round the blackout curtain.

"Let me see that!"

I showed him. He turned crimson and started shaking.

"Look at that!" he roared. "What is it? Is that supposed to be a position line? Is this your fabulous Decca?" It was mine now, apparently. "We're nowhere near there!" He stabbed his finger at the position line on the chart. "It's crap! It's crap! It's bloody dangerous!"

"It's got to settle down, Captain."

"I'll settle the bloody thing down!"

In a fury, he started slamming the receiver box with his fist. The box lurched to one side on its housing, the lights went out and all the dials went slack, the hands flopped down to six o'clock.

"Look at it! Look at it! I told you it was a piece of shit!" he screamed. "We will never, ever, use that bloody thing again!"

He came it a final punch and stormed back out into the wheelhouse. I followed shortly afterwards, in time to see him start beating one of the broken radar sets. The fog lifted not long afterwards, thankfully, and I was able to plot the ship's course the old-fashioned way.

After rounding Cape Finisterre, we made our way across the Bay of Biscay, a day's run, then came round further west at the Ushant rocks to head into the English Channel. The wealth and power of Great Britain was built on maritime trade and naval dominance over the centuries; the English Channel was the corridor of that power.

It was hard not to be moved, not to feel that strength when steaming towards the Casquets, the group of dangerous rocks west of Alderney with its distinctive light buildings. The Casquet rocks are the scene of many a maritime tragedy, the most famous probably being the SS *Stella*, a cross channel passenger ferry that ploughed into the rocks on a foggy afternoon on Maundy Thursday 1899, sinking in ten minutes and drowning half the passengers and crew.

Nelson's ships used to gather in strength in the southern channel, blockading the French ports in the Napoleonic wars: 100-gun first rate ships of the line, second rated 90-gunners, third rated 80-gunners, hanging in the early morning mists like wraiths, calling the enemy out to fight. It was only the first three rates of ships that were thought powerful enough to fight in the line of battle. The lighter 40-gun frigates harried the opposition in hit and run attacks all along the coast.

As we steamed further east we picked up the Isle of Wight to the north, which sheltered the seat of British naval power, Portsmouth, a maritime stronghold since Henry VIII, the architect of the Royal Navy, was on the throne. Later we passed Newhaven, famed as the main embarkation port for troops and equipment going to the continent in the First World War: what tragedies there, hundreds of thousands of one-way passages.

Later still we came to the funnel of the Dover Strait, twenty-two miles of the most intense maritime traffic in the world. Ships are marshalled into traffic separation zones, eastbound to the south, westbound to the north. In the zone it was fine as far as through traffic was concerned; we were either overtaking or being overtaken. Sometimes we encountered a hopelessly equipped and badly staffed ship, an old flag of convenience wreck using twenty-year-old charts that didn't show the zones, crashing around on the wrong side of the channel, scattering other ships, enraging everyone.

The crossing traffic frayed our nerves; ferries roared at us at speeds of over twenty knots, swinging round our stern too close, always safe but always frightening. Smaller coasters didn't care; they blundered and wandered and were not fazed by a close encounter, were not concerned about the havoc they wreaked or by all the bowels they caused to twitch and shake.

And the pleasure yachts, how we hated them. Like most professional deck officers, I had an immense respect for round-the-world yachtsmen, the professional sailors who pitted themselves against the oceans, immensely brave people. But pleasure yachts, 'yachties' as we called them, would make my blood boil with the way they acted in close waters. Steam gives way to sail, says Rule 20 (a): 'When a power-driven vessel and a sailing vessel are proceeding in such a way as to involve risk of collision, the power-driven vessel shall keep out of the way of the sailing vessel.' How they loved that, the pleasure sailors, the four-weeks-a-year seaman, the weekend dinghy pliers, the boozy floozy carriers, the oilskin-wearing maritime wannabes, all cluttering up the sea as they sailed on righteously, relentlessly, clogging the shipping lanes, asserting their rights, cooking up potential disasters as big ships were forced to swerve round them.

Few seemed to have ever read Rule 20 (b): 'This rule shall not give a sailing vessel the right to hamper, in a narrow channel, the safe passage of a power-driven vessel which can navigate only inside such channel.' I never met a deck officer who didn't loathe these people and their antics, and who at times would have run them down, laughing, if they could have gotten away with it. Worst of all were those small sailing boats who skittered about to get as close as possible so they could wave at us, in a comradely nautical way. Wave? They made us so angry, we wanted to run out the fire hoses and blast them as we passed.

Rotterdam anchorage. A couple of months in Nigeria had taken its toll. We had very little in the way of stores, nothing in the way of mail from home. The agent had done a comprehensive job in the arrival procedures, with a small fleet of boats descending on us as soon as we dropped the hook. The only people allowed on board initially were the customs and immigration staff, although clearance was quick and the Q flag was hauled down, signalling a general scramble up the gangway.

The agent was first, carrying a briefcase and with a large bag slung over his shoulder which we suspected was the mail. Next was the food stores man, eagerly met by the chief steward. Then there was the bunker oil barge, the fresh-water barge, a big barge from spares and repairs, the chandler, a delivery of new cargo wires, a painting barge and a host of others. Our cargo from Rotterdam was all electrical goods and the cargo lighters would be arriving the next day to start the loading.

Letters from home, I had nothing momentous. A couple from my mother together with some bills she forwarded, although it was always grounding to look through the window and into a different world. The married men with children walked around misty-eyed, and made arrangements with the agent for a shore boat so they could go to the Seaman's Mission and call home. We watched the food and drink being loaded with greedy eyes, knowing we would feast well that night. The Old Man received a message to fly to London immediately to help sort out the tail end of the legal row that was still rumbling on following the argument and the arrest of the ship in Warri. He carried out a brief handover to the chief mate and said that he should be back the following day.

The chief mate, as acting captain, started his temporary command in a pompous way by insisting upon regular checks on the anchor, and thirty-minute fixes on the chart to confirm we weren't dragging the hook, despite the flat calm weather. There was an expulsion of hot air as he strode around the bridge, thinking up commands. He was mulling over whether he should issue an order for logging VHF radio checks every watch when I suggested, with a straight face, that we have a fire and boat drill while at anchor. He looked at me sharply but then, to his credit, broke into a grin and said:" I'm getting a bit carried away with all the power, aren't I?"

We all got a bit carried away that evening though. The fridges had been stocked up with Oranjeboom lager, and several bottles of Gordon's gin were placed in the bar, together with Captain Morgan rum for the chief mate/acting captain. We acted excessively, the night was hazy. The chief engineer was determined to enjoy a last thrash before his wife joined him in Hamburg, after which he would be expected to behave himself. The party progressed raucously round the ship, from the saloon to the bar to various cabins. At midnight I awoke in my cabin, mouth dry, tongue like a furry creature, empty beer bottles littering the place, bookmarking where the party had passed through.

I looked in on the bar before going up to the bridge for my anchor watch; they were all still at it, going strong and making a racket. We felt we deserved a night of excess after our trials in West Africa.

When the chief mate came up to the bridge to take over at four o'clock, he was looking pale. He listened to me in a distracted way before suddenly rushing out on the bridge wing to lean over the side and vomit copiously. He came back into the wheelhouse with an embarrassed and apologetic look, strings of vomit and clumps of expelled food lining his beard. I was repulsed and went to my bunk, no longer feeling like going down to the bar to join the party stragglers. It was the right decision to make, as I was on cargo watch later that morning and needed to be on the ball for loading the electrical goods.

Just before lunchtime, I was leaning over the side watching the cargo lighters and nursing a mug of coffee when I saw the agent's launch approaching. In the bow, dancing like a madman, was the Old Man. He started hallooing as the boat came closer. There were various boxes and bottles stacked around him, and he was gesticulating with what looked like a crate of fresh peaches. He swarmed up the gangway as soon as the boat came alongside and thrust the crate at me. It was indeed a crate of fresh peaches.

"How about that, then?" he demanded. "Fresh peaches! And I've got four bottles of champagne, some Cadbury's chocolate and today's newspapers!"

I congratulated him on his eclectic mix of gifts. It transpired that the company had given him the champagne in appreciation of his holding everything together during the problems in Warri, he had bought the chocolate and newspapers at the airport, and he had told the agent to pick up a box of fresh peaches as they passed though the market near the quay on their way to the launch.

Hamburg was Germany's busiest port and lies 15 miles up the River Elbe. We picked up the pilot at the head of the estuary and steamed upriver at 12 knots. The Elbe is wide and deep with several islands in the lower stream, and there was a constant flow of traffic in both directions. As we approached Hamburg, near Finkenwerder where the old U-boat pens still lie with the vessels entombed in cement, a band struck up the British national anthem. Their job was to play the national anthem of every ship that passed by.

Hamburg was a vibrant place, vivid, wild, a major shipping port with a red light district like no other. The Reeperbahn area in St Pauli district held sway as the premiere European attraction for a no-holds bar night out. The history of Hamburg is one of strife and conflict, like much of Germany. Two thousand years ago the Romans reported a settlement on the site, although Emperor Charlemagne officially founded the city in the 9th century. Over its first four hundred years of existence it was sacked by the Vikings, burnt by the Poles and captured by the Danes, and its population was driven to near-extinction by the Black Death. It grew into a major trading centre and was member of the Hanseatic League, a trade and defence alliance of northern European cities. The place went through religious battles in the 16th century as the citizens embraced Lutherism; in the 19th century it was conquered by Napoleon, then burned down again and finally ravaged by cholera. Hamburg stuttered in the First World War although didn't suffer too much damage, but then was all but destroyed by RAF firestorm bombing in the Second World War, after which it rose yet again. You can't keep the Germans down.

I took the first cargo watch and saw to the stowage of the steel girders we were taking on board for Abu Dhabi. Duncan and I had agreed to work day-and-day-about in port. The charters had supplied a supercargo whose job it was to plan everything; he and the chief mate spent much of the day in conference. The last shift ended at eight in the evening with the next one starting at eight the next morning. I was expecting to spend the night on board as duty officer, but the mate had no interest in going ashore himself and gave me leave to go instead. His wife Susan looked at me speculatively, but I was going on a serious pub crawl and didn't want to be saddled with chaperone duties, nice lady that she was and however disappointed she might have been with her husband for not taking her to see the bright lights. My cargo watch finished at 20:00 and I cleaned up and hoofed it into town to find the others, thinking that with luck I would be able to root them out in the Reeperbahn.

Our berth was on the south side of the river and it was a long walk round the docks, crossing the river by the old footbridge upriver of the wharfs and then cutting back through the northern dock complex. It was dark and mostly quiet; the area had a slightly threatening feel, as most big old ports do. Occasionally, I would come across the odd soul or a small group of people, and I treated each encounter guardedly.

There was a remarkable incident, which sits in my mind as an exemplar of the German people. Not far outside the docks, I came to a pedestrian road crossing with the light on red. There were no cars, the rush hour was long over, the streets were quiet. Standing on the deserted pavement in front of the deserted road, patiently waiting for the pedestrian light to turn green, were three Germans. One was a traditional *hausfrau* in her sixties, big and beefy, clothed in black, wearing a black hat, a tough-looking no-nonsense women who had seen war and strife and hard times in her lifespan. The second was a woman in her late thirties, well-groomed, elegantly dressed, assured. The third was a young man in his early twenties, a punk rocker, grubby, denim-clad, strewn with chains and safety pins, spiky hair standing erect. They stood together in a line without speaking, waiting for the red man to turn green.

I did what any English person would have done on coming to a quiet, deserted road to cross: I walked across it.

The three Germans went wild. *"Nein! Nein! Sie können nicht! Sie können nicht! Das licht ist rot! Das licht ist rot! Nein!"* A matron, a modern woman and a young punk – they all screamed at me in outrage. They couldn't understand me crossing the road without permission. They must have thought I was mad, or a criminal. I waved at them from the other side, which infuriated them still further. The three generations of Germans, different to look at, different in their values, but all obedient to the lights.

The Old Man disgraced himself in Hamburg in a quite shocking way, even for him. My night on the town had gone well. I had ambled around by myself for a couple of hours, taking in the sights and sounds, keeping my eye out for the others. I was happy in my own company, the area was vibrant, throbbing, there was plenty to look at. The patchwork of streets around the main Reeperbahn thoroughfare was studded with dozens of bars, brothels, music venues, sex clubs. The streets were thronged with packs of young men, sailors, tourists; it was unlikely there were many locals except those who worked there. People were noisy, boisterous; many were drunk. I had a notion of the sort of place I would find my shipmates in: somewhere loud but not deafening to the point of inhibiting conversation, busy but not crushing, with music but not a music venue, dark and slightly edgy, just a bar, not a restaurant, perhaps one of the places that projected blue movies which the clientele ignored, against the wall.

I finally ran them to earth in a bar off Davidstrasse, making a racket and teasing the barmaids: Duncan, Peter the leci, Peter the second and Sparks. I put on a mock-serious face and told them I had been despatched to find them because the ship was sailing early following a change of orders. We walked as far as the taxi rank before I exploded with laughter. They railed; drinks were on me. The night was enjoyable, the German lager was good, we ate bratwurst rolls in the street when we felt hungry, prostitutes cooed at us from doorways when we passed. We got into a scuffle with a belligerent Dutchman who was looking for trouble, although he had little chance as Duncan dumped him on the floor, knocking the wind and fire out of him. He sat up and waved his hands in surrender; we helped him to his feet and he bought us all a drink.

At two in the morning we'd had enough and took a taxi back to the ship. We went to the bar for the obligatory nightcap and found a bright group, the Old Man, the chief, the chief mate and his wife, all in a merry mood. We sat there for another hour and then started to drift off. Soon, it was me, Sparks, the Old Man and Peter the leci, who was asleep on the daybed. The Old Man started to moan again about our time in West Africa, about being arrested because the company had agreed a dodgy charter, about being 'abandoned' there without food. He then started a rant about the company providing us with only meagre rations in Rotterdam, even though our main stores had been arranged for Hamburg. He wound up the rant further, slurring away, attacking everything that our Hong Kong owners were doing, or not doing.

He decided we were being treated badly and it just wasn't good enough. He decided to call up the company in Hong Kong and give them a piece of his mind. We laughed and I egged him on, not thinking he would do anything. But he did. He ordered Sparks to get Hong Kong on the radio. Sparks tried to talk him out of it, he looked at me, I shrugged. Sparks and the Old Man went off to the radio room, I woke Peter up and we went off to our cabins.

There was a pounding on my cabin door. It seemed I had barely dropped off, but I looked at my watch and saw it was 06:30. I unlocked and opened the door; Sparks stood there looking worried.

"You'd better come up to the radio room, Simon – the Old Man's gone crazy," he said.

"Why me? Call the mate or the chief engineer."

"I can't get an answer from the mate. The chief told me to bugger off."

I felt like doing the same, but decided to go up and see what was going on.

It was bad. I stood outside the radio room with Sparks and listened to the Old Man talking to the radio.

"Iss no good enough. You hear me? Iss no good enough! We have had an arrrwwful time in Africa and iss juss no good enough."

"OK, Captain. I get the message," said the voice at the other end, sounding exasperated.

"You donn unnnerstan. Iss not good enough. Juss no good enough."

"Captain, I understand and I'll talk to you later today."

"The food we loaded in Rotterdam was poor … poor. Piss poor. We've been two months in an arse of a place and now we're off to another arse of a place. A pair of arses. It's not good enough."

"Captain, go to bed. I'll speak to you later."

Sparks whispered: "That's the company superintendent the Old Man is speaking to. He's just been saying the same thing over and over again for the past twenty minutes."

I nodded. I had guessed as much. It seemed that the Old Man, drunk as a lord, had decided to call the superintendent, his boss, in Hong Kong and give him a piece of his mind.

"Yeah, yeah. I'm going to bed, but … iss not good enough you know. We're not arses, you should treat us better."

"Goodnight, Captain."

"And iss your fault. Iss not good enough … you're an arse."

"Goodnight, Captain."

Sparks and I scuttled out the way as the Old Man went lurching down to his cabin.

"There'll be hell to pay over that," I said to Sparks.

He nodded.

There *was* hell to pay. The agent came aboard the next morning and said that the superintendent was on the early morning flight from Hong Kong and would be here later today. The Old Man looked worried.

"How bad was I, Second Mate?" he asked.

"Pretty bad, Captain. You just kept telling him that it wasn't good enough."

"Was I insulting him?"

"You called him an arse."

"Oh … God."

The superintendent came aboard that evening, looking mean and in a bad mood after a long flight from Hong Kong. The hospital bed had been made up for him to stay in. He was a hard-eyed grizzled man in his early sixties, twenty years' experience as master before being appointed superintendent. We could hear him roasting the Old Man from the next deck down, threatening him with the sack, referring to past misdeeds, telling him this was his very last chance. Most of us felt sorry for the Old Man, but the chief mate condemned him, shaking his head at the Old Man's unprofessional way of acting. He had probably been hoping the Old Man would have been sacked so he could assume command.

"He should act in a more dignified manner," said the mate.

This from someone who was vomiting into his beard the other night, I thought.

The Old Man remained subdued for the next week, until his natural ebullience lifted him up again.

After Hamburg we sailed on to Bremen, back round the north German coast and up the Weser River. Bremen enjoys fame or notoriety, depending upon your point of view, for the events of 1919 when the Bremen area declared it was a Soviet Republic and named itself the Revolutionary Republic of Bremen. It didn't last long though; four weeks later it was smashed to bits by the Freikorps, the seed corn of the Nazi party. Hundreds were killed. The Weser was another U-boat haven in the Second World War.

More steel in Bremen, long girders again, which were loaded in the bottom of the holds with a lot of smaller steel items packaged in tough wooden crates to be stowed in the tween decks. The German dockers were organised and had the reputation of militancy, from their revolutionary roots no doubt. Not that they ever actually ceased work, they just shouted and gesticulated a lot and often walked away shaking their heads at our English foolishness. There were two shifts: seven in the morning until three in the afternoon, and three in the afternoon until eleven at night. All the work was carried out by shore cranes so we swung our derricks out over the water side of the ship. We had three loading gangs which arrived at the bottom of the gangway exactly three minutes before the start of the start of the shift, before walking briskly onto the ship.

Duncan and I were leaning over the rails next to the gangway the first morning, watching them come aboard. Duncan said they looked as if they were marching; I said that I expect the Polish ships get worried. We sniggered together at our infantile humour. The German dockers marched past and eyed us cautiously.

Duncan took the first day's work from seven in the morning until eleven at night, which allowed me to spend the morning bringing the charts up to date. We had received sheaves of Admiralty chart corrects on our arrival in Hamburg, about four months' worth. Nautical charts are corrected all the time, with new lights and buoys, revised depths, wrecks and dangers, traffic routing systems, shoals, buildings on the shore, radio beacons and anything thought worthy of note. Chart correcting is an ancillary job given to the navigator, the second officer. I didn't dislike it; chart correcting was a task to get immersed in and shut out the world. I had my own set of fine-nib chart pens, black ink and magenta, and strove to make the changes as much like the original print on the chart as possible. Ships like the *Funing*, tramping anywhere for charters, carried worldwide chart portfolios, unlike liners that only carried the portfolios for the routes they plied. I brought all the European charts up to date first, leaving the more distant portfolios until afterwards.

After lunch I decided to visit the city. I was getting changed when the chief mate collared me in my cabin.

"Do me a favour, Second Mate. Take Susan with you. She's driving me crazy and I'm too busy to get off the ship."

My heart sank. I was planning a stroll around the town for a couple of hours and then meeting Peter the leci for a few drinks. I would feel a bit hampered, but it would have been wrong to refuse.

"Sure, Chief Off, my pleasure," I said, knowing Peter would be irritated. He didn't have a lot of time for the mate's wife.

In Bremen we had a telephone fixed at the top of the gangway, as we did in most European ports, so we asked the chief stevedore to telephone for a taxi to take us into town. It wasn't far, but we wanted to get maximum value for the time we had. Susan and I had different tastes. She was keen to visit the Boettcherstrasse, a street full of arts and crafts shops, and the Hachez Chocolatier, which had been making chocolate goodies for sweet-toothed Germans since the 1890s. For my part, I wanted to walk around the Schnoor Quarter with its medieval shops and narrow crooked streets, as well as visit the Becks Brewery, Bremen's most famous son. We both wanted to see the Rathaus, the historic town hall. We traded: she gave up the chocolate factory and I threw out the brewery, after which we spent a pleasant couple of hours walking the Boettcherstrasse and the Schnoor Quarter, before rounding off the sightseeing at the fifteenth-century Gothic Rathaus.

Culture done, it was off to the Ratzkeller in the basement of the Rathaus, local Becks for me, German riesling for Susan. Most German wines were grown 400 miles away in the south-west of Germany, along the French border. I felt my choice of drink was more apposite, Becks being brewed less than 400 yards away on the banks of the Weser.

Peter the leci arrived at six o'clock and I could see the disappointment etched on his face when he saw the chief mate's wife. I shrugged, he sulked. We all drank too much, drifted round a few noisy bars, ate a bad meal, arrived back at the ship at midnight. I delivered a staggering Susan to the mate, who gave me a dangerous look before packing her off to bed. The ship's bar was quiet but I had drunk enough anyway. The day ended with a flat feel, as such days often do, after the music stops and the beer has run dry.

Contrary to the old sailor motto about women on ships being unlucky, wives at sea were a force for good, in my experience. Officers and crews on British cargo ships and tankers at that time were virtually 100 per cent male. Passenger ships had female staff to a limited extent, although these tended to be in passenger care rather than working the ship: they were excursion organisers, entertainment staff and the like. There were females at sea in the Eastern European fleets, although these were huge hairy women who we made cruel jokes about. A female Russian captain or a female Polish chief engineer usually looked so frightening and mighty that we barely them regarded as female. The first flag bearers of female participation in the British Merchant Navy were starting to make themselves heard, although they had a hard time, constantly harassed and derided. A few pursued the life anyway, which they believed was worthwhile. I had taken over from a female second mate a few years previously and I knew of a couple of female radio officers doing the rounds. Overwhelmingly though, it was a male environment, with the exception of wives who went to sea with their husbands.

Rules varied from shipping company to shipping company about who could take their wife and for how long. Some companies only permitted the senior officers to be accompanied, others allowed all officers the privilege, although for no more than six months a year. There were rarely more than two or three wives on a ship at any one time. The crew were never permitted to travel with their wives: the standard of crew accommodation was too poor for two people to share a cabin, and the shipping companies were not going to enhance it to an acceptable standard for the occasional accompanied trip.

Generally speaking, wives at sea lightened the load. They brought an edge of civilisation to men who would otherwise have descended in manners and behaviour. Some would flirt, which was acceptable; others would stray, which was not. Some wives were quiet and mousy and remained out of sight in their cabin, almost as creatures of their husbands. Others were spirited and joined in everything. A wife who participated would run the bar and organise games and competitions. She would also, by Herculean effort, drag the conversations away from the perennial cycle of talk that travels back and forth between men at sea: drink, previous ships, outrageous occurrences involving drinking and humiliation and someone getting their just desserts, or all three. The conversations and shipboard life took a broader swathe when wives were involved, and we were all the better for it.

On the *Funing* we had two wives sailing with their husbands. Susan the chief officer's wife, who had been on board for some time, and Brenda the chief engineer's wife, who joined the ship in Bremen. They could not have been more unalike. Susan was young, in her twenties, slim and pretty and auburn haired; she laughed a lot. Brenda was more mature, in her late fifties; she was chunky, her blonde hair was from a bottle and she had a waspish edge. Brenda didn't like Susan, which I suspected was driven by wistful jealousy because Susan was young and pretty while Brenda was older and lumpish. Susan didn't like Brenda because she put her down and squashed her at every opportunity. The battle lines were drawn.

Brenda, being the wife of a man with four gold stripes, assumed her husband's rank and was spiffily superior to other officers, and in particular to other officers' wives, in this case Susan. It was usually a bad tactic for a wife, who had no true status on board a ship and was signed on as a supernumerary, to try and lord it over the ship's officers. I had seen it happen on several occasions over the years and the situation invariably ended badly. Humiliation was lurking in wait for Brenda, to spring out just when she least expected it. Susan was a bit of a coward and rarely fought back when Brenda was crushing her from her husband's exalted position. She usually just walked away with moist eyes, leaving Brenda gloating with satisfaction at the vanquishing.

Brenda's downfall came one night in the ship's bar in Bremen. She had just seen off Susan with a barrage of withering remarks, telling her variously that she was stupid, immature, dull, plain and a nuisance to everyone on board the ship. Susan fled. The rest of us went quiet and we smouldered with dislike of Brenda. Brenda was sitting at the bar, mildly drunk, looking hugely self-satisfied. She held out her glass imperiously to Peter the leci, who was behind the bar.

No delicacy from Peter: "I'm not serving you, you fat slapper!"

Brenda reared up. "How dare you! I am the chief engineer's wife, I'll have you know!"

"Aye, well if you were the chief engineer I wouldn't be speaking to you like this, but you're not, you're just a supernumerary … and a rude bitch."

Brenda turned to me. "Second Officer! Are you going to let this … *electrician* speak to me like that?"

I said: "Peter. Did you call Brenda a fat slapper?"

"Aye."

"Did you call Brenda a rude bitch?"

"Aye."

"Did you mean it?"

"Aye."

I turned to Brenda and said: "Sorry Brenda, Peter thinks you're a fat slapper and a rude bitch."

"And an ugly old cow," said Peter.

"And an ugly old cow, apparently," I added.

Brenda sat there and went puce, then flung herself off the stool and stormed out the bar. We were expecting the chief engineer to come down and start a ruckus, but he never appeared. He made an appearance the next day though, with a bruised mouth and a black eye. Brenda had obviously given him a good beating to vent her wrath.

We picked up our Thames pilot in a choppy sea at the North East Spit Pilot Station off the top corner of Kent. Pilotage was compulsory for ships of our size from there inwards.

The Thames is one of the great rivers of the world. It's not a mighty river, not as long as the Nile or as wide as the Amazon or as powerful as the Congo or as sweepingly graceful as the Danube. It's not even the longest river in England. But it breathes history. Drake and Raleigh sailed up the Thames to impress Elizabeth I; Hawkins and his privateer band slipped out through the mudflats to hunt down their prey; Nelson's battle fleets gathered off the Medway estuary; clippers came in from the Far East with their cargoes of tea; Darwin sailed on his journey that changed the view of life on earth; square riggers set off bound for Iquique to bring back nourishing phosphates; the great ironclad battleships paraded there at the turn of the century; magnificent ocean liners called in at their zenith; the *Bismarck* hunters of the Second World War gathered and plotted; and all the ships that brought in the wealth of the biggest empire the world has ever seen. Cook, Bligh, Henry Morgan, Julius Caesar, Angles, Jutes, Saxons, Vikings, Normans: they all sailed up and down the Thames, past Shoeburyness Headland, past the Isle of Grain and Holehaven Creek and into the meanders. They sailed past Gravesend ferry and Dartford and the Rainham marshes, past Bexleyheath, where the highwaymen would shoot your eyes out for a bag of coin. Then up and into the close reaches, into London and the wide swing round the Isle of Dogs, then finally the Tower of London squatting on the bank with a thousand bloody secrets, watching all the comings and goings along the Thames for the past 900 years.

The London docks at Tilbury was our last port of call before we headed off to the Persian Gulf. Tilbury was part of the Port of London Authority and was then the main London port. There wasn't much at Tilbury before the docks were built: the Romans were there, but then they were all over that part of England, Tilbury is mentioned in the Domesday Book as Tilberia. Queen Elizabeth I reviewed her troops at East Tilbury, and there has been a ferry running across to Gravesend on the south bank since medieval times, but that's about it. Its sister port Gravesend has a bit more history about it: Stone Age and Iron Age settlements, the Romans, an 800-year-old market, burnt by the French during the Hundred Years War, fortified by Henry VIII, bombed to bits by the Germans in the Second World War.

The historic older docks further upriver had virtually closed, derelict and silent, dead or having the last rites read, either filled in or just sitting there with grand plans for marinas and the regeneration of the surrounding inner city areas. In the early Victorian era, the main London docks were all near the city around Wapping, Rotherhithe, the Isle of Dogs and Tower Bridge. There were two main dock companies, the London & St Katherine Dock Company and its rivals, the East & West India Docks Company. As the nineteenth century progressed, ships became larger and as transport links were improved it became less necessary for ships to come so far upriver. The London & St Katherine Dock Company built a huge complex at East Ham: the Royal Docks. These were a tremendous commercial success. Trade boomed; it was the largest enclosed dock area in the world, containing 250 acres of water. Seething with envy and keen to get back at their rivals, the East & West India Docks Company retaliated through its parliamentary contacts, and was granted permission by Gladstone's government to build new docks at Tilbury, 25 miles downriver from the Tower of London. The first ship called there in 1886. Since then, Tilbury has relentlessly pulled traffic downstream, forcing the successive closures of all the old docks – the East India docks in 1967, St Katherine's in

1968, Surrey Docks in 1970, West India Docks in 1980 and finally the grand Royal Docks, which had been winding down and was in the process of closing that year, 1981, when we arrived at Tilbury. Tilbury had been progressively modernised at the expense of the old docks, and now had a container terminal, a paper terminal and a grain terminal. Tilbury had everything. Tilbury ruled supreme.

We were due to be in Tilbury for a week, topping up our cargo for the Middle East. The British dockworkers were heavily unionised and in were defensive mode after Margaret Thatcher's union-bashing forays. We were warned not to antagonise them, as it was thought they would walk off at any opportunity. The work was painfully slow, the Tilbury shop stewards determined to demonstrate that they would never be bested by capitalist lackeys such as us and insistent upon squeezing meaningless protocol out of every situation. The crane drivers all had a friend, from some earlier union agreement, in the cab, which caused the work to be even more pedestrian than it needed to be while they chatted. We mostly let them get on with it, just concentrating on making sure the right cargo was loaded into the right place. We took on quite a bit of deck cargo, some steel structures and a few containers, all loaded by shore cranes. There were also a couple of crated luxury cars, which we had earmarked as deck cargo even though the shippers were insisting they should go below deck. This caused a bit of a squabble until space was finally found in one of the tween decks.

My cousin Penny lived not far away, and so I visited and spent the evening there, imper-sonating a civilised man with decent values. Penny and her husband were schoolteachers

The author as Second Officer

with young children and a nice house; I was a spendthrift who drank too much and had accumulated nothing of value in my time on earth. We got on well, though, and I enjoyed the evening, eating thoughtfully prepared food and drinking wine that was too good for me. The next day they visited me on the *Funing* and I showed them round. I don't know what they thought. Probably: 'My God! Is this his life?'

Later that week I hired a car and drove to the small village outside Oxford where my widowed mother lived with my younger brother Anthony. Mum was fine. Dad had been dead four years now. Anthony was only sixteen and still at school, although he was already showing the potential to overhaul me in maturity by having a steady girlfriend. My elder brother Peter was with his partner in their flat in London; they were both up and coming bankers. Me? I had a string of utterly meaningless encounters to my list of credits; I couldn't even remember the names of most of the girls I had known, only Annie. I went back to the *Funing* feeling barely adequate.

Our passage to the Persian Gulf was interrupted by orders to call into the Loire and pick up 5,000 cases of wine and 500 cases of brandy in St-Nazaire for Abu Dhabi. At first thought this seemed an odd cargo for the Middle East, where the people were denied alcohol through religion, although it was apparently for the expatriate community over there, who worked hard to correct the balance, drinking for their countries. St-Nazaire should have been a relatively quick call, but only half the cargo had arrived when we moored so we had an idle time for two days. We were able to wander the town and eat *plats de fruits de mer* in cafes on the harbour front while guzzling wines from the Loire Valley as directed by the *patron*.

The passage to the Mediterranean was uneventful, with a quiet crossing of the Bay of Biscay, which we were thankful for because of our deck cargo. The last time I had crossed the Bay going south we went into the teeth of a storm, the deck cargo was ripped from its restraining wires and we spent a dangerous night trying to stop it careering round the deck and smashing up the ship.

There was an unseemly row between the Old Man and the chief engineer as we were steaming along the Algerian coast. It had been a hot summer that year and it warmed up further as we passed Cape Finisterre, where the Old Man gave orders to change into half and halfs: blues trousers with tropical shirts. Two days later we were steaming along the coast of Algeria when the Old Man decided it was warm enough to change into whites and also turn on the ship's air-conditioning. The captain was a tropical man, having spent most of his seagoing career in the Far East. He disliked the fussiness of full blues and was more comfortable in whites. So was I, in fact, as were most of the others, although not the chief engineer. He thought it was too cold to be in whites and far too cold to have the air-conditioning turned on. Now, the reality was that it was Brenda who didn't want the air-conditioning turned on and what Brenda wanted was what they both wanted.

In my observation, women feel the cold more than men, particularly as they age. It's not uncommon to see a man in shirtsleeves while his wife is wearing a jumper and coat. Brenda was a cold person, always wrapped up in several layers of clothing, and it was pretty clear that she was the emissary of the demand for no air-conditioning. I heard the Old Man and the chief shouting at each other in the Old Man's cabin one afternoon. Shortly afterwards the Old Man came banging and slamming onto the bridge.

"I don't know what's wrong with the chief!" he said.

I shrugged.

"It's bloody baking, and he's moaning about being in whites!"

There was no denying that it was hot along the north African coast, mid-eighties Fahrenheit.

"I certainly think we should be in whites, Captain." I said, diplomatically.

"What about the AC, though? The chief thinks it's too cold for the AC to be turned on!"

He went out onto the bridge wing and looked at the thermometer.

"Look! 83°F! We're off the coast of Africa in the summer, its eighty-three in the shade and the chief thinks it's too cold for air-conditioning! Unbelievable!"

I grunted. I never liked air-conditioning myself and would have been happier just leaving my porthole open.

The Old Man pressed me. "Well? Do you agree?"

"Most people would think it's warm enough to have the AC on, sir."

"Too bloody true!"

He stomped off.

The Old Man over-rode the chief and demanded the AC be turned on. The chief found various technical reasons why that couldn't happen. The leci needed to check it first for safety reasons, although he had another priority job; the coolant level was unsatisfactory; the drainage was blocked; the pressure was too low; the fuse box was arcing. The reasons were variously untrue or exaggerated, but the chief had the upper hand, being the senior technical man on board the ship. The chief's excuses caused the Old Man to gnash his teeth and glow with rage.

Finally, when he calmed down, the Old Man played his trump card by saying he was cabling the agent in Port Said to supply an engineering team to come on board and fix the AC while we transited the Suez Canal. The chief couldn't let that happen. First he would be exposed as a fraud, and second it would be a damning admission of his poor engineering skills if he had to have a shore engineer come and fix his machinery. Shortly afterwards, the AC started working, although the chief announced that it would need to be switched off every day for a couple of hours for 'necessary maintenance'. This necessary maintenance was always carried out after lunch, leaving the Old Man to swelter and curse in the heart of the day as he tried to take his afternoon nap. They both acted in an infantile manner, the Old Man going around without a shirt saying that he couldn't bear the heat, the chief in a jumper, shivering theatrically. Both sides strove to win support, but the game of life aboard ship is riven with politics so I sweated and shivered as needs be, depending upon who I was talking to, and kept out of the argument as best I could. The bickering lasted all the way to Suez, when the chief finally gave up and conceded that it was hot enough for the AC to be turned on properly.

When we arrive at Port Said, our agents came aboard and announced they weren't expecting us for another couple of days and so hadn't booked us into the southbound convoy. We headed for the roads to anchor, where Old Man took his time giving the agent a roasting for being slack. After my afternoon watch, I sat on the boat deck with a few others, drinking cold beer until the sun went down, watching the northbound convoy exit and the southbound ships line up without us, to start their transit. We spent a day swinging round the hook, before being taken in the convoy the following afternoon.

The canal transit was uneventful. We tagged on the end of the eight-ship convoy at four o'clock, which meant that we should expect to exit the Port Tewfaq end at breakfast time the next morning. The traffic in the Suez Canal was managed on a one-way basis, although passing was allowed at the Ballah Loop, where the waterway splits into two channels. Half way along its length, the canal widens into the Great Bitter Lake, where one convoy would anchor to allow the other to pass from the opposite direction. From start to finish, the 120-mile canal transit took us about sixteen hours.

The Suez Canal was owned and run by the Suez Canal Authority, which in turn was owned by the Egyptian state. When the canal first opened in 1869 it was jointly owned by the French, who had built it, and the Khedive of Egypt, who was the local head of state. Britain opposed the whole idea, seeing it as threat to its maritime dominance, and tried to sabotage the project, although without success. Once it was there to stay, Britain plotted to take control by first purchasing the Egyptian government's shares and then, in 1888, arranging for the Treaty of Constantinople to determine that the canal would be open to all nations, and placed under British military protection. The French were apoplectic, claiming the British had engineered the treaty. The canal remained under British control until it was nationalised by Egypt's President Nasser in 1956.

Our transit on the *Funing* was to be predominantly at night and we took our canal searchlight on board not long after passing through the harbour walls at Port Said. The searchlight, operated by one of the local canal boatman, was fixed up in the bow to shine our path. When I came up for the midnight watch we were just exiting the Ballah Loop and I could see the northbound ships across the sand in the moonlight. We headed down to pass Ismailia, the city that sits more or less at the midpoint of the canal, entering the Great Bitter Lake in the middle of my watch. I went onto the fo'c'sle head with the bosun to drop anchor, after which we stayed there, leaning on the rails and chatting, watching the northbound ships slide by. Half an hour later, the Old Man called us on the squawk box and gave instructions to weigh anchor.

Port Tewfik was at the southern end of the canal and we dropped the pilot the next morning as we passed the harbour heads. By the time I surfaced and came on the bridge in the middle of the morning, we were well into the Gulf of Suez, steaming south at full speed, twelve hours from the Red Sea, steaming for the Orient.

5

Return to the Orient

The Orient. The East. I always liked the word 'Orient' because it conjured up such an exotic image. Of course the Orient is only east to someone living in the west. The term comes from the Latin words *oriens*, which basically meant anywhere east of Rome and denoted the direction from which the sun rose.

Having defined the Orient as the East, at least to someone in the West (the Occident) we then have the different categories of East. There is the Near East, the Middle East and the Far East. It was the British who coined these phrases during the heyday of the British Empire, when London looked at its eastern possessions and spheres of influence and took its cue from Rome by referring to them in terms of their proximity to the British Isles.

The Near East used to mean the countries from Turkey to Afghanistan, including Egypt, the Lebanon, Iraq, Iran and all the Gulf states. The term Middle East sprung up in mid-Victorian times among scholars, and originally only referred to Mesopotamia, that corridor of land between the Tigris and Euphrates rivers in Iraq, the birthplace of much of modern civilisation. Over the years, the term Middle East has become expanded to take centre stage and now includes all those countries formerly known as the Near East.

The Far East is a general reference for those places near the Pacific edge: Japan, China, Korea, the Philippines, Thailand, Indonesia, Malaysia and Singapore. Between the Middle East and the Far East lies a group of countries including India, Pakistan, Sri Lanka, Burma, which don't have an 'East' reference. This bloc used to be referred to as the Indian subcontinent, although it has more recently been awarded the label 'South Asia'. All of this was very loose with much overlapping. Curiously, within these designations Russia and later the Soviet Union were always excluded. When deciding what was east and what was further east, the British always felt that Russia and all its satellites stood very much alone, not forming a part of any group.

For me though, the East began when we passed Perim Island in the Bab al-Mandab Strait at the southern end of the Red Sea, and swung our bow to head across the Gulf of Aden and out into the Arabian Sea.

It wasn't that I didn't like the Middle East; I just didn't like the parts I'd been to. But as for the unfathomable mysteries of the Arabic culture, the vastness of the Empty Quarter on the Saudi peninsula, the temples and icons and remnants of cultures that had disappeared thousands of years ago – I hadn't seen any of those. My Middle East experience was bleak oil jetties from my tanker days: baking heat, dust, soulless modern buildings and an anti-western sentiment. Similarly, I had no great feeling for the Indian subcontinent. I had been round the Indian coast on a couple of occasions, but I didn't know it well.

It was always the Far East for me. I loved the Far East. Singapore was my second home, I had lived and been to school there as a boy and returned many times since on various ships. Hong Kong, too, had been my stamping ground over the years, as had the Philippines, Borneo, Indonesia, Taiwan and Japan. I felt drawn to the Far East; I always felt good when we crossed the 100°E line of longitude, and felt I was coming home when we did.

As the *Funing* came abreast of Socotra Island, I yearned to set a course for the Eight Degree Channel, to slide between the Maldives and the Laccadive Islands, then cant south to Dondra Head on the southern tip of Sri Lanka and on for the Malacca Strait. Instead, we rushed along the coast of South Yemen, then Oman, heading for where I didn't really want to go, heading for the inferno of the Persian Gulf.

At the western side of the South Yemen coast, not far from the Bab al-Mandab Strait, is the port of Aden, which had been under British administration, together with the surrounding area, for 130 years. Ships on their way to India would lie off Steamer Point, the entrance to the harbour, to pick up supplies for the rest of the voyage. To the west of Aden port was Little Aden, where BP built a huge oil refinery to replace its assets following the Iranian nationalisation in 1951.

The Aden Protectorate started to smoulder in the late 1950s and finally erupted in armed protest against the British presence in the 1960s. After a bloody ten years the British government pulled the troops out in the late 1960s in a sea of recriminations, leaving behind a place that became South Yemen, full of hostile factions battling it out. In 1970 South Yemen swerved sharply to the left and a Marxist government was formed.

Refugees flooded out to North Yemen. Bad luck for BP, which lost its refinery again.

The coast of South Yemen was unrelentingly brown, rough, barren; low hills sliding down into the sea. The coast shelters a vast interior where less than 3 per cent of the land is considered arable. There is not a single river in the country that flows year round. Steaming along the coast, it was like travelling along a moonscape. Oman was the same, desolate and wasted, little to see until we turned to the north, when the coastline became even more rugged, although there was more life.

The bleakness of the South Yemen and Oman coastline made the green sea seem sharper in contrast, almost emerald in colour. The sun sat as a bright white orb in a blue-white sky, the colours scourged by dust blown out from the desert interior.

We steamed north through the Gulf of Oman towards the entrance to the Gulf. Although newsreaders referred to it as the Strait of Hormuz, navigators always called it the Quoins, after the two islands, Great Quoin and Little Quoin, which sit in the middle of the strait. We passed the Quoins on a bright afternoon, ready to swing south down the coast of the Emirates for our first port, Abu Dhabi.

The Quoins are always busy because that it is where the traffic is funnelled in and out of the Gulf. At that time nearly half the world's oil passed by those two islands.

The seas were thick with tankers, a lot of them immense. Ships of 200,000 tonnes deadweight were common. The largest in the world in 1981 was the *Seawise Giant* at 564,500 tonnes; she was 458 metres long, over 1,500 feet. These were known as VLCCs, Very Large Crude Carriers, taking crude oil to the big refineries in Europe and the East, where it was cooked to produce methane and propane, aviation spirit and high grade white oils, black oils and diesels, bitumen and tar. These behemoths sit 65 feet in the water and have to stay in the deep channels; we normal-size vessels had to keep out of their way. I had served on a VLCC as third mate, and when I left I vowed, 'never again'. Most of the ships we saw were tankers, those going into the Gulf were high out of the water in ballast, those coming out were deep down to their marks. There were always a few Arab dhows in sight, the traditional wooden sailing vessels with their lateen sails, unchanged for centuries.

Going through the Quoins in the early 1980s was a more tense experience than it had been a few years previously. To the south of the strait lies Oman, and to the north is Iran. The Iranian revolution in 1979 had caused the overthrow of the shah and the end of the fifty-year Pahlavi dynasty. What then followed was the creation of the Islamic Republic of Iran.

Singapore at Night

The new republic immediately turned against the US and Great Britain as representing the evils of the world. The US was referred to as the Great Satan, while Britain was rather woundingly referred to as Little Satan. In any event, steaming through the Quoins as one of the Satans, with Iran less than twenty miles away, was always a sobering experience. On the morning watch Duncan heard derogatory muttering about Satan on the VHF.

As we swung round to head down towards Abu Dhabi in the late afternoon, there was an occurrence which caused a tremendous row over the VHF airways. A heavy European accent – we speculated a Pole or a German – started making obscene comments about the Grand Ayatollah Ruhollah Khomeini, the then clerical ruler of Iran. The remarks were nasty and designed to hurt, involving the ayatollah committing unspeakable acts with small boys. The reaction and rage from the Iranian shore stations was ballistic, with screaming threats to hunt down, arrest and execute the perpetrator. Once the screaming died down the Polish/German voice would repeat its obscenities, stoking the rage to greater heights and ever more awful threats. We kept a strict VHF silence, not wanting to become involved in any way. It was good theatre, though, and I hung around at the end of my watch to keep listening.

I may not have liked the Gulf much, but I admired the history and culture of the area. The place is the cradle of civilisation. Sumer, one of the world's oldest civilisations, developed in what is now Iraq, between the Tigris and the Euphrates rivers in 5000 BC. These two great rivers flow into the northern end of the Gulf. The Sumerians had an effective economy and a functioning civil service 4,000 years before the ancient Britons had even learned to paint their faces blue to scare off demons. The Persian Empire held sway for centuries before Alexander the Great passed through the area, and a few years later the Romans were in town, as usual. The whole place was a perennial hotbed of war between the Arab peoples to the west and the Persians to the East. A thousand years ago, Arab mathematicians, astronomers and wise men led the world, the beauty of the poets was unmatchable, the Middle East gave us art that made the west look shabby.

What mattered in the Gulf now, though, was oil. In the early 1980s, the Gulf states held over 50 per cent of the world's oil reserves and accounted for 25 per cent of world production. Oil was all that mattered, oil was power, oil allowed all the Gulf countries to set the throttle of the global economy by controlling the price.

We were headed first for Abu Dhabi, in the Emirates. Before oil, the Gulf was famous for pearls, and the Gulf pearl divers were the best there were. Abu Dhabi was big in the pearl trade. Great Britain had had a presence in the Gulf since the middle of the nineteenth century, with bases along the Trucial coast. This was inside the Gulf and comprised part of Oman, together with what was then a collection of Arab sheikhdoms. Britain governed the Trucial States as a protectorate until 1971; after the British pulled out those states formed the United Arab Emirates.

Oil had been discovered in the Gulf in the 1930s, and this had changed the way in which the big European powers regarded the area. The oil companies poured in. But then most of the Gulf countries nationalised the British, French and American oil assets in the 1960s and 1970s, allowing the wealth to be retained by the locals, even though usually only by a few of them. Abu Dhabi was growing fast and the population was around 250,000 in the early

1980s. There was a lot of activity and a lot of building, hence the demand for the steel we were bringing.

Bad news awaited me in Abu Dhabi. The chief officer received a message that he was being relieved at our next port of call, Kuwait. A new chief officer would be joining. I was bitter. By that time I would have been on the ship for nearly four months and had been expecting promotion. I had my Master's Certificate of Competency, and I felt the job should have been mine. I complained to the Old Man, who shrugged in a 'what can I do?' manner. I sulked, I slammed about for a few days – all to no avail of course. I wrote a letter to Hong Kong asking why I wasn't being promoted.

The chief officer kept me company in my bitterness. He was also put out; he didn't want to leave, and he wanted to remain on board for another couple of months. I suspected that he was hoping the Old Man would disgrace himself further, thus allowing his promotion. We sat in the bar and bemoaned our fate. At least Abu Dhabi wasn't a dry state.

After Abu Dhabi we went north to Kuwait, another city state on the make, oil-rich, religious, intolerant, no sense of humour or forgiveness. The bar was sealed, and Susan and Brenda were told to make sure they covered themselves up properly. We checked our calendars and pictures to make sure they wouldn't appear to be too *risqué* for the religious police who patrolled the ship, the 'ayatollahs', as we called them. The sailors were told to take down any pictures of naked women they had pinned to their bulkheads.

There was a map of the world in the ship's office which offended the ayatollahs because it showed Israel. One took a black marker pen and obliterated it in a vicious scribble.

After a few days, Peter the second engineer was given a warning notice by the ayatollahs because he was judged to have 'homosexual pornography' on display. This pornography turned out to be a cartoon rugby calendar, one picture of which showed a group of rugby players larking about in the communal changing room bath. Peter was ribbed cruelly. The Old Man said he resented having a disgusting pervert on board and that he was considering putting Peter on a separate table by himself in the dining saloon because no one wanted to eat with him. The chief said he was thinking having him chaperoned whenever he was in the engine room as he didn't want him alone with any junior engineers.

We all goaded Peter endlessly; we called him every unpleasant name we could thing of: an uphill gardener, a shirt-lifter, a fudge-packer, a back-door man and a host of similar derogatory terms. Peter became very upset, denying that he had any homosexual leanings, robustly declaring his heterosexual nature. His denials and agitation made the baiting of him even more fulfilling for us, and the sport went on for several days until it eventually ran its course.

We stayed three weeks in the Gulf, discharging our steel. Towards the end, the agent in Kuwait told us that Hong Kong had agreed a new charter and we were to steam to Durban to pick up sugar and steel for Japan, along with chemicals and machinery for Penang, Singapore and Hong Kong. The charter was with the Chinese. The chief mate handed over to his relief, who came aboard shortly before we sailed. We had a muted leaving party, toasting the mate and Susan with lemonade now that the bond was sealed. One of the ayatollahs kept sticking his head round the door to make sure we weren't spiking our drinks with a hidden bottle of the wicked stuff. We weren't, not wanting the hell and shame of a Kuwaiti prison cell. Full bunkers were taken on board in Kuwait before leaving, oil not being a problem in that part of the world.

After dropping the pilot we set course south-east for our two-day run to clear the Gulf. The waters had a steady stream of tanker and gas carrier traffic heading in and out of the big Gulf ports: Mina-al-Ahmadi, Bandar Mahshahr, Bandar Shahpur, Bahrain, Doha, Umm Qasr, Dammam, Abu Dhabi, Dubai and Bandar Abbas. The busiest area was at the head of the Gulf from Kuwait round past the hectic Shatt al-Arab waterway to the inlet for Bandar Mahshahr. The Shatt al-Arab was a 150-mile stretch of river that acts as the border between Iraq and Iran, formed by the confluence of the Tigris and Euphrates rivers.

Most of the ships we encountered in the Gulf were well navigated and we had no incidents. There was over a billion dollars of oil cargo afloat in the Gulf at any one time, which made the ship owners and charterers focus on good manning standards, despite the general deterioration that was taking place in the established fleets.

I always enjoyed seeing the Persian Gulf while heading south-east. I felt the sea was cleaner, the landmarks clearer; there was more sea life and bird life. All this was nonsense, of course; it was the same as it had been on the way in, I was just glad to be heading for the exit.

A large eagle took up residence on the foremast spar for three days, venturing out for dinner in the fish-rich waters of the Gulf from time to time. The Old Man was a bit of a bird buff and he identified it as a Pallas's band-tailed fish eagle, a male, a huge prey avian that breeds in central Asia. The Old Man said it was on early migration. We named him Naki after the Iranian island of Nakhiloo, which we were steaming past when he joined us. I studied him in the afternoons through my Francis Barker binoculars, watching his bright eyes, watching his white head snapping from side to side as he in turn studied his world. Naki had a light brown breast merging to a dark brown shaggy body, and when he sighted his prey and launched off the spar, his six-foot wingspan opened and he spread his tail to display a distinct white stripe, then shot towards his victim like a missile. Naki was magnificent. He stayed with us until we were well into the Arabian Sea, then flew out one afternoon to fish and never came back.

When we came abreast of Ras al Hadd, the headland which is the easternmost point of Oman, we turned to the south-west for the twelve-day passage to Durban. We wouldn't make landfall until we reached the Comoros Islands at the head of the Mozambique Channel, apart from a brief sighting of Socotra Island off the tip of the Somali coast.

The Comoros reminded me of the Canaries in that they were spectacular volcanic islands rising high out of the ocean and visible a long way out on a clear day. Most of the islands had taken independence although one remained an overseas *département* of France. We passed through the islands and into the Mozambique Channel on a bright cloudless afternoon, flying fish skipping across the water, fleeing from underwater predators, birds out from the islands wheeling overhead.

The Mozambique Channel is the wide swathe of water between the island of Madagascar and the African mainland, about 200 miles wide at the narrowest point, widening to 500 miles at the southern end. Madagascar, to the east, had been an unwilling French protectorate for seventy years, until granted independence in 1960. When the French took control in the 1890s they had a seven-year resistance battle and lost a lot of troops, mainly to disease, before finally winning the day. The Madagascan royal family were exiled to the small island of Réunion. The enthusiasm of the French to take governance of the island was mainly driven by their desire to prevent the British doing it. They were concerned that the British Empire had expanded hugely in the African continent by hoovering up most of east Africa, from the Sudan to the Cape. Madagascar's long geographical separation from the mainland has resulted in plant and animal life development that is unique to the island. Some 90 per cent of all life on Madagascar is found only on the island.

To our west was Mozambique, which has had a bloodier recent history. The place began to be settled by the Portuguese in the sixteenth century when traders and adventurers took over Arab concessions and trading posts. The indigenous people became increasingly resistant to Portuguese rule, formalising their discontent in 1964 with the formation of the Mozambique Liberation Front, FRELIMO, a Soviet-backed Marxist guerrilla movement. The Portuguese rulers didn't take kindly to resistance and in the fifteen-year bush war tens of thousands of people were killed. In 1974 there was a revolution in Portugal and the military junta was overthrown. FRELIMO assumed control of Mozambique. I had been in the main port of Lourenço Marques a couple of weeks before the Portuguese revolution and returned four weeks afterwards.

What a difference. On my first visit, I had seen how brutal the Portuguese police were in their treatment of the local Africans; they carried *chicotes*, heavy hippo-hide whips about three feet long, which they used to move people along where necessary. But when I returned, the police stood around helplessly in small groups as the Africans strolled into the European-only shops and hotels with impunity, smirking, daring the police to say anything. Lourenço Marques was renamed Maputo. Over the next eighteen months, a quarter of million Portuguese fled across the border to Rhodesia and South Africa, and Mozambique collapsed into chaos.

Now, when we steamed past on the *Funing*, the country was in the grip of a ferocious civil war between the governing FRELIMO and the new guerrilla resistance army, RENAMO. Tales of unspeakable horrors seeped across the borders.

When we arrived at Durban we had to anchor on the roads for a couple of days before berthing at the north side of the harbour, just a quick hop over the railway tracks to the city centre. The north side of the harbour was a better place than Island View on the south side, which necessitated catching a ferry across the harbour. Island View was also renowned for sailors being mugged when they were on their way back in the small hours.

We berthed in the late afternoon, with cargo loading due to start the next day. The estimate for our stay in port was a fortnight. The mate was quite happy to stay on board that first night and let me and Duncan go ashore for the evening. Durban was familiar ground to me; I had called there several times on tankers and cargo ships. Whenever I visited there we had always stayed for some time – always several days, sometimes several weeks. I had managed to become involved in two car crashes there in the past: once as a cadet when a drunken South African giving us a lift ploughed his car into a roundabout, and once as third mate when I hired a car and lost control late one night, whacking it through a shop window. Duncan wanted to hire a car this time, but I was wary, so we walked up to North Beach and sat on the veranda of a hotel at the foot of West Street, drinking Castle beer and watching life pass by.

After a while we fell in with the boisterous table next to us, a group of white Rhodesians who had left the country when it had become independent the previous year and changed its name to Zimbabwe. They refused to call themselves Zimbabweans. They were in turn both bitter and maudlin about the loss of their country. Violence hovered in the air, and Duncan and I were careful with our words.

Later in the evening we took a taxi to the Smugglers Inn on Point Road with a couple of the Rhodesians. The Smugglers was a renowned late-night drinking den, dark, rough, a real dive. A woman was singing badly to rowdy cheers. We stayed until after midnight. The Rhodesians started a fight, but we kept out of it.

We finally returned to the ship in the early hours. The others were gathered in the bar, the Old Man was telling a tedious shaggy-dog story about a defrocked vicar; we had all heard it a dozen times. Duncan jumped in at the end and stole the punch line: "he lost his faith, because every time he went to work it was the same old story."

Everyone groaned. The Old Man looked wounded and irritated at being upstaged.

The loading went slower than planned. Our steel and drums of chemicals were unloaded from flatbed railway carriages and deposited on the quay before being swung on board by the shore cranes. Occasionally the train bringing the cargo would be delayed up country and I would amble around listlessly in the heat while the dockers lay on the deck in clumps, waiting for the next goods train to arrive.

Some mail arrived before we left: two letters from home for me, one from my mother bringing me up to date with the happenings and an envelope packed with bills. I also had a letter with a Hong Kong postmark, from the company. I was to be appointed chief officer on my next ship, the *Coral Chief*, a container liner on the Far East to South Pacific trade. They wanted me to take over at the end of February, which meant that I would get over two months' leave if I could get off before Christmas, hopefully in Hong Kong.

The worry of being stuck as an over-qualified second mate receded. If I hadn't been promoted I would have left the company. Getting a berth wasn't as easy as it had been five years previously; jobs were much thinner on the ground. I wasn't that worried, though, because I had all the ingredients that really mattered: youth, health, qualifications, experience and optimism.

Three weeks in Durban and we were done, loaded to our marks. We slipped our moorings after lunch one day and swung out towards the east. The ship was very stiff because the heavy steel placed a disproportionate amount of weight in the bottom of the holds. We had loaded the drums of chemicals in the upper tween decks to raise the centre of gravity as much as possible to counteract the steel, but the *Funing* was still very stiff.

Essentially, there are three points that control the transverse movement of a ship, the rolling of the ship. The first point is the centre of gravity, through which the downward gravitational force of the ship is expressed. The second point is the centre of buoyancy, which is the centre of the underwater area through which the upward flotation force of the ship acts. The third point is known as the metacentre, which is the fixed point about which the ship the ship moves, similar to the swinging point of a pendulum.

So, if a ship has a low centre of gravity because most of the weight is in the bottom and a low centre of buoyancy because the ship is loaded well down into the water, the metacentre tends to be very high. A high metacentre means that there is a huge righting force every time a ship is made to heel over from the movement of the sea. This large righting force causes the ship to come back upright with a jerk. When a ship is loaded like this there is no smoothness to the roll; the ship is made to lean over by the force of the waves then snaps back upright, leans again, snaps upright again. This is a stiff ship, and it has an uncomfortable motion.

Not as uncomfortable as a tender ship, though; the opposite in fact. A tender ship has a high centre of gravity and a small righting force, usually brought about by the holds being full of lightweight space-hungry cargo – goods in cartons perhaps – and a lot of heavy deck cargo. When the ship heels over it hangs there loosely, before slowly and reluctantly rolling upright again. The movement of a tender ship is disconcerting; it feels as if the vessel is not only going to fail to come upright but is going to carry on rolling over and just flop under the sea. The desirable state is between the two, which is what the chief officer aims for when working out the loading plan. It wasn't the case this time, though; we went across the Indian Ocean as a very stiff ship indeed.

There are two possible ways to go from Durban to Penang. The first is south of Madagascar, north of the islands of Réunion and Mauritius, over the top of Sumatra and down the Malacca Strait. The alternative is south of Madagascar, south of Réunion and Mauritius, through the Sunda Strait between Sumatra and Java, then up the east side of Sumatra, northwards through the Malacca Strait. My preference was the first, going north of Sumatra and then down the Malacca Strait. It was the more direct route, it was half a day shorter and it avoided the island-hopping we would have to do if we went through the Sunda Strait and came up from the south. I found it hard to believe that the Old Man was even considering the southern route, but then he was an old-time Far East man who knew the currents and weather, and he had his reasons. In any event, after deliberating he told me that we would go north anyway.

The passage to Penang was 5,300 miles, which at 15 knots would take us fourteen and a half days. I spent a couple of hours laying off the courses, running close to Madagascar and within radar distance of Réunion and Mauritius. From Mauritius we would head east-north-east until we were past the atolls and reefs shoals of the Chagos Archipelago, after which we would pull round to the north-east and head for the tip of Sumatra. Traffic would be light until we reached the Malacca Strait, and no adverse weather systems were in evidence. We were anticipating a good voyage, albeit uncomfortable if we hit heavy swell from the south, because of the stiff roll the ship would give.

The Old Man became uncharacteristically gloomy after we passed Madagascar. Like many exuberant people, he would very occasionally become dispirited and his buoyant personality would collapse. He had been mooning about for a couple of days when he collared me at the end of my watch one afternoon and told me that he needed to speak to me in my capacity of ship's medical officer. The medical officer role was a position that generally fell to the second mate.

We went down to the dispensary where he informed me that he was depressed. I listened to his tale, arranging my features to appear wise and informed. From what I could make out, the Old Man's low spirits were brought about by a resurgence of worry over his antics in Hamburg when he had called the company superintendent in Hong Kong, given him a piece of his mind and told him he was an arse. I tried to talk him up, telling him the matter was done and forgotten. He didn't accept this, being convinced that the company might take further action against him when he went on leave. He thought it probable that he would be asked to report to the head office in Hong Kong on the ship arriving there, to discuss any residual issues surrounding the legal wrangling that had taken place in Nigeria. He had convinced himself that once in Hong Kong he would get a proper roasting and might even be dismissed.

I continued to display a bright and cheerful tone, believing this was the best way to bring him round. I gave him a bit of Omar Khayyam, thinking that would buck him up. "Come on, Captain. What's done is done. 'The moving finger writes and having writ moves on. Nor all thy piety nor wit shall lure it back to cancel half a line, nor all thy tears wash out a word of it.' That's the way to look at things. Accept you made a mistake and move on."

"That is not in any way helpful, Second Mate. I came to you for some treatment, not a bloody poetry recital."

"Unborn tomorrow and dead yesterday. Why fret about them if today be sweet?"

"Enough of that crap! Give me some sulphadimidine."

"Sulphadimidine is for infections, Captain, not depression."

We consulted the *Ship Captain's Medical Guide*.

"See?" I said, jabbing my finger at the page, which read: 'For the treatment of acute infections such as pneumonia and tonsillitis'. "It's not for depression."

He said: "I'm sure that's what I had before."

Ever on the lookout for medical fakery, I wondered whether the Old Man had an infection he wanted to keep secret and was trying to get sulphadimidine under another flag. I thought this unlikely, though, as he looked so depressed. I read through the book more.

"Ah, here we are, page 218: Depression. It says that in cases of depression I need to be patient, tactful, firm, apply common sense and be sympathetic."

"I'd hardly call waffling Persian poetry at me any of those things," he grumbled.

"Page 219; this is more like it. If you have mild depression, I should talk to you frankly and make you see your troubles in a new light. I should then make sure you get a good night's sleep and give you a couple of sedative tablets. Do you think you have mild depression, sir, or is it more advanced?"

"Go on, what does it say under advanced?"

"Right, here we are: advanced depression, although not to a dangerous level. Treatment: a few days of complete rest with sedatives before returning to duty. How does that sound, Captain? How about a few days off?"

"It sounds unrealistic, I'm the ship's master; it's not as if I can go away for the weekend," he said glumly. "Is there anything else?"

"There is. Major and severe depression. I quote: 'In the case of a patient who appears to be frankly insane, and who is dangerous either to himself or others, continuous and close observation must be maintained until he can be transferred. If ordinary sedatives are not sufficient, it may be supplemented by chlorpromazine three or four times a day.' Hmm, what do you think, Captain?"

"I'm not insane!" he said indignantly.

"I wasn't suggesting you were," I said. "I was just wondering if it was chlorpromazine you had last time, rather than sulphadimidine."

"Well, whatever it was I'm not bloody well being treated for insanity, that's for sure."

We sat in silence for a while.

I said: "I do have one idea, sir."

He said: "What might that be, Second Mate?"

"Why don't we go down to the bar and polish off a few bottles of Castle beer?"

Pause, then a smile from him: "Good idea. Lead on."

I never thought myself to be a particularly good medical officer.

One Monday we had a boat and fire drill. The Old Man felt we should have a complete exercise rather than the usual mustering. The timing was to be was ten in the morning, which everyone hated. Usually they tended to be at 16:30, which meant a slightly early finish for the day workers, didn't disturb those taking an afternoon nap and didn't really interfere with the ship's routine. Ten in the morning interfered with my navigational routine, wrecked the morning's maintenance work by the deck crew, interfered with the steward's cleaning regime, annoyed the cook and his staff, and wreaked all sorts of havoc down below in the engine room. Still, a full boat drill and fire exercise was going to take the best part of ninety minutes so at least it wouldn't conflict with those going for pre-lunch watering in the bar.

Smack on ten o'clock the ship's hooter gave the general alarm, seven short blasts followed by one long one. We all trooped out in our lifejackets, which at that time were the bulky kapok-filled versions as approved by the Department of Trade. We had four lifeboats, two on each side, skippered by the Old Man, chief mate, second mate and third mate. They were all pretty basic open boats, banks of oars and a hand-cranked diesel engine.

The procedure was to release the gripes, the locking wires that held the boat fast, then lower the lifeboat down to the boat deck so we could all pretend to climb in. One of the sailors climbed in to screw in the plug before we lowered it, in case some mishap landed the boat in the water. I then signalled to lower away until the gunwales were level with the boat deck. The Old Man was on the bridge overseeing everything, I called him on the walkie-talkie.

"Number 3 lifeboat down to the boat deck, Captain."

"Get your men in it, Second Mate."

"Pardon, sir?"

"Get everyone in the boat and ship oars. This is a full drill," he commanded.

I noticed the ship was slowing. I thought, Good grief, he's going to launch the boats. The sea was flat calm.

I turned to the crowd. "OK everyone, in the boat. Wait until it's secured first."

There was the expected grumbling. I had two ABs pull the boat close in with wires to minimise the gap, then climbed in first to show example. The rest followed. The boat started swaying.

"Everyone sit down. Sit down."

Down they sat. I left two ABs on the boat deck to release the boat as needs be. They would lower the boat using the release lever and then climb down the monkey ladder.

"Raise oars!" I shouted to the sailors in the boat. They hoisted the oars so they stood vertically. "When I give the order," I said to the two ABs on the boat deck, "let the boat swing out and then throw the monkey ladder over."

They nodded.

"We're all ready to go, sir," I said to the walkie-talkie.

"OK, Second Mate. Start the engine, test the lifeboat radio and check the water, stores and pyrotechnics, then wind the boat back up and secure it. I'm just going to send the mate's boat down to the water."

"Aye, aye, sir."

We all smirked, relieved that we wouldn't have the task of dropping our boat into the sea and then winding it all the way back up again. That was such a back-breaking task it had to be shared by all. The mate was probably fuming.

The third engineer powered the engine with a few turns of the handle, and a couple of us wound the dynamo on the lifeboat radio until the signal light glowed.

"Engine started, Captain. Radio in order, Stores and water all correct."

"Good show, Second Mate. Bring the boat back in and secure it."

We stowed the oars and all hopped out, the last man unscrewing the plug to prevent the boat filling up when it rained. The winding in was enthusiastic; we were all keen to watch the entertainment with number 2 boat, the mate's boat, when it was dropped into the Indian Ocean.

Our boat secured, we all ambled round to the other side of the boat deck to watch the show. The mate's boat was in the water by then but still attached to the wire falls. The Old Man bellowed form the bridge: "Let go! Take a turn round the ship!" The way was off the *Funing* now and she had almost come to a halt. The mate was shouting at his men. They released the falls, the boat set off, the engine died. The mate screamed at the second engineer, the second engineer screamed back at him, the junior engineer started swinging the handle. We all chortled, safe up on the boat deck.

"Start the engine!" shouted the Old Man helpfully.

"We're trying to start the bloody thing, Captain!" We heard the mate's voice crackling through the Old Man's walkie-talkie handset.

It wouldn't start. There was lots of accusatory shouting and arm-waving as the lifeboat drifted astern. The *Funing* was still making about 2 knots. I heard the telegraph ring on the bridge, the ship started to shudder, the Old Man had rung half astern to stop the ship dead in the water. The wash boiled around the stern area; we watched with glee, waiting for it to hit the lifeboat. When it did, the little boat bucked and bobbed. The mate had just order the oars to be lowered. One sailor lost his grip and the oar slipped into the sea. The mate howled with rage. It was a great theatre.

Half an hour later all the boats were back in place and secure. The mate looked hot and angry; he was red-faced with irritation and snapped at anyone who spoke to him.

The fire drill wasn't as strenuous as the boat drill, but it was more frenetic, with people rushing everywhere. The Old Man declared a fire in the paint store under the centre accommodation, and we all set about saving the ship.

As second mate, I was in charge of the breathing apparatus so I had one of my team mask up and don the oxygen bottle set, then parade up and down for a while. I decided that this was too tame, though, so made him jog up to the bridge deck and back to demonstrate how quickly the oxygen would be used up.

The mate directed the actual fire-fighting, which consisted of two hose parties. They connected the hoses to the seawater main on the deck, then blasted water over the side, each one testing the big brass nozzle to make sure it threw both a long jet and a diffused spray as it was turned. There were four men on each hose to control the huge pressure that rushes through; one person couldn't control a hose on his own. I had tried once as a cadet and been flung all over the place, to the hilarity of those watching.

The standard fire-fighting tactic was to have both hose teams performing together, the spray team creating a cooling wall of water to allow the jet team to get close to the fire without being cooked.

The chief steward and his team strapped the junior messman into the stretcher and lugged him up to the hospital. One of the stewards slipped and dropped his end at one point, whacking the messman's head on the deck, which amused the onlookers but caused an indignant yell from the patient.

Duncan let off a couple of fire extinguishers that were nearing their refill dates, one foam type and one of the dry powder ones for electrical fires. Until recently, we had put someone in an asbestos fire suit and gloves during the drill, but this had now been banned; post-war medical research had revealed that asbestos was deadly to the lungs and so most shipping companies had disposed of these fire suits in the 1970s. The fire suit we had to wear when I was a cadet even had an asbestos hood, for more certain early death presumably. I read up on asbestos at a later date and discovered that the Roman Pliny the Elder had written a treatise on the dangers of working in asbestos mines nearly 2,000 years ago. I found it disillusioning that modern medicine was so slow to catch up.

After the fire was declared extinguished, the hoses were rolled up and re-housed, the extinguishers refilled, the breathing apparatus and stretcher stowed away. It was half past eleven and the crew were shuffling around trying to look busy, hoping they wouldn't get put back to work for the half hour until the lunchtime break. The Old Man decided to round things off with a man overboard drill. This pleased most people, as it was always an interesting spectacle. The ship was brought back up to full speed, the bosun and a couple of ABs took a chunky wooden crate onto the starboard side of the main deck, then looked up to the bridge and waited for the Old Man's signal. The rest of the ship's company clustered around on the main deck and boat deck, waiting for the signal. The Old Man dropped his arm, the bosun and his men heaved the crate overboard and a huge chorus rose from all of us watching: "Man overboard to starboard!"

I ran up to the fo'c'sle head with the bosun and several crew members, while Duncan and the Old Man up on the bridge performed the classic man overboard manoeuvre. The first task was for Duncan to pull the wooden peg out of the starboard bridge wing lifebuoy, releasing it to roll down its chute and into the sea. As the buoy dropped it pulled a Schermuly smoke signal canister with it. The release pin for the canister was lashed by a rope to a fixed point on the ship. As the rope went taut it pulled the release, and the Schermuly canister burst, releasing brilliant orange smoke. The smoke lasted for 15 minutes. The man who had fallen overboard would hopefully see the smoke and swim to the lifebuoy, and the ship then would turn back and head for the smoke. In practice, the Old Man didn't want to waste a good lifebuoy and so Duncan had detached the Schermuly canister beforehand, yanked the release line and flung it into the sea.

Simultaneous with the release of the lifebuoy, a number of other actions took place. The ship was put hard-a-starboard; one man was ordered to climb the mast on the monkey island, and another to climb the foremast, both to act as lookouts; a call went down to the engine room to put the engines on standby; the general emergency signal was sounded, seven short blasts and one long; and the man overboard flag, O for Oscar, was hoisted.

Some authorities said that the engines should be immediately put on stop so that the man overboard wouldn't get chopped up by the screw, but most deck officers thought that was pointless. On a typical ship travelling at speed, it takes about ten seconds for the man who falls over at the mid-length to reach the point where he is passed by the propeller. By the time the telegraph is rung and acknowledged, the duty engineer will only have a few seconds to stop the propeller turning, which simply cannot be done. The best chance the man overboard has on hitting the water is to immediately strike out to swim as far away from the ship as possible in the limited amount of time he has before the tumult of water around the propeller area sucks him down and in and around and around, drowning him or mangling him or both. At the same time the ship is turned towards the side where the man went over, to swing the stern away from him.

Next, the Old Man and Duncan executed a Williamson Turn. The *Funing* was allowed to go 60 degrees off course to starboard and was then put hard-a-port to come right round to the reciprocal course. If done right, this should put the vessel heading straight back towards the man overboard position. If the manoeuvre worked, we should be back at the overboard position within 12 minutes.

We were all very tense; to us it was the real thing and the wooden crate had life. The day was calm and visibility was good, we could see the smoke almost dead ahead, as it should be. We searched for the crate. The lookout on the foremast mast saw it first and shouted down.

The Old Man put the engines on slow ahead. The chief mate already had the lifeboat down to the boat deck, ready to launch, all thoughts and feelings of his earlier lifeboat frustrations forgotten. Engines on dead slow. The wooden crate drifted down our starboard side, 30 yards away. Stop engines. Our man overboard was deemed saved. We all cheered. It was good seamanship, and everyone was proud.

I had a strange experience early one morning on the twelve to four watch. We were in the middle of the Indian Ocean, south of the Chagos Archipelago, about halfway on our voyage to Penang. It was the middle of the watch, just after two in the morning. The sea was deserted of ships, no lights on or below the horizon, just us alone in the centre of a dark circle. It was a warm night, a balmy night with no wind, no moon, just the light from the brighter stars flung down into the sea, reflecting back. The swell was minimal and the ship barely rocked as we cleaved through the water. There was a hint of bioluminescence along the hull and in the wake. I was dressed in tropical uniform, white shirt, white shorts, white socks, light shoes.

Some second officers on the midnight to four watch took advantage by dressing more casually, although I never did, I liked the order, I liked knowing exactly what I was doing. Everyone on board was in their bunk except me and the quartermaster/lookout above deck, the third engineer and the duty fireman down below in the engine room. I allowed the lookout to go down to the crew mess for a fifteen-minute break. If we had been in busy waters I wouldn't have permitted him to go without a relief, but in the middle of the Indian Ocean it was fine.

I had been in the chartroom, working on the next stage of the voyage under the dim yellow lamp that hung over the chart table, laying off courses from Penang to Singapore. Every ten minutes I would go out onto the bridge to make sure the lookout was awake, to scan the horizon myself and make sure he hadn't missed anything. I would first lean against the forward ledge until my eyes were re-accustomed to the darkness, then walk to the end of each bridge wing, searching through 360 degrees. I always looked 5–10 degrees above the line of the horizon, because the light sensors in our eyes are at the periphery of the pupil and so looking above the line of the horizon gave the best chance of seeing any new lights.

I stayed out on the bridge now that the lookout had gone down for his tea, sipping my mug of coffee and condensed milk, intending to return to the chartroom when he reappeared.

A sudden wind sprung up and blew through the wheelhouse, a cold wind, almost a chill wind, causing me to shudder. It seemed strange and I couldn't understand what had caused it, I assumed we had passed through some minor weather front, a cold front, even though there had been nothing in the met observations to suggest that, and nothing in the cloud cover. Whatever it was, it was cold. I walked over to the starboard side and pulled the big heavy teak door shut, sliding it closed on its runners, then walked over to the port side and did the same. The wind stopped blowing through.

A few minutes later I walked into the chartroom to pick up my cigarettes. When I came back to the wheelhouse, less than thirty seconds later, both doors were open. Odd. I pulled them both closed again and slid in wooden wedges, assuming the gentle motion of the ship had caused them to move. I reached for my coffee then realised I had taken the mug into the chartroom and left it there.

Back to the chartroom, back out onto the wheelhouse. The doors were both open again, the wedges lying on the deck. I strode out onto the bridge wing, looking for the lookout, thinking he was playing some sort of game. No one was there; he was still below on his tea break. I shut both doors firmly, I snapped on the brass retaining hooks, I hammered in two wooden wedges to each door, I tried yanking on them; they didn't budge. The doors were as securely closed as they could be and shouldn't work themselves loose again.

The crash came several minutes later. And what a crash it was. Like a thunderclap. I was leaning against the glass window at the forward part of the wheelhouse, gazing into the inky blackness, lost in idle thoughts when both of the big heavy bridge wing doors exploded open. The brass hooks snapped out, the wooden wedges flew through the air. The sea was flat and the ship was barely moving. And then, the creeping cold slid in and wrapped itself round me in an icy blanket, it made me gasp, I lost my breath, I couldn't move, I couldn't hear, chill fingers crawled into my mouth, I started to choke, there was something awful all around me. Five seconds perhaps, maybe only three, and then it was gone and I broke into sweat in the warm Indian Ocean night.

I lit a cigarette, my hand shook. My mind conjured stunted shapes crouching in the dark on the bridge wings.

And what was it, what could it have been? I've speculated ever since. Did we pass over the spot where a ship once foundered, lost with all hands, was this the last gasping place of a hundred drowned sailors? Did a man die here once, alone and abandoned, fallen overboard unheard and left to shriek and rage and panic in the dark waters as his ship receded and the white-tip sharks began to circle? Had we run over the ocean graveyard where whales go to die?

Perhaps I had just been half asleep with my imagination running to idiocy. I didn't spook easily, I didn't get scared. I didn't believe in ghosts. I left the doors open for the rest of the watch, though, and was glad when the lookout returned.

We came abeam of Pulau Weh Island in the early hours after thirteen days at sea, coming in from the Andaman Sea. Pulau Weh is the island off the northern tip of Sumatra and marks the entrance to the Malacca Strait. The place has always been strategically important and has a good harbour at Sabang, the principal port. I had been there once, years before, and remembered it as a sleepy, slightly shabby place, pleasant with a mix of population who smiled a lot and who were mainly Muslim.

As we leant on the bridge wing in the dark and watched the lights, the Old Man told me that the harbour at Sabang was to be dredged out to have a major oil and container terminal. Good for Sabang – no more sleepiness, though. From Pulau Weh it was a day's run across the top of the straits to Penang.

The island of Penang is part of Penang state and is one of Malaysia's larger islands. The thirteen states in Malaysia are mostly ruled by their own sultans, with the exception of four,

Penang being one of them. It used to be part of the much larger state of Kedah although the then Sultan ceded it to the British in return for becoming a protectorate against marauding armies from Siam and Burma. To seal the deal, the British representative, Captain Francis Light, also married the Sultan's daughter. Light named the island Prince of Wales Island and the main settlement Georgetown after the then young heir to the British throne.

There were subsequent squabbles with the Sultan, particularly when the British government failed to honour Captain Light's bargain, which he had made without consulting them, to defend Kedah against an attack by Siam. The matter was eventually settled with a perpetual annual payment being made to the Sultan of Kedah, which continues to this day. Penang became part of the Straits Settlements under British rule, and remained so until independence was granted in 1957. It wasn't a happy place for a lot of the British rubber planters who passed through though, due to the huge number of deaths from malaria, earning it the over-used title 'white man's grave'.

We only stayed in Penang for a day, discharging chemicals and picking up transhipment cargo for Singapore. All my visits to Penang had been short ones and I was disappointed that I had never had the opportunity to have a stroll around the streets of Georgetown.

The Malacca Strait separates the Indonesian Island of Sumatra from Malaysia. Wide in the north, the strait narrows at the southern end to a very busy patch of water in the approaches to Singapore, the city-state island sitting at the toe of the Malay peninsula. Nearly all traffic to and from the Far East uses the Malacca Strait, making it one of the world's busier shipping areas. The exceptions are ships coming from the far south, Australia or the southern Indian Ocean, which sail through narrow gaps in the Indonesian archipelago, usually the Sunda Strait.

I was in a bar in Singapore once when someone standing next to me, acting as an old sea-dog and an obvious imposter, started banging on about how he was caught in the Malacca Strait in thick fog one day, with ships passing him so close he could touch them. I thought, Hmm. Fog is a phenomenon of colder climes, and happens when moist air comes into contact with a cold surface that cools it down below its dew point. There is as much chance of getting fog in the Malacca Strait as there is running into an ice-storm in the Persian Gulf.

The Malacca Strait climate is monsoon: the south-west monsoon from April to October and the north-east monsoon for the rest of the year. The word monsoon comes from the Arabic *mawsim*, meaning seasonal. The prevailing monsoon sets the direction of the wind and weather; sometimes the monsoon winds can blow for days unabated. The wettest months in the Malacca Strait are October to March, during the north-east monsoon. The rest of the year tends to be drier, although precipitation can still occur during the south-west monsoon when the air blows in over Sumatra and heats up to build huge thunderheads, which cause the rain to come sluicing down in the afternoons.

So, in the Malacca Strait there can be torrents of rain at any time of the year, sometimes so heavy it blocks visibility. But never fog. I didn't contradict the old sea-dog though – I let him have his bark.

It was a day's run down the strait to Singapore. As we left in the mid-afternoon a massive thunderstorm rolled over the coast, the sky went as black as doom, lightning flashing and slashing across the cloud, the rain coming down on us in heavy rods. The navigation in the Malacca Strait was reliable, thankfully, with well-tended lighthouses and buoys to mark the islets and shoals.

There was a constant flow of shipping of all types. An old Hong Kong flag passenger ship limped along, northbound for Saudi Arabia with a full cargo of pilgrims. The pilgrimage, the *Hajj*, is a religious duty that every able-bodied Muslim who can afford to journey to Mecca should go on once a lifetime. Once done, the pilgrim can call him or herself a *mustati*.

In contrast, a modern Cunard liner rushed past us with a cargo of fat, rich westerners on their own pilgrimage to exotic meals and tax-free shopping. Once done, they would have photographs and videos and obscure carvings, their own relics to impress the neighbours.

A Ben Line ship on her way home, a Dutch Nedlloyd liner on her way out. A procession of Shell tankers: black oil carriers, white oil carriers and supertankers. A small group of Royal Navy ships on a fly-the-flag voyage of the East. Container ships, car carriers, general cargo ships, bulkers, tankers, warships – they all passed us by. Closer to the shore and all down the Malay coast were small fishing boats riding the waters, the occupants lifting a lazy hand in salute if we passed close. The traffic stepped up as we neared the Singapore Straits.

When we arrived in Singapore we received bombshell news: the *Funing* was to be sold to the Chinese. That brought a general glumness of mood. When a crew signed on a ship, they always felt it was 'their' ship; they felt it belonged to them. A ship's crew tended to think, quite unreasonably, that they had some sort of rights to or control over the vessel. This feeling was probably brought about because the ship was our home and as such we believed we had a say in the matter. We didn't of course, nor could we or should we – but that didn't change the way people felt.

It was not dissimilar to the feeling when a Marconigram arrived to advise that someone would be paying off the ship at the next port. There was joy and elation at going home of course, usually exaggerated, but at the same time there was also a tinge of sadness at what was in effect 'leaving home'. Curiously, I had this feeling even when I disliked the ship and was keen to get off.

We were all sad that the *Funing* was being sold, sad because no one liked to see the fleet diminished and sad because … she was being sold. But it was the way of the commercial world and it was the way of ships. Sooner or later all ships die, they are either sold, or scrapped or they sink and disappear beneath the waves. A bit like people really; not exactly the same, although there is a parallel.

Our orders were that after finishing the charter in Yokohama we would be dry docking in Moji, at which time the ship would be overhauled and transferred to the new owners. My thoughts of being home for Christmas disappeared; no one would now be relieved before the sale. Homecoming was looking nearer mid-January for me.

Singapore came and went. The place was changing fast. I had been at school in Singapore as a teenager, at which time it still had the vestiges of British rule by way of the organisation, the police uniforms, the cars, street names, the grand old buildings and the general ambiance of the place. But by the early 1980s, the island was driving at full speed for modernity in every way. Huge modern buildings were springing up, there was an emphasis on pride in the nation, hygiene initiatives were purging the grubbiness out of the streets, though taking away a lot of colour and character at the same time. The government was becoming increasingly intolerant of dissension. It wasn't an oppressive state, but the place didn't have a comfortable feel about it.

I had a stroll around the port area. The sailor bars in Anson Road near the docks were all closed. Connell House, the old colonial style Seaman's Mission founded by the merchant navy engineer Matthew Connell, where I had stayed on many an occasion, was now a government building. The street markets were quieter and pristine, the men all had short haircuts, the women looked demure, and no one chewed gum or shouted or acted in a disorderly manner. Few people smiled. I went back to the ship feeling disappointed, with the ghosts of the near past now seeming far away. During our stay in port, surveyors and representatives of the new Chinese owners came aboard and painstakingly went through every space in the ship, making their list of repairs for the dry dock.

We headed for Hong Kong. The quickest route was to head for the coast of Vietnam, passing east of the Paracel Islands then across to Hong Kong, keeping well off the Chinese island of Hainan. The trouble with that route was the Vietnamese Boat People. After North Vietnam overran the armies of South Vietnam in 1975 to win the war, there had been a steady trickle of people fleeing the country by boat. In 1978 the trickle turned to a flood and the flood to an exodus. The Vietnamese government did nothing to stem the flow. Thousands died in unseaworthy boats – estimates are that more than a quarter of a million people died.

The strategy of the boat people was to try and get to a better life, anywhere south of Vietnam. Indonesia, Malaysia and the Philippines were the closest countries, but they didn't want the boat people and wouldn't let them land. The other target area for the boat people was passing ships. If one went near the boat people would make distress signals to try and get picked up, hoping that the ship would then land them for resettlement.

In the late 1970s and early 1980s it was a major problem. Ships started steaming by, sometimes throwing stores overboard as they passed but still passing by. A lot of shipping companies gave their ships orders that on no account were they to pick up boat people. Because there were so many and the refugee camps established in Malaysia and Indonesia were full, ships bringing more people in were being turned away. Resettlement in other countries was slow. Some boat people became desperate; if they sighted a ship they would start to sink their boat, thinking that the ship would then have to pick them up. Some did. Others steamed on by.

Our standing orders from the company were to try and avoid the areas where boat people would be found, which was the western part of the South China Sea. If we did encounter any we were allowed to drop supplies although should avoid picking them up as that would then mean we had to find somewhere to drop them off. The exception was if we passed a boat that was in obvious distress, in which case we should stop and rescue them, bringing them on board.

Although by 1981 the flood had been reduced to a trickle again, there were still occasional bursts, and with this in mind we took the longer passage to Hong Kong, along the coast of Sarawak and through the Palawan Passage south of the Spratly Islands, then turning north. The voyage took a day longer than it would have done going via Vietnam, but in the practical sense it was the route we had to take.

Hong Kong was frantic. We picked up a mooring buoy south of Stonecutters Island and then the health and immigration officials descended upon us. Once we were granted pratique, the Q flag was hauled down and the second wave of visitors arrived in their boats and barges: customs, the company agent, food stores, bonded stores, the chandler, the water boat, the bunker barge, engine spares, an engine room bilge-cleaning gang, the head stevedore, the unloading gangs, the cargo receiver's representative and sundry others. Ominously for the Old Man, two senior head office officials arrived and headed for his cabin, to give him a more measured roasting no doubt. Other smaller boats started to arrive, mostly containing wives and children and friends and relatives of the Chinese crew.

Victoria Harbour teemed and buzzed, every imaginable water craft on the move, the Star Ferry ploughing its way between Kowloon and Hong Kong Island, the Macau hydrofoil tearing across the water, passenger liners lying waiting for their berth at the Kowloon terminal, deep sea cargo ships coming and going, anchoring in the roads or mooring to buoys. There was a clutter of small craft: barges and lighters and bum boats and transporters. Chinese junks bruted their way through all the traffic on their way to and from the mainland.

Hong Kong was then sixteen years from the date it would be handed back to the Chinese. No one knew what would happen, and there was a mix of optimism and trepidation. Assurances from the Chinese government were being treated with scepticism. Next year would be a crucial juncture because most commercial leases had a fifteen-year duration and businesses wanted to stay light on their feet and not get locked into an environment that would prevent them from trading effectively. There was talk of some of the big taipans relocating their head offices and assets to London or Bermuda. All this added to the excitement in the air, giving it an extra frisson. Hong Kong raged with activity.

The estimate for our stay was four days. An hourly ferry was laid on to run us ashore, giving a choice of two stops: Ocean Terminal in Kowloon or Hong Kong Island itself. I had a night ashore with the two Peters. We went to a couple of bars off Nathan Road in the centre of Kowloon, then took a taxi to a restaurant we had been recommended to visit in the Chinese area of Mongkok. There were no other Europeans and the menu was in Chinese only. The waiter affected not to understand English. We made signs that he should bring us a good meal of his choosing then sat there drinking lager, wondering what we were going to be fed. The meal was fine: shark's fin soup, steamed crab in a hot sauce, spiced chicken, sweet and sour pork, plates of vegetables, bowls of rice. We ate too much, drank too much. Afterwards, bloated, we strolled the length of Nathan Road to the waterfront and caught a ferry to Hong Kong Island, acting loudly in the bars of Wanchai until we realised we were making fools of ourselves.

On the second day, two of the sailors went to see the mate to tell him they would be unwelcome in Japan due to some past confusion involving their lack of understanding as to

Dry-dock in Japan

what was permitted to be imported and what was prohibited. The mate blasted them for not telling him about this earlier. The personnel department managed to get a couple of ancient company men as replacements, and the two errant smugglers were paid off. The company looked after its men.

We slid out through the East Lamma Channel in the late afternoon of the fourth day, a much lighter ship now, setting course for the Taiwan Strait then on to Japan. Our last trip.

We changed into blues as soon as we left Hong Kong. Most ships would have changed uniforms before we arrived, but the Old Man clung resolutely to whites for as long as possible. It became steadily colder as we went north to Japan, and by the time we reached Oshima Island, on the run in to Tokyo Bay, the temperature was in the low forties Fahrenheit, about 5°C. We swung in through the Uraga Channel at dawn and entered the bay to pick up our pilot. There was no respite in the bay; it was in a state of permanent maritime rush hour, ships coming from every point of the compass, overwhelmingly Japanese coastal traffic with a minority of deep sea ships picking their way through. Small coasters went past us at an alarmingly close distance. On the bridge of a ship in Tokyo Bay – and for that matter anywhere in the Japanese Inland Sea – it was important to hold your nerve; these were not places for the timid.

We berthed at Yokohama docks quickly, efficiently, tying up on the south side. People swarmed on board, and the Q flag was down in minutes. Six days in Yokohama and we would be done, according to the agent. The likelihood of him getting that wrong was remote. The bosun and his men started to open the hatches. The dockers stood in groups and waited; they were smartly dressed in matching overalls and helmets. Some wore the curious soft boots with a divided toe which are liked by the Japanese and laughed at by some Europeans.

I walked around the deck with the mate; several dockers gestured at us and made a racket, laughing. Taking the mickey, I thought, calling us round-eyes, apes, barbarians, confident that we would have little or no understanding of Japanese. They were right.

Yokohama was one of the busiest ports in Japan, along with Tokyo, Kobe, Nagoya and Osaka. Yokohama had come up with a rush since the end of the feudal Edo period in the 1850s, when Japan opened up to the world. Up to then it had been a modest fishing village. The modernisation of Japan required industrialised cities and major trading ports. Yokohama established trading links with all the major powers and grew exponentially. It was destroyed twice in the twentieth century, once by the earthquake of 1923 and again when it was flattened by American bombing in 1945. The city recovered quickly on both occasions.

I went ashore with Peter the second on the first night. He hadn't been there before and said he had a yen to see the place. I yukked, even though I'd heard the pitiful joke a hundred times before; I was an old Japan hand.

We went off to Chinatown and found to our surprise we were continually accosted by Japanese, who all said much the same thing: "We no rabbit! We no rabbit!" This probably happened a dozen times, in the street, in bars. When approached in the street, it was usually with the formal politeness of the Japanese, first smiling to catch our eye, bowing, smiling, bowing more, saying a couple of words and then … "We no rabbit!" In bars it was a different event. The clientele were already warmed up when we walked in and they dispensed with the politeness and formalities, no bowing, just launching straight into the 'We no rabbit!' routine.

Peter and I had no idea what these people were talking about and felt all we could do was politely agree that they were not rabbits. It was only when we returned to the ship that we were told that Japan was in a state of uproar over the departing remarks of a European ambassador who had recently finished his four-year tour of duty. When asked what he thought of the Japanese people, the ambassador had replied: "The Japanese people work like slaves and live like rabbits." This caused bafflement at first, and then, unsurprisingly, indignation. I thought it curious, though, that of all the people who had come to us to deny they were rabbits, no one had ever said: "We no slave!"

We acted more eccentrically as the end drew nearer. In the officers' bar stood a large fibreglass bird, a sort of giant deformed toucan, three feet high with disproportionately long legs and a massive beak. Several years ago someone had stolen it from outside a shop, where it had been placed as a charity mascot, and brought it back to the *Funing* as a trophy. It now stood serenely, ridiculously, at the end of the bar. It was painted bright red with a yellow beak and legs and had acquired the name of Percy. As we milled around the bar area, Percy was often in the way and was moved around constantly, sometimes moved to the back of the room, sometimes placed on the bar top in a place of honour.

The Old Man and Peter the leci liked Percy and would occasionally hold witless conversations with it. Most others, including me, ignored Percy as a foolish statue although we tolerated its presence. Duncan despised Percy, often kicking him over, bullying him. In a conversational lull, he would sometimes round on the creature, punching it in the beak, saying: "Take that, you beaky bastard!" and Percy would go clattering onto the deck. The Percy lovers would howl in protest.

One evening in Yokohama, Duncan and I were the last men standing in the bar after a long evening. It was two in the morning.

Duncan said: "I've had enough of that bloody bird," before storming out. Five minutes later he returned with a hacksaw, laid Percy on the bar and sawed his legs off at the base. Percy then sat on the bar top gently rocking on his torso. We choked with laughter; it seemed the funniest thing we had ever seen. There was genuine outrage the next day at Percy's dismemberment. I was blamed, which I vigorously denied. No one believed me. Duncan joined in the condemnation to camouflage his guilt.

Percy's days were numbered following his de-limbing. Not long afterwards, again late at night, the conversation turned to the practical difficulties of drinking a yard of ale. Most of us had tried to drink one at some point and we all felt expert, even though we had no official glass yard to prove our prowess. We agreed the bar should have its own yard, or some such substitute. Our eyes fell on Percy. We sawed the hollow beak off. It was a perfect substitute: the beak of ale. The Percy lovers went potty when they saw beakless legless Percy on the bar the next day. The sad carcass was flung away – but the beak was retained and our beak of ale competitions became a regular late-night event.

If you stay in Japan for any length of time you become a bower. Japanese formality demands that people greet and acknowledge each other by bowing. The protocol is too complex for most westerners to absorb. Suffice to say there are circumstances where a bow begets a bow and so you bow back, which begets another bow, and so on. When two people meet they sometimes bow and nod back and forth for some time, smiling at the same time. Sometimes it seems as if it will never end.

Basically, bowing is a mark of respect, not a mark of subservience. Some westerners make asses of themselves over the bowing protocol. There's no need to bend over 90 degrees, like an actor taking a curtain call, and then hang there until released. If someone is going to do that, they might as well go the whole hog and prostrate themselves on the ground, as if they were at the court of Kyoto during Edo times.

Bowing in Japan is generally done with the body, not just from the neck. But if you have met the person before and they're not your superior, or if they're a shop assistant, waiter etc, it's normal to give a relatively short dropping of the head in greeting, acknowledgement or thanks. It's important to drop your eyes because it's thought rude to retain eye contact throughout. Meeting someone for the first time demands a bow which is held for half a second or so, angling the body about 15° forwards from the hips, keeping the back and head in a straight line. Meeting someone who is an obvious superior – your boss, or parents in law – requires a similar bow, but to about 45°, and holding it for a bit longer. Allowances are usually made for *gaijin* who don't know any better.

Anything more than that is either obsequious, or an apology. Someone might perhaps make an apology bow after running into someone's car. A massively obsequious bow might be performed by a man trying to get on the right side of his girlfriend's father.

The repeat bowing is brought apart by the ensuing conversation. Someone will bow when meeting, then might bow again after receiving a compliment and bow once more in acknowledgement of a request. Each bow in turn solicits a return bow.

After a week of constantly meeting Japanese people, it was impossible not to bow. I became a pretty good bower; most of us did. Peter the second was a bit grandiose, sweeping his arm with a flourish as if he was attending the court of Versailles, but we generally did well, keeping our hands by our legs, as normal. We even started bowing to each other, in jest at first but then more in habit.

We had Christmas in Yokohama. It isn't a public holiday in Japan, so we had our blow-out on 23 December, the Emperor's birthday, which is. It was a rarity for all of us to sit down for Christmas dinner together. I had been away at sea for quite a few Christmases although they tended to be at sea itself rather than in port, which meant that there were always some people on watch. In Yokohama one of the crew was on gangway watch, and Duncan and I were on call in case anything arose. Nothing happened, though, and we spent the afternoon feasting and the evening drinking and playing games.

The meal was gargantuan – too much food for the greediest of men – and the drink was never-ending. We wore paper hats and told idiot jokes. I did rounds of the ship in the mid-afternoon, making sure the mooring lines were properly tensioned, the gangway was safe, making sure the watchman was awake and sober. I walked the decks and the hatches and the accommodation, checking for fires. Everything was fine. Duncan did the same in the early evening and we both did a turn of night rounds. Regular rounds were barely necessary although it was good practice and I needed a break from the festivities, as well as some leg stretching.

There are four main Japanese islands, the largest Honshu where most of the big cities and ports are located, along with 80 per cent of the people. The other three are Hokkaido in the north, and Kyushu and Shikoku in the south. After leaving Yokohama, we headed for Moji, which is situated on the northern part of Kyushu.

The island of Kyushu is mountainous and volcanic with a lot of agriculture. Only 10 per cent of Japan's population lives there, mostly in the industrialised northwest part, which is where Moji is located. From an aesthetic viewpoint, Moji could have been Kobe or Yokohama or Nagoya or Osaka or any one of the big Honshu city ports. Vast swathes of factories, concrete, chimneys, pipework, railway yards, storage depots, cars and trucks and noise and people rushing everywhere. Everything was concrete and grey, not a blade of grass in sight.

We anchored in the bay for a day while they prepared our dry dock. There was no cargo remaining in the *Funing* at this stage, and the mate had arranged the ballast to conform to the builders' requirements for docking. We inched into the dock in the early morning, the pilot taking care to ensure the ship was positioned dead centre. Once the stern was in the dock, gates were closed and the water pumped out. Mooring lines held the ship in place and she gently settled onto the long line of wooden keel blocks that lay along the bottom of the dock. She settled firmly and steadily, which was always a relief when docking. No matter how carefully the docking plan had been worked out, there was always a nightmare fear that the ship would not settle properly and would topple over against the dock wall.

Then it all started. We felt instantly redundant. The dockyard workers who came on board were working for the new owners, not for us. We are there to watch what was being done, to record any damage, to guide people round the ship, to make sure the gear not going with the sale was separated and safeguarded. They painted out the name as one of the first moves; the *Funing* became the *Pin Jiang*. Seeing the change gave me a bleak and homeless feeling.

Duncan and I went ashore in the evening. There wasn't a lot to see; several small Japanese bars, hot cramped places, overheated. We couldn't stay in any one place for more than half an hour, after which we emerged gasping for air into the chilly Japanese winter night.

Most of the bars had a karaoke microphone. This was long before karaoke had caught on in the west. From time to time someone would pick up the microphone and wail tunelessly for a bit. Leaving aside the exoticism, oriental music, be it Japanese, Chinese or Korean, was something I struggled to appreciate. Most of the singers sounded as if they were in pain, one performer so dreadful it sounded as if he was being tortured.

In one place we were exhorted to perform, the clientele looking as if they wanted to be entertained. We leafed through the usual Frank Sinatra and Dean Martin choices before having a bash at 'Fly Me to the Moon'. I thought we did pretty well and the locals smiled and clapped although they wouldn't let us have another go, which was hurtful. I expect the reality was that they found our singing as bad as we found theirs.

We stayed out late and ended up arguing about nothing as we walked back through the quiet shabby streets near the port. The death of the *Funing* hung over us and snatched away our mood, leaving us ill-tempered and intolerant. The next day Duncan was still very cool to me, although I couldn't remember exactly why this was. I had obviously been more unpleasant than I remembered.

New Year's Eve and New Year's Day were public holidays and all dockyard work ceased. We had little work to perform; all we did was amble around and record the work that had been undertaken. I took a couple of day trips. I was told that Kokura Castle was worth going to: a grand place that had been built in the seventeenth century for the Kokura clan, subsequently burnt down during the wars with the Chōshu clan in the mid-nineteenth century. I was under the impression that it had been restored, but there wasn't a lot to see.

I went for a wander around Yomira Park, where the locals gawped and small children ran after me making a din, calling me *gaijin*, foreigner. I had wanted to see the notorious prisoner of war camp south of Moji, but this wasn't in any of the guides and when I questioned the agent and chief stevedore, both of whom spoke good English, they assumed a bovine gormlessness and affected they knew nothing.

Day after day we watched the *Funing* become just a memory. The colours were changed, the public notices were replaced in Chinese, alien food was brought on board, the bar was to be closed and converted to a couple of cabins. There was no handover to the Chinese officers – they just took over.

On the tenth day we were all paid off, our discharge books stamped. A net was spread on number 3 hatch coaming into which our baggage was deposited, to be swung ashore and loaded on the bus waiting on the quay. The bus took us to the station where we caught a fast train to Tokyo. We were to stay in Tokyo overnight and fly home the next day. I was going to London with Duncan and the two Peters. The Old Man lived in Australia, the crew were bound for Hong Kong. The chief engineer and his wife were planning to go sightseeing in Japan for a few days before flying home.

That evening we went out for a meal with the agent and two of his sidekicks. They took us to a yakitori restaurant near the Ginza. Yakitori restaurants mostly serve skewered grilled chicken and pork with vegetables. The agent probably thought such low cooking was just the thing for us *gaijin*. He was right; we wolfed it down enthusiastically and drank saké (rice wine) and Kirin beer, occasionally getting up to do a turn on the karaoke, to the cheers of our own party, if nobody else's.

As we drank more and the conversation relaxed, the commonality accentuated our differences and we quizzed each other. The agent started to press me as to what we British actually thought of the Japanese people. I gave him an honest answer: I said that I thought the Japanese were a complicated people, proud, nationalistic, ferocious in war (he liked that), honourable on the surface although deceitful (he didn't like that), hard-working, disciplined, slaves to their masters, fastidious, clean.

His take on the British: honourable, decent, unhygienic, warlike, aggressive, soft centred. He candidly said that most Japanese regarded Europeans as being further down the evolutionary scale than Asians and particularly so from the Japanese.

He then quickly went on to say that they regarded black people as further down the chain still, almost to the point of seeing them as a different species. The Japanese referred to black people as *doujin*, *dou* meaning dirt. I think he told me that in case he thought he had upset me by his comment on my weak advancement on the scale of human development, thinking I would be pleased if he told me I was ahead of the Africans.

I asked him to explain *gaijin*. Was it an offensive term or not? He said *gaijin* meant an outsider, a non-Japanese. It was a factual term, not an offensive one, although it was often used dismissively, in which case it was derogatory.

There were similar terms to describe westerners in other parts of Asia. In Hong Kong, the Cantonese term is *gweilo*, which means 'foreign devil' and is specifically offensive. Some Hong Kong Chinese tried to cleanse the wound by saying that it actually referred to pale skin, but that always sounded like a back-foot explanation to me.

The Thai people called us *farangs*, meaning 'foreigner'. This was meant to be descriptive and non-offensive, although thin-skinned Europeans often took umbrage because they believed it was a term use to specifically underline the difference of westerners.

I was never bothered by any of these names and my preference of the three was to be called a *farang*, which I thought sounded quite dashing.

The agent asked me what insulting terms we used for Japanese. I told him that Jap and Nip were fairly common, although these were diminutives of Japan and Nippon and were not true insults. He was very keen to understand proper insults though, so I gave him slant-eyes, butterheads, Tojos and yellow bastards, which were all I could think of. This seemed to satisfy his curiosity. He replied in kind by giving me some key derogation for the British: hairy barbarians, round-eyes, big-noses and apes.

We nodded in mutual understanding. He felt that 'Tojo' was a bit cruel whereas I wasn't too keen on hairy barbarian because it highlighted my poor evolutional pedigree.

At midnight, the others left the restaurant to go back to the hotel, although the agent and I stayed and drank saké until the early hours while the place closed around us. We toasted each other, toasted each other's countries and toasted the foolishness of men.

6

Up with the Gods

England in late January, Heathrow airport. We said our goodbyes: me, Duncan, Peter the second, Peter the leci, jaded from the flight from Tokyo, fourteen hours including the departure and arrival formalities, and we all went our separate ways. I hired a car and set off to the small village in Oxfordshire where my mother lived. The English winter countryside was bleak and grey, studded with patches of snow. There was an air of disenchantment and defeat, a January feeling. Hitler was badly advised – he should have invaded Britain in January, it would have been a walkover. I sped up the M40 in my Vauxhall Chevette hire car. I had wanted to get a smarter vehicle, but the prices at Heathrow were so outrageous that I was reluctant to go beyond the Chevette band.

When I arrived home, I replaced the Chevette with a gold Ford Capri as my wheels for the duration and then started with my usual pattern of leave. First, it was hello to all and sundry, diluting my tales, downplaying my antics.

I loathed telling stories of the sea to people who hadn't been there, people I had no empathy with, people with whom I had no connection. In the tales I did tell, they probably thought I was lying anyway, not that I gave it much thought. I just wanted vapid talk with no strain, I wanted to go to the Wheatsheaf and play darts and pool with the young men and play cribbage and shove ha'penny with the old men and go to clubs after the landlord called last orders and stay out until the early hours. I wanted the idle conversation and all that went with that.

I had two months before joining the *Coral Chief*. I wasted too much time at the start, though, squandering it in profligate evenings in Oxford and London and wherever else took my fancy. Eventually, I fuelled myself with courage and rang Annie. I blathered, she was receptive. No rejection. Phew. We met in Bristol a couple of days later. I strived to behave and avoid making myself look oafish, although I lacked the social manners of shore society. I knew myself all too well, I knew I had the capacity to let myself down given half a chance.

I went to Bristol regularly over the next few weeks, staying in bed and breakfast places, in small hotels, in larger hotels, sometimes in my car. I saw Annie whenever she allowed, I tried to balance a vigorous pursuit without letting it tip over into the realms of stalking. Sometimes we met three or four times a week. I met her family, I met her twin sister Bernadette: alike but different. They didn't seem to despise me, which was a relief, although I learned sometime afterwards that her mother had warned her against sailors, warned her about what a bad sort we were, warned her against my potential wickedness while away at sea. Wise Mother.

My world tilted. Nothing was the same again. My past life started to appear as ragged and cheap, my values and pursuits worthless. After five weeks I asked Annie to marry me. She hesitated. She started to weep. I thought I had blown my chances, but she was happy. Women had always baffled me and have continued to. She didn't want me to stay at sea for ever, though. I didn't want to stay for ever, either. I wanted a job in pilotage or port management. She said yes. My world tilted more.

The next night we plotted strategy in the Ship Inn, appropriately named, for me to speak to her parents. I wasn't looking forward to it. My voyages over the past decade through gales and storms and the edges of typhoons and hurricanes seemed tame compared to this simple discussion. This was something that could blow up in my face and wreck my world. When we met with her parents, I made a pompous speech and asked for their blessing. Her father was decent enough and congratulated us, as did her mother. We all toasted the event. God knows what her parents really thought, though. Probably: 'You're marrying a sailor who you hardly know? You must be mad! He'll be up to all sorts of things when he's away.' And things like that, I expect.

The rest of my leave passed with me practising the art of conducting myself better – simple things, really: mannered conversation, not drinking too much, keeping my sea life to myself for the most part. I met all of Annie's seven brothers and sisters. They inspected me and I inspected them back. I was deliberately reticent in my conversations.

I took my mother and my brother Anthony out to dinner at the Bear in Wallingford one evening and announced that I was getting married. Mother said, "Who to? Do I know her?" She didn't. I explained. Annie came round to meet the family a few days later, as nervous as I had been when meeting all her tribe. I hyped up the nervousness, acting like a cat on hot bricks, but things went well. She charmed.

We made plans. I would go back to sea on the *Coral Chief* as chief officer and when I returned we would finalise our marriage plans for the following spring. After we married, Annie would come away to sea with me for a trip or two, and then we would decide how to move forward. I would try and get a job on the cross channel ferries or in port management or something close to home. My deep sea days were numbered – eighteen months, perhaps two years. Only disaster would take me beyond that.

The company gave me a fortnight's notice to fly out and join the *Coral Chief* in Sydney. I would be away five months. It was the end of February, I should be back in August, ten weeks' leave, then back to sea and home again in time to get married in April, on Grand National Day. I left all the preliminary arrangements to Annie and went back to sea.

⋆ ⋆ ⋆

Sydney, Australia. Sydney is Australia's largest and oldest city, founded as a penal colony in 1788 by Captain Arthur Phillip and named after the Secretary of State, Viscount Sydney, the man who was the brains behind convict settlement in Australia. The district surrounding what became Sydney had been settled by the indigenous aborigines for tens of thousands of years, but the arrivals from Britain soon put paid to that. The aborigines died by the thousands of European diseases, and those who survived were hounded out of the area. There was some aboriginal resistance to the settlers over the following thirty years; they armed themselves with spears, clubs and boomerangs although the British authorities countered by adopting the well proven tactic of gunning them down.

For many years, Sydney vied with Melbourne for the position as the leading Australian city. Melbourne held number 1 position during the gold rush boom years of the Victorian period, but then Sydney assumed dominance at the beginning of the twentieth century and has retained it ever since.

The agent's runner met me at the airport and told me the *Coral Chief* wasn't arriving for four days. I was put up in the Top of Town hotel on the edge of Kings Cross, the bar and red light district of Sydney.

Kings Cross was bright, gaudy, noisy, full of bars, cafes, strip clubs, nightclubs, restaurants and eating houses. The area was renowned for its drug problem and was the headquarters of Sydney's criminal godfathers. The streets were thronged every night, mostly with younger people, mostly men. In the late evening there was a lot of drunkenness, a few fights. The police roved around and gathered at potential hotspots. Desperate-looking junkies lurked and begged, street prostitutes cooed at passers-by. It was, frankly, the sort of place I had grown used to over the years, it was familiar turf and I felt quite relaxed.

I explored Sydney over the next couple of days: I visited the opera house and took a ferry across the sound to see the harbour bridge. On the first evening I was determined not to consign myself to the lowness of Kings Cross and instead went to the Rocks, the smartened-up historic district by the waterfront, to eat seafood in a restaurant overlooking the water. Smartly dressed Australians sipped wine and ate shellfish around me, while I did my best to ape their behaviour.

On the second day I went down to Bondi Beach to watch the surfers and to swim in the shallows, before lying in the sun to read for a couple of hours. The second evening I succumbed to Kings Cross, drifting around the bars and the bright noise, making transitory friends over a few beers, returning to my hotel at midnight, weaving.

I liked Australians for the most part, they were straight-talking and decent, I liked their sense of humour. It seemed to me, though, that there was an underlying lack of confidence that often manifested itself in challenge and assertion. Most newspapers and magazines could be relied upon to provide a variation of the same story: a family who had lived in cold and unemployed misery in a ghastly council estate in Blackburn had emigrated to Australia and they now live in a house with a pool near the beach. They are brown and happy and their kids love it and the husband has a fabulous job and the wife plays tennis and they enjoy

Coral Chief in Sydney

a barbie at the country club every weekend. All these stories seemed to me to have an air of desperation, as if the author was saying: 'Look, it's so great here, it's so much better than anywhere else. Agree with us! Agree!'

In the conversations too, there was a lot of the same:

"It's great here, mate."

"Dunno how you stand that English weather."

"No class barriers in Oz, mate."

"We have Christmas on the beach you know. You poms couldn't do that, could you?"

"We're great at cricket. We're a country that loves its sport."

"We're great at rugby."

"Everyone plays tennis in Australia."

"We Aussies are straight-talking people."

"We Aussies love the outdoors."

"You ever thought of moving out here to live in the sun, mate?"

And it was a great country, and I loved it. But I could sense a delphian meaning every time someone was fishing for a compliment. I could feel a sensitivity to the unspoken a ccusation that Australia was in the middle of nowhere at the wrong end of the civilised western world.

When the occasion arose I would bait an Australian, which would usually be taken in good spirit although it could cause the temperature to rise.

I would ask, innocently: "When was it you Aussies stopped hunting aborigines on horseback? Was it the 1920s?"

"We never hunted Abos on horseback! That's bullshit!"

"Oh. Did you just hunt them with dogs then?"

"No we bloody didn't! We didn't hunt them at all!"

Or

"Is it true you can't get proper newspapers over here under two days old?"

"We don't want your bloody English newspapers! We've got our own!"

"But that *Sydney Morning Herald* is more like a comic, isn't it?"

"No it bloody well isn't!"

I found the best way to really wind up an Australian man was to question their manhood.

I would say: "I read the other day that Australia has an above average proportion of homosexuals. That really surprised me – I never would've thought it. Do you think it's the sun that's over-developing the homosexual gene?"

"That's bloody rubbish! That's crap! Where did you get that from? We're not poofs! It's you poms who are the poofs!"

"I think I read it in the *Sydney Morning Comic*."

"Bullshit! Bullshit! That's a lie!"

Usually though, the Aussies I met were laid back and didn't rise to the bait – most of them turned the tables on me, in fact. But when one did rise, it was great entertainment.

There was a turn of drama when I checked out of my hotel. I'm not a great one for going through bills although the total seemed a bit stiff so I looked through it more carefully before signing: my employers were fastidious in analysing expenses and I didn't want anything bouncing back on me. My bill had been loaded, dozens of drinks and several meals had been added. I tossed it back to the man who was checking me out. He started to look nervous. I asked to see all the chits I had supposedly signed, which made up the bill. He had a hurried conference with his colleague and they disappeared.

Eventually they came back with a large pile of chits. I identified two-thirds as bogus and asked to see the manager. They swiftly removed the offending chits and said it wasn't necessary to call the manager and they would be able to sort things out. I suspected they had given their pals my room number and told them to make merry on it, thinking I was too casual to notice. They would have probably got away with it if the loading hadn't been so excessive. I told them to take everything off the bill with the exception of the room hire and I wouldn't take it any further. They did so without arguing, which was a good result.

The agent picked me up and took me to the quay where the *Coral Chief* had just berthed. The *Coral Chief* was a container ship. A container ship? I had never thought I would serve on one. I had spent the last six years on older conventional general cargo ships that carried break bulk cargoes and stayed in port for days on end, sometimes weeks. I had been in pursuit of a way of life at sea that was dying all around me. In hindsight, it was a foolish quest. I hadn't wanted to accept the disappearance of something that was going, going, gone. I should have read more Plato: 'Change is the only constant in life.'

The *Funing* was the last conventional general cargo ship I ever sailed on. The dying of the light? The light was out. From now on it was container ships for me.

The *Coral Chief* wasn't a large ship by the standards of the day: 6,373 gross tons, 390 feet long with a container capacity of just over 600 TEU. The *Coral Chief* had been built at the Shimizu dockyards in Japan five years previously, and was of a size designed to visit the smaller South Pacific ports. The 600 containers were carried mostly in the holds, where they were slid in on steel guides to ensure they ended up in neat secure stacks. We also carried containers two high on deck, locked in position by steel pins to stop them falling over the side. The ship had a gantry crane that rode on rails which ran down either side of the deck; the crane operator climbed up a ladder to the operating cab positioned on the top span. In the Australian ports shore cranes were sometimes used, although in the South Pacific islands the ship's gear was a necessity.

I went up to introduce myself to the captain. He was a loud and manic man who thrust a can of Foster's lager into my hand in greeting, despite it being only ten-thirty in the morning. I signed on and spent the rest of the day having a handover from the departing chief mate. Despite my best endeavours to look relaxed and confident, I was a first trip mate and he could probably sense my unease.

The chief officer, or mate, has a significant role aboard ship: he or she is the senior deck officer and second in command, a watch keeping officer at sea, in charge of the deck crew and in charge of the cargo work. As the whole reason for a cargo ship's existence is to carry cargo, the chief officer's position is crucial.

The role of chief officer is more than just a step up from second mate; it's a step across the barrier. The four senior officers on board are the captain, chief officer, chief engineer and second engineer. The captain and chief engineer have four gold stripes, and the chief officer and second engineer have three. These people are the 'big four' who run things. The chief mate runs the ship above decks, and the second engineer runs everything connected with the mechanics of the ship. All the other officers report upwards to the mate and the second, who answer to the Old Man and the chief respectively.

Beneath the big four sit the bulk of the officers, the second mate, third mate, sometimes a fourth mate and several cadets, together with corresponding ranks on the engineering side. There are several other officers in different departments, all two stripers: the radio officer, electrical officer and catering officer. Sometimes these three also have a junior officer beneath them. Then below the officers are the crew.

On the *Coral Chief*, which was a modest-size ship, there were eleven officers and twenty-two crew members. The big four tended to find themselves sticking together to a large extent. But having spent most of the past six years as second mate, I instinctively felt I had more in common with the middle-ranking officers – although it soon became apparent to me that they thought otherwise. There was a barrier, and I was on the other side. So I found myself more in conversation with the Old Man, the chief and the second. I was up with the gods now.

There are several fundamentals to cargo carrying at sea. A ship needs to stay upright to be able to move through the water efficiently and safely, which means that the cargo must be distributed more or less equally on either side. If too much cargo is loaded on the port side then the ship is going to list to port. Sometimes the cargo distribution has to be unequal to some extent, in which case sea water will be pumped into a ballast tank on the opposite side to bring her upright.

Similarly, if all the heavy cargo is loaded at the fore end of the ship then she will tip forwards too much, known as 'down by the head.' The reverse is true as well, and a ship will not sail well either if she is too far down by the stern. Ideally, most ships should be loaded so they are slightly down by the stern to start with. This is because the bunker fuel oil burnt by the engines is stored in tanks around the stern area, which means the ship starts to gradually tip further forward as the voyage progresses.

As mentioned earlier, the other crucial aspect is vertical weight distribution. If all the heavy cargo is on the top, the ship will become unstable and topple over. Conversely, if all the heavy cargo is at the bottom then she becomes too stiff and the subsequent sharp corrections to the roll can cause structural damage.

All the load and discharge planning was done by an Australian supercargo in the Australian ports. The order of discharge was worked out for us and we were given plans showing where each container was to go. I carried out check calculations on the shipboard stability calculator, a machine in the ship's office, although I didn't have to organise the cargo distribution.

In the islands it was different, and everything fell to the chief mate. It all looked pretty straightforward and it all was pretty straightforward, but my nerves were wracked with nightmare fantasies of me bringing about a dangerously loaded ship that toppled over and sank.

The ship's run was the three major ports on the eastern Australian coast – Melbourne, Sydney and Brisbane – then up to the Islands. What we referred to as the 'Islands', was that area where South-East Asia joins the South Pacific: Papua New Guinea and the outlying islands in the Bismarck Sea. Our main ports on the New Guinea mainland were Port Moresby, Lae, Madang and Wewak, after which we went to the western end of the Bismarck Sea, calling at Kimbe and Rabaul on New Britain, Kavieng on New Ireland, and Kieta on Bougainville. The voyage turnaround was billed as twenty-eight days although the engineers told me the *Coral Chief* frequently broke down frequently, and on all the recent voyages the ship had ended up being stuck somewhere for several days while repairs were made.

The *Coral Chief* officers were mostly British; the deck and engine room crew were from Papua New Guinea and the cooks and stewards from Hong Kong.

Papuan crews were a new experience for me. Papuans are Melanesian people, who are from the western part of the South Pacific, as opposed to Polynesians who are from the central and eastern part of the ocean. Melanesians are strong, solidly built, woolly-haired and darker in complexion than the Polynesians. The *Coral Chief's* crew were amiable; they worked hard and caused little trouble, unless they had been drinking, in which case they tended to fight amongst themselves. The departing mate warned me to keep an eye on the drinking as there had been trouble on a couple of occasions.

★   ★   ★

We left Sydney and steamed north for the day's run to Brisbane, the capital city of the state of Queensland, keeping in sight of the land for most of the journey. There was a constant flow of coastal traffic, particularly around the coal and steel port of Newcastle, where big bulk carriers laden to their marks came out of the Hunter River. We kept about ten miles off the coast, the navigation was straightforward with few dangers and it was well lit at night. The Old Man scribbled in his night orders book that he wanted to be called as we approached the Newcastle area. I called him at four-thirty in the morning but it was quiet with little shipping movement so we drank coffee and traded stories for twenty minutes or so before he went back down to his cabin.

North of Newcastle the places were more dependent on tourism and agriculture. Port McQuarie was a big city that people retired to, its main claim to fame being the home of Australia's largest koala bear population. Coffs Harbour was known for bananas and beaches. All the way up the coast we were passing landmarks with striking names: Bungaree Norah Point, Sugarloaf Point, Crowdy Head, Cape Byron. The sea became busier as we neared the Queensland border and came up to the Gold Coast, the sun-seekers' mecca. Then it was Brisbane, the largest city in the state of Queensland and the third largest city in Australia.

Most of the places between Sydney and Brisbane, including Sydney and Brisbane in fact, had sprung up as penal settlements in the late eighteenth and early nineteenth centuries. The British decision to start shipping convicts to Australia had its roots in the industrial revolution in the second half of the eighteenth century.

At that time, Great Britain started to surge ahead, converting an economy based on manual labour to one based on machines and engineering. This displaced a lot of workers and caused unrest across the country. The prisons were soon full and so the penal system started using 'prison hulks', old decommissioned warships moored offshore, to cater for the overflow. Then, someone had the bright idea of stowing the convicts on working ships instead, because these had the added attraction of being able to transport them to another part of the world.

Viscount Sydney was given the responsibility of planning convict transportation. He was Home Secretary at the time, although it isn't clear whether he was the architect of the idea or just the manager. Sydney gets the credit anyway. The man on the spot in Australia was Governor Phillip, who devised the internal processes to make it all work.

Convict transportation suited Britain for a number of reasons: it cleared the country of criminal riff-raff and political agitators, it gave Britain a reason to annex the eastern half of Australia, which countered French expansion elsewhere, and it provided a labour force to develop the new acquired country.

The colonies in America had been lost after Great Britain was defeated in the American War of Independence in the 1770s, which meant that shipping prisoners across the Atlantic was no longer an option. Slavery was under pressure from liberal forces, but the shipping of cargoes of convicts to Australia was agreed to be a good idea all round.

Once there, the convicts had a relatively free time compared to a lot of penal conditions elsewhere in the world at that time. Not that many were locked up, because there was nowhere to run to, although they were made to labour under harsh conditions and were subject to various cruelties. Penal transportation to Australia lasted until the middle of the nineteenth century, by which time the country was largely settled and the convicts had done their bit.

An Australian who can now claim convict ancestry is envied as a blueblood. People on the make like to boast about their convict heritage; for a politician it's worth a ballot box of votes even if the claim is a bit thin. About 160,000 convicts were transported from Britain over a fifty-year period, mostly English, a good number of Welsh and Irish, a few Scots and a sprinkling of bad people from all over the Empire. About 25 per cent were female.

Brisbane had grown from yet another convict settlement; it was difficult to find a place on the east coast of Australia that hadn't. The entrance to the Brisbane River is shielded by two islands, which together form a large sheltered natural harbour, Moreton Bay. The pilot boarding area was to the north of the bay and we had to steam outside the islands, where he waited in his fast launch, the red and white pilot flag fluttering in the morning breeze. It was early March, the tail end of the southern summer, the pale blue sky cloudless from horizon to horizon. All the signs were for a cooking hot day.

Our berth was a couple of miles up the Brisbane River on the north bank. The pilot guided us up there slowly. There were no available shore cranes and so we had to use our gantry. We moored the ship and the crew made ready for cargo work, taking the locks off the gantry crane and readying the lifting gear. The stevedores tried to lift the first container, but the crane broke down. The crane was always breaking down. We stared at it helplessly. On a conventional five-hatch general cargo ship there were four derricks to each hatch, that's twenty cargo lifting devices for the ship. But on the *Coral Chief* there was only one gantry crane and when it broke down all cargo work came to an immediate halt. The fore and aft transporting would stick or the transverse movement of the hook would jam and judder or the wire would snag or one of the electric motors burn out. The chief engineer would get his team to fix it if they could, although sometimes the problem was insoluble and a shore engineering team from the manufacturers would be called out to take the thing apart and reassemble it as necessary.

On this occasion, the chief summed it up with a pithy technical opinion: "It's buggered." We told the agent to arrange for shore engineers from Mitsubishi to come out and do their magic. In the meantime, the stevedore gangs left, the container stacking trucks drove off and we were left to hang around in the quiet. I set the crew to rigging stages over the side and painting the hull. Stages are ten-foot-long narrow wooden platforms with cross handles near either end: ropes are wound round the cross handles to allow the stage to be raised and lowered. A couple of men climbed onto the platform with their paint tins and brushes and lowered themselves into position. The crew painted away in the quiet of the hot tropical day. Most sailors like working on stages; I certainly did when I was a cadet.

There was decent restaurant not far from the ship where a few of us went during the three days the engineers took to rebuild the crane. We ate huge platters of shellfish and fish with names that were strange to me, washed down with icy beer. They were lively evenings that went on late – but I wanted to get on, I wanted to get on with my new job.

On the second day, I received the provisional cargo loading orders for the New Guinea ports, so I sat in my office and calculated where everything would all go. It was the usual South Pacific fare: coffee, tea, cocoa and copra, with a few containers of general goods.

Working out the loading plan wasn't that challenging; it was a case of ensuring they were positioned to allow the Melbourne containers to come out first, then the Sydney ones next and finally those for Brisbane.

It was a bit of a 3-D jigsaw but nothing that couldn't be overcome with a bit of application. The important issue was ensuring that the centre of gravity would keep the right relationship with metacentre at all times. If the centre of gravity was above the metacentre the vessel would tip over. This risk could sometimes be a problem with ships like the *Coral Chief* because of the high deck cargo, which raised the centre of gravity. When this looked as if this might happen I would calculate how much water to pump into the double-bottom ballast tanks to bring more weight into the lower part of the ship. The first time I carried out the planning it took me a couple of days. I changed my mind frequently, did all the maths several times, produced endless sheets of colour-coded plans and bored the other officers with explanations of the complexities of my work.

Eventually we left Brisbane and headed for Papua New Guinea. When going north from Brisbane there are two routes to choose from, the inside route between the Queensland coast and the Great Barrier Reef, or the outside route, heading east into the Coral Sea until clear of the Barrier Reef before turning north. We went by the Reef route.

The north-east Queensland coast is a fragmentation of reefs and islands and rocks. The watch keepers of a deep sea ship going inside the reef cannot take things lightly, because if the ship drifts off the course line she is courting disaster. We swung round Fraser Island and headed north-north-west, past Rockhampton and Mackay, past the Whitsunday Islands, until we were abeam of Townsville where we turned to starboard and went out through a gap in the reef and into the Coral Sea. The vista was spectacular, blue-green seas broken by white strips as the breakers rolled over the submerged reefs. We could hear the crash and hiss of surf as we passed.

The Great Barrier Reef is a mass of living coral formed over millions of years. It was a spectacular natural phenomenon that attracted people from all over the world. From a seafarer's point of view however, it's a peril in waiting. Reefs have no compassion, nor do the creatures that lurk within them. Ships have been ripping themselves to bits on the Great Barrier Reef for as long as there have been ships. When we went through the reef, there was a lot of sea life; birds wheeled overhead and flying fish skipped across the surface. Sharks skulked in the shallows although we rarely saw them, sometimes just a flash.

The run to Port Moresby took just over four days, which allowed us to settle into the sea-watch routine. I had the four to eight watch, which suited me. After I finished at eight in the morning I had breakfast with the Old Man, the chief and the second. Being up for five hours brings on an appetite, and I wolfed down juice, melon, bacon and eggs, sometimes kedgeree, toast, tea. We always talked ship's business at breakfast. Lunch and dinner tended to be more social with wider conversation but the breakfast discussion was always to address the day's work and the problems that needed to be solved.

After breakfast I alternated between working in the ship's office and walking round the deck, checking the crew's work and discussing matters with the bosun. In the late morning I tried to give myself a half hour to relax in my cabin, to read and write letters. I was in the bar at midday for a couple of cold beers, then lunch followed by an afternoon snooze. The evening four to eight watch was broken by dinner, with the third mate relieving me for half an hour. In the evenings, we congregated in the bar, talking, drinking, playing cards.

Every third night was a film night. I went to my cabin by ten, read for a bit then turned in for the night. I was woken at quarter to four in the morning, back up on the bridge at four, a mug of wake-up coffee was given to me by the lookout, a grunted conversation with the second mate for ten minutes or so. There was comfort in the routine.

Port Moresby is the capital of Papua New Guinea, the largest port and the only place of significance on the southern coast. It was always our first port of call in the islands, after which we went east through the Jomard Passage, a narrow strait separating the Coral Sea from the Solomon Sea, which needs to be passed with care, particularly if there is a ship coming from the other direction.

The Jomard Passage is famous for the Pacific War incident in 1942 when the Japanese fleet slipped through to invade Port Moresby, precipitating the battle of the Coral Sea between the Japanese on one side and the Americans and Australians on the other. The Japanese won the battle in terms of ships damaged. On the US/Australian side there were five sunk, five damaged, nearly a hundred aircraft lost and a thousand people killed. The Japanese lost three ships, one damaged, seventy aircraft downed and six hundred and fifty men killed. Despite their victory, these were the first serious casualties inflicted on the Japanese and, if not the turning point of the Pacific War, it broke their step and checked their confidence.

The discharge and loading went well in the islands. There were minor changes to the plans, but nothing radical. In all the ports, the gantry crane behaved itself, the weather was fine, the crew stayed sober and obeyed me, there were no delays and the cargo that arrived was mostly what I was expecting. I began flirting with the notion that the job was too easy. Then we got to Madang and it all went wrong.

A large part of the lighter copra cargo that I had planned as deck cargo was replaced by heavier cocoa. This caused the centre of gravity of the ship to rise. As the gantry crane loaded each new container the ship started to heel over more and more. I furiously pumped water into the double-bottom tanks to bring more weight into the bottom of the ship to counteract the problem, but I couldn't get it in fast enough. The situation became worse. The ship was tipping over too far, there were still twenty containers to go, and as each one came aboard the *Coral Chief* heeled over with a jerky lurch, each one like a stake through my heart. The Old Man came out and stood next to me on the deck.

"Don't tell me we have a problem, Chief Officer."

"It should be fine, Captain."

"Should be?"

"Will be. The copra has been replaced by cocoa so it's shortened the GM. We're taking more water into the double bottoms to counteract it. The ship might feel a bit loose for a while but it's fine."

"Hmm."

"If it gets too bad, I'll tell them to hold off loading the final boxes for a while until we fill up the double bottoms more."

"No you won't. We're not delaying our departure. Get it sorted out."

He walked off. The lurching heel increased. The water going into the double bottoms was acting to bring down the centre of gravity but the temporary free surface effect was actually making matters worse. Free surface effect is when liquid sloshes back and forward in a tank, causing even greater instability. The free surface effect wouldn't disappear until the tank was full and the water was pressed up against the tank top.

I became gripped with fear. In my mind I saw the *Coral Chief* slumped against the quay, unable to right herself. I saw myself dismissed in disgrace, ending my days as permanent second mate on some wretched South American river steamer, not trusted for cargo responsibility. Sweat leached out of me, I smoked furiously, I contemplated whether I should dash off to my cabin and start drinking.

The last container came aboard with a mighty heeling of the ship. A lot of the ship's company were out on the deck now, watching and silent. I imagined they were all staring at me accusingly. I did my best to look as if everything was exactly as I had planned. The looseness gradually came out of the ship as more water was pumped in. The Old Man asked me if all the double-bottom water would take us below our load lines. I told him of course not. Close, though.

In Lae, letters arrived. I had a huge stack; Annie had written every day. I felt chastened and immediately stepped up my own letter writing. I had received my first lesson in pre-matrimonial responsibility. The mail service in the smaller places of New Guinea was not that reliable. There had been a recent scandal when the mail built up to such an extent that an official in one sorting office was reported as having burnt all the undelivered letters to bring things up to date. The story grew legs and became ever more fantastic, although whatever kernel of truth there was didn't inspire confidence.

The pile of letters I received set the course of things for the voyage; the agent would bring the mail on board and three-quarters of it would be mine. People made jokes, I tried to look modest, I told myself they were jealous, I felt proud. There were a few who never made jokes and didn't talk about letters from home; these were the people who nobody ever wrote to.

On average, it took about twenty days for a letter to arrive from home, sometimes a bit quicker in Australia, a bit slower in the islands. Letters were all written to the head office in Hong Kong, where they were bundled together with business correspondence for the ship and then despatched to the agent at our port of call. Sometimes letters could hang around in Hong Kong for a while and so twenty days was about what was expected. Taking into account the distance, twenty days from the UK was about 600 miles a day, which didn't sound too bad.

In some ways, it seemed that our ship, as all ships, was like a mini-kingdom, a self-sufficient floating country in which we had our own governance, internal security, finances and foreign policy. We made our own electricity and water, we traded our food, we made our own entertainment, we engaged in commerce. We had our own politics and endured our own scandals, crises, rumours, intrigue, espionage, violence, disasters. We rewarded the good and punished the bad. We were a fiefdom in thrall to our masters: our controllers, our owners. As in all fiefdoms we sometimes cheated and lied and only told our controllers what they needed to know, or what we thought they needed to know. Ours was like a medieval structure with a king, prince, dukes, earls, viscounts and barons, then all the masses, the peasantry. The king's word was the law and we had no recourse. When he said: 'Off with his head!' we dragged the victim to the block.

And the players?

The king. Captain, the master, the Old Man, 47, Welsh, twice married. Stocky, selfish and prone to tantrums. Lively company but manic and often overbearing, potential to lose control when drunk, had an obnoxious side, had a history of making a fool of himself. Tactless, sometimes cruel. A good seaman with an overload of self-confidence, although I suspected he had a weak streak that could let us down in a crisis.

The prince. The chief officer, the second in command, Chief Mate, Mate, Choff, me, English, 28, turning one of life's corners, engaged to be married, introverted. Some people thought me a big-head with little sympathy for others, both of which I thought were unfair. Drank too much. Enough said.

A royal duke. The chief engineer, Chief, 41, Scottish, married. Short and bull-like, ginger-haired, thick glasses, small moustache, pale, quiet. Slow but clever, unflappable, stolid, reliable. A bit dull on the surface but more interesting after digging down. Portrayed himself as equal to the Old Man, but everyone knew he wasn't. Thinking he should be king, and resenting the chief officer as prince. Accompanied by his wife, a perpetually miserable person much older than him.

A baron. The second officer, Second Mate. English, 26, single. Medium height, slow moving, Mexican moustache, poor conversationalist. Beady black eyes which fixed on people in an unsettling way. A dull man with a weak laugh, never smiled with his eyes. Drank a lot and became unpleasant, a lecher, a plodder. Good at his job when sober.

A knight. The third officer, Third Mate. Pacific Islander, 26, married. Short, coffee-coloured, immensely strong. Inveterate liar, but entertaining and good company. Inferiority complex, easy to like. Drank too much and frequently let himself down. Generally unreliable.

A duke. The second engineer, Second. 32, single. Medium height, weedy frame, permed hair, strong tan, thick moustache. A ditherer, out of his depth, insecure. Flashy dresser, expensive tastes. Hard to dislike.

A baron. The third engineer, Third. English, 25, single. Tall and scruffy. Long-haired, pallid and unfit. Nervous, habitually bit his nails to the quick. Sarcastic, critical and intolerant. Good company for short periods. Very good at his job, hard-working. A lonely man. Unpopular.

A knight. The fourth engineer, Fourth. New Zealander, 24, single. Small and merry, pale and ginger. Happy, quiet, clever, interesting, no ambition. Stylish in dress. Not a leader, would make a poor senior officer. Likeable.

A baron. The radio officer, Sparks. 39, English, married. Tall, lean, healthy, moustache and glasses. A sleek man with a good intellect. Independent character, no leader but no follower either. Hard to like or dislike.

A baron. The electrical officer, Leci. 32, Scottish, single. Short, bulky, bearded, drank like a fish and usually became incomprehensible later in the evening. Insular. A loner.

A knight. The chief steward. 51, Hong Kong Chinese, married. Short, busy, always grinning, obsequious. Fractured grasp of spoken English, a bully to his men. Socialised with the crew, not the officers.

The serjeants at arms: the petty officers, the bosun and storekeepers, keeping order, acting as the interface with the officers.

And the peasantry, the crew, the broad mass of everyone else.

This was our world.

☆　☆　☆

The mainland New Guinea ports and the offshore islands all had their own character. Kavieng on New Ireland was a pretty place. We arrived at sunrise, the light gleaming off the coral patches, a handful of outrigger crews waving us in, and Kavieng suddenly appeared among the trees, a few white buildings near the beach, the jetty jutting out like a hand clutching at civilisation. All around was verdant and quiet.

There was a cargo delay and we were there a day and a night. In the evening, a few of us went to the Kavieng Club, the European hangout that was peopled by Australians and British and Germans who all slyly talked against each other. They made a big show of signing us in the guest book. The club was part beach bar and part yacht club, old photographs of cricket teams hung on the walls.

We had a barbecue meal and drank lager with the club members then beat them at darts, which they didn't seem to like. There was a sadness about the European clubs in these Pacific outposts; the members wore blazers and celebrated the Queen's birthday with forced enthusiasm, as if reaching for something they never had.

On the way back, much later in the dark, we were walking down the beach road and came across lots of big crabs running out from the sea. We chased after them; the Old Man and I caught a couple and took them back to the ship to boil for a late supper, holding them by the claws like prizes.

There was a nasty turn in Wewak when the Papuans got drunk and started fighting with the Chinese. The spark was the Papuan perception that the food was poor and the Chinese cook was making no effort. Bottles and chairs were used, blood was drawn and the crew mess was generally smashed up. There were more Papuans than Chinese, but the Chinese were tough. The second mate patched up the warriors, mostly bruises, loose teeth, a broken nose, one had damaged his hand. Nothing too serious. The Old Man stopped the crew's grog for a week, which they accepted without protest.

Port Moresby was gaining a reputation of being an unsafe place because it drew people in from all over New Guinea, which in turn caused a lot of tribal mixing. The consequent rivalries, coupled with too many people chasing too few jobs, gave birth to sporadic violence, usually short and brutally resolved although sometimes there were more prolonged battles.

A lot of the crew had their families in Port Moresby, and the ship would become overrun with relations once we were alongside. Small kids ran around the alleyways shrieking while the women sat by the top of the gangway jabbering noisily in *Tok Pisin*, the most common of the 850 Papuan languages. In Port Moresby, the ship had a carnival feel.

Occasionally we would be in port at the same time as one of our sister ships, up from Australia or down from the East, which precipitated a party to celebrate the arrival of familiar faces from previous trips. There was a punch-up among the officers one evening when the ambiance slipped and a surfeit of beer caused people to speak their mind too openly, but I missed the fireworks, having gone to bed an hour beforehand. The third mate looked a mess in the morning, with his ballooned lip and missing tooth. The crew sniggered at us, probably thinking we should have our grog stopped for a week too.

In the day it was always hot in Port Moresby, hot and bright, so bright the white buildings hurt to look at. A lot of people sat around in the dirt, a lot of dogs ambled around then sat and scratched. The water in the harbour was brown-green. Stone Age canoes lay next to smart yachts. The jungle rose up on the hills all round, thick green. The yacht club was dying on its feet through lack of members. Some wooden huts had sprung up nearby. Sometimes it seemed to me the jungle was creeping back down the hill to take over again.

Lae was the second largest city in New Guinea after Port Moresby, although it was comparable in terms of the volume of exports. It was the end point of the road from the New Guinea Highlands, along which the produce of the fertile interior was transported. We picked up a lot of coffee from Lae, some cocoa and a bit of copra. Lae was billed as the Garden City for its floral beauty, although I always thought that was over-egging the description. It was certainly a prettier place than Port Moresby and far less criminalised, even though it was in turn becoming less safe. There was a rise in Raskol gangs throughout Papua New Guinea. Raskol is the *Tok Pisin* derivation of 'rascal'; they were violent gangs that recruited their members from the army of unemployed that congregated around the bigger cities and settlements. They had strong connections with the Australian marijuana trade and indulged in carjacking, kidnapping, rape and murder. Raskol gangs were building up around Lae, although it was still deemed a safe enough place to walk around in the evening. The biggest danger was probably the potholes in the road that were deep enough to break a leg. There were a lot of small wooden shops run by Chinese shopkeepers who pretended not to own them so as to not upset the locals, who owned nothing – with the exception of the fat cats, who owned virtually everything.

On the streets of Lae there were men down from the Highlands with tattooed faces and holes in their ears big enough to put your fist through, stocky men as solid as boulders, flat feet too wide to wear shoes, teeth stained red with betel nut; they lived on the edge of town in houses made from sticks and leaves and plastic sheets.

We would occasionally go for a drink in the big hotel in Lae, which called itself 'international' because it served three different types of beer. On the occasions I went to the edges of the town I was bitten by insects as large as walnuts. In the late afternoon it rained, big fat drops as hot as tea. And always the green jungle loomed behind us, dark green, so dark it was almost black.

Madang was probably my favourite port of call in New Guinea. The settlement had been founded by the Germans in 1884 and named Friedrich-Wilhelmshafen. In Madang there were palm trees on both side of the winding creek, the water was clear blue and I could see right through to the river bed. Clustered along the bank were the old German wharfs with sleepy-looking wooden warehouses on which were painted the names of ships that had visited over the years: *Riverbank* 1975, *Hupeh* 1978, *Sinkiang* 1979. The older paintwork was too faded by the sun to read. The *Coral Chief's* name was on there somewhere. Canoes and small boats moved up and down the creek as slowly as reptiles. Along either bank were huts and houses and a hotel with a pool, all with roofs made from dried palm fronds. One of the wharfs was sad and deserted, with grass growing up through the cracks, and was leaning at an alarming angle towards the river. In the evening big fruit bats flocked out of the jungle, whispering overhead while we watched them. Madang was quiet in the day, silent at night; it was a place where no one hurried or worried.

In Rabaul, the main port of New Britain, we had a barbecue on the boat deck during a cargo lull. The Old Man marshalled a herd of friends and acquaintances on board in the late afternoon. Among the guests were two New Zealander couples, who the Old Man offended by telling inappropriate jokes.

"How do you tell if a girl is from New Zealand? Pat her on the top of her head and see if her knickers fall off!"

That went down like a lead balloon, as did the one that followed: "How can you tell if a Kiwi girl is wearing American knickers? One Yank and they're down!"

His *pièce de résistance* was: "How many Kiwi girls does it take to change a light bulb? Three! One to hold the chair, one to hand me the light bulb and one to give me a blow job while I have to do the job for the silly cows!"

The Old Man roared with laughter at his offensive jokes, but he was the only one laughing. The rest of us looked embarrassed, the guests either smiling nervously or standing with frozen faces. One of the New Zealand women, a big brown beefy matron, stormed off, her husband scuttling after her obediently.

"Come back," shouted the Old Man, "I haven't patted you on the head yet!" She turned and flung a stream of unrepeatable oaths, her sun-ruined face twisting with hatred as she screamed at him.

The Old Man was impervious, turning to us and saying: "Don't you just love the Kiwis?" then: "Come on everyone, let's get the nosebags on! Plenty of grub for everyone now Jumbo's buggered off!"

Our barbecue was a typical ship's model constructed by the engineers: half an oil drum laid sideways on legs with a section of engine room grating fitted into it to grill the food on. The second mate lit the fire then heaped it with coals, which were soon burning furiously. The idea, of course, as is the case with any barbecue, is to wait until the fire dies down to a bed of hot embers and then put the food on. But we were too impatient and greedy and heaped on the steak and sausages and chicken, which quickly blackened in the flames while staying raw inside. The Old Man started eating it immediately.

Watching him wolf down uncooked chicken made my throat thrunge with liquid, and I had to turn away. Few people could bring themselves to eat anything after that spectacle, with the inevitable result that everyone started to drink too much and act foolishly. When the singing started I went to bed, well aware of my capacity for making a fool of myself in such circumstances and mindful that my presence was required for cargo work, which would be starting at seven the next morning.

Several of the crew came from the small islands in the Bismarck Sea, and when we steamed past they would all hang over the side and yell and wave at any canoes, which usually contained their friends and relations. A lot of Papuans had overtly Christian names that seemed to favour the letter J: Jude, Jesus, Jellico and Jeremiah. The naming regime was a gift of the missionaries.

The Papuans ate raw fish when it was available. This wasn't an intricate sushi-type dish of the type prepared by the Japanese; they just ate the fish raw and live. The first time I saw this was when we were alongside in Kimbe and the bosun climbed down a monkey ladder to buy some fish off an outrigger canoe whose owner was shouting up to boast of his wares. The bosun selected a fish, a fat-bodied silver-scaled fellow about fifteen inches long, still twitching. He just bit a huge mouthful out of the still twitching body and chewed away. Another sailor clambered down and the bosun offered him a bite. Chomp. Another fist-size mouthful. The bosun saw me watching and waved the fish in my direction. I politely waved a 'no thanks' to him, which caused an explosion of laughter from the crew who were lined up along the rails watching. The bosun and the sailor took turns to bite the flesh off the body of the fish until just the head, tail and backbone were left, at which point they tossed the remnants over the side.

Overall, in the Islands I preferred the smaller places we visited: Madang, Wewak, Rabaul, Kieta, Kimbe, Kavieng. These were all in that part of Papua New Guinea and the outlying islands which had been a German protectorate until the end of the First World War.

At the turn of the twentieth century, New Guinea was controlled by three European powers. The Dutch had the western half and administered it as part of the Dutch East Indies, the British had the south-eastern part and ran this through their dominion of Australia, and the Germans controlled the north-eastern quarter, christening it Kaiser-Wilhelmsland. The Germans also had possession of all the offshore islands surrounding the Bismarck Sea as well as the Solomon Island chain. But then all German overseas territories were confiscated after the First World War, and many German names were anglicised in a show of spite: New Pomerania became New Britain, New Mecklenburg became New Ireland, Friedrich-Wilhelmshafen became Madang – and the German Shepherd dog became the Alsatian.

Several German names in the South Pacific survived, though, the best known probably being the Bismarck Sea and New Hanover Island. All the ports along the coast had been founded during the German period, and people of German stock were still very much in evidence. The ports were all well planned and well organised, they had the later Australian insertion of a yacht club and they all now had a group of Chinese traders. Among the Chinese was always someone who ran a restaurant, which we visited when we had the chance, to eat exquisitely prepared seafood and drink cold South Pacific lager.

☆　☆　☆

The Australian ports had their own character too, very different from those of the Islands. Our time there seemed to be defined by industrial action and repairs to the ship. For a service billed as twenty-eight days, we hung around a lot, to the probable fury of the owners in Hong Kong. The unions were strong. So we anchored off Melbourne for two days during a tug strike. We sat at anchor for three days off Brisbane during a dock strike. We wasted two days in Sydney following a walk-off over an overtime squabble.

Then there were the breakdowns. We had continual breakdowns; our breakdown cycle was probably more reliable than the twenty-eight day cargo cycle. Five days in Melbourne for the gantry crane, a day in Sydney, two days in Brisbane. Then the big one: a major boiler problem halfway across the Coral Sea going north. We limped back at 3 knots to Cairns, the nearest port. It took us four days. Our water was rationed, no laundry, no showers, hardly any water to wash in. The tap was turned on for an hour a day. We all turned grubby and smelly. We were all irritable.

Brisbane was my favourite port of call in Australia. The people were laid back and friendly, the seafood was outstanding and we enjoyed ourselves in the local pubs. The place was girding up for the Commonwealth Games later in the year, although everyone seemed very relaxed about it. The crew enjoyed Brisbane too much, getting into trouble. On our second visit three of them were thrown in gaol for fighting. I went with the agent to get them released the next day. They were ashamed and apologetic, but we all knew it would happen again.

Sydney was popular with all of us, although I found it a city that had all the clothes but didn't know what to wear. Should it dress as British, American or Australian? The British elements were the older buildings, the civic organisation and the established areas, which to me were the more attractive parts of the city. The American influence was the modern thrust in the brash new buildings and the business district, together with the fast food joints and the never-ending advertising prattle about money: making money, getting more money, making your business make more money, starting a business and making money. The Australian persona seemed weaker than it should have been, sitting between the two, looking baffled, veering more towards the US. I liked Sydney; it was a good place to eat and drink and wander round, and the local company was always enjoyable, but I felt it needed to exert itself a little more.

Then there was Melbourne, a scruffy city, more industrial than Sydney. More Birmingham than London, more Detroit than New York. It liked to style itself as a cosmopolitan mix. The biggest group by far were those of British heritage, although there were a lot of Mediterranean and Middle Eastern peoples: Italians, Greeks, Maltese, Turks, Lebanese, Egyptians, Iraqis and Iranians, which gave the place an interesting buzz, especially in the evening. The aborigines were poorly represented and kept to the fringes of the city. We had several days in Melbourne on a couple of occasions, I bought boomerangs as gifts to take home and a cassette recorder to play the tapes that Annie was now sending me.

'Looks like war, doesn't it?' From April until June 1982, our conversations either started with the South Atlantic war or moved onto it. We listened to the BBC World Service daily.

The Argentinian occupation of the British island of South Georgia was followed by a full-scale invasion of the Falkland Islands at the beginning of April. The small Royal

Marine contingent was overrun and the Falkland Islands were renamed the Islas Malvinas. The Argentinian public was ecstatic; its military dictator General Galtieri was fêted and transformed overnight from despised autocrat to national hero.

Britain was shocked and outraged. General Mario Menéndez was appointed as the Argentinian governor. One of his first moves was to make the Falkland Islanders drive on the right, which caused even more outrage. British Prime Minister Margaret Thatcher ordered a military mobilisation to recapture the Falklands. The Royal Air Force bombed the runway at Port Stanley to prevent the Argentinian garrison being built up further. In three days, the Royal Navy assembled the biggest task force seen since the Second World War and it was despatched to the South Atlantic at full steam. South Georgia was re-taken before the end of April.

British Merchant Navy ships were being requisitioned and the news was that up to fifty ships could be enlisted. We all wanted to be one of them although there was little chance; we were the wrong type of ship on the wrong side of the world. The big name vessels took the headlines: Cunard Line supplied the world's premiere passenger liner, the SS *Queen Elizabeth II*, to serve as a troop carrier, and P & O contributed the SS *Canberra* and the SS *Uganda* as troop carrier and hospital ship.

For the ten weeks of the conflict, from the beginning of April until the Argentine surrender in mid-June, the war was our all-consuming interest. The radio, television and newspaper coverage was good in Australia, although we had to scrabble for news in New Guinea. The sea and land fighting began in earnest in May. When the Cunard Line ship *Atlantic Conveyor* was blown up we all felt the injury. When General Menéndez surrendered to the British commander in the middle of June, we had a party like no other. Our baser natures emerged, ugly nationalism ruled the day, we cheered our men and we jeered at the enemy.

General Galtieri resigned in disgrace on Argentina's humiliating defeat. The subsequent internal investigation carried out by the Argentinian army recommended that he face a firing squad for his incompetence, although he was instead sentenced to twelve years in prison. Margaret Thatcher won the next British election: to the victor the spoils.

We had Easter crossing the Coral Sea, and a grand meal was planned that evening. Usually, the third mate would relieve me for dinner but this time I arranged for a tray of food to be brought to me on the bridge so he could enjoy the feast. I ate prawns and chicken and sliced beef off the chart table. I even had a glass of wine, the only time I had ever taken alcohol on watch since I had been to sea. Of course, I had been mildly drunk coming on watch on a few occasions during my dark younger days, but I had never actually drunk alcohol before in my duty hours.

After the end of my watch at eight o'clock, I took a torch and did rounds of the ship, checking the deck, looking for loose containers, looking for any problems. The sea was flat calm, there were no clouds in the sky and I could clearly see the sharp constellations of Leo and Virgo, the stars dropping their light down into the dark sea. I walked through the crew quarters, the Papuans were in the mess, drinking and playing chess and draughts, loud music thumping in the background. The Chinese were in the cook's cabin, making a racket, screeching at each other. The officers were in the smoke room, replete, talking quietly and recovering from the meal. The ship was happy and peaceful, the mood was just perfect.

I took a cold can of Fosters from my fridge then went and sat on the poop deck by myself, watching the wake fall away into the gloom, feeling the warm night air blowing on my cheek, reflecting on my good fortune.

The Coral Sea could be fickle, though. On one voyage we had six large trucks as deck cargo. A late season tropical revolving storm came blasting across the sea, heading for the northern tip of Queensland as we were coming south from Wewak. I went on deck with the bosun and his men, and we put double lashings on all the trucks, lashings on the anchor cables, lashings on the lifeboats. All the dogs on the watertight doors were hammered shut and we rigged lifelines and battened down the whole ship as best we could. The Old Man slowed the vessel, keeping us north of the 10°S latitude line, hoping the cyclone would go rushing past us towards the Torres Strait. It did: relief all round.

Mid-voyage, the shipboard atmosphere started to change. We had a new cook, who was dreadful. He ran up a flag to show the quality of his fare with the first meal, which was a ham steak wearing a thick overcoat of grease hiding poorly cooked fat and gristle. The food stayed at that standard; bad food, shockingly bad. We were served chicken with the blood still weeping. Everything was drenched in grimy grease. All flavour was smothered by garlic.

We complained to the Old Man but he saw nothing wrong, he had no interest in food. He just shovelled down whatever was put in front of him. The cook could have fed him an old boiled dog and he would have eaten it just the same. The Old Man told us there was nothing wrong with the food and to stop being so fussy. I bypassed the Old Man and went to see the chief steward, telling him the standard was unacceptable. The chief steward threw up his hands and said it wasn't his fault, he had been sent a cook who couldn't cook, he had been given poor food at the last stores pick-up.

We all started boycotting the meals, cooking ourselves bacon and egg sandwiches in the pantry. As soon as we arrived in port, the officers rushed ashore to eat, bringing back food for those on duty. The Old Man asked me plaintively why everyone had stopped coming into the dining saloon. I told him it was because the food was so unspeakably bad that no one could stand it. Eventually, he became fed up eating by himself and hauled the cook up to his cabin, telling him that his monthly bonus was being stopped until things took a turn for the better.

While the cook struggled to improve, things became worse elsewhere. The crew were getting drunk more often and fighting among themselves, so the Old Man decided to have a crack-down on their behaviour. He stopped their beer ration. They became sullen and worked slower. He retaliated by stopping them bringing their girlfriends back to the ship. They became even more sullen and resentful, muttering darkly whenever an officer passed. He threatened to stop advancing them money so they wouldn't even be able to go ashore.

They went silent, they glowered, they worked slowly, started late, sat around a lot. People predicted disaster. A German ship trading on the Papua New Guinea coast and crewed by Papuans had mutinied a few months previously when the officers had resorted to the same tactics. In the end there was violence, two officers were hospitalised, the ship was blacklisted by the stevedore gangs in Port Moresby and Lae. Eventually, the owners had to replace the Old Man and chief officer.

I had a long meeting with the bosun and deck storekeeper. They were both surly and taciturn. What made it worse for them to bear was the Old Man's own enthusiastic boozing in port, bringing shoals of his loud friends back to the ship late at night. I bullied the petty officers, telling them they would never work on one of the company's ships again if they didn't start working properly. I told them the Hong Kong owners would replace them all with Chinese crew and they would be finished. That worried them. They pleaded with me to ask the Old Man to lift his restrictions. I said they needed to behave better if they wanted some of the restrictions lifted. I told them I would do what I could if I saw a demonstration of effort for two days, after which I would speak to the Old Man. They agreed. They worked like never before, early starts, late finishes, short smoke-o breaks, short lunch. The Old Man was impressed. I moved in to do my Fletcher Christian bit.

I said: "This is them saying sorry, Captain. You've won."

"Yes, I have. That's the way to do it, an iron fist! That'll teach 'em, bastards!"

"We need to ease up on them now, Captain."

"What do you mean?"

"I mean, they're apologising. You need to acknowledge in kind or there'll be a reversal and then things will go completely downhill. Remember what happened on that German ship a few months ago."

"Yes. They beat the shit out of the mate and second mate, as I remember," he said.

"Yes, Captain, that's right. Let them have a light grog ration and see how it goes," I suggested.

"Hmm. We'll see."

The Old Man allowed them two beers a day per man, which was plenty because the non-drinkers traded with the drinkers. After a couple of weeks of good behaviour he told the deck officers to turn a blind eye to girlfriends. The ship recovered.

The Old Man was a difficult character, charming one moment, unhinged and screaming the next. He was easily bored and needed something to arrest his wandering mind, otherwise he would go on a mission that gave grief to all and sundry. He would carry out deranged activity. In Brisbane he visited a Polish ship and brought all the ship's officers back with him for a guided tour of the *Coral Chief*, then became angry because the chief steward couldn't arrange enough food to feed all fifteen of them. Most of the Poles ended up in the bar, drinking all our grog on the Old Man's page.

A new internal telephone system was installed in Australia, and the Old Man discovered that if he dialled zero it connected to the loudspeakers and he could broadcast all over the ship. There was no stopping him. He gave pointless updates, instructions, orders, observations and used it to summon people to his cabin. But when they arrived they found the summons was usually for no real reason.

The author as Chief Officer

One morning when the second mate was a couple of minutes late for his watch he gave him an unnecessary public telling off using the loudspeaker system. Even the Old Man's defenders thought that was a poor show. The second mate was beside himself with rage at being so publicly humiliated.

Not long afterwards, the system began to get abused. Odd noises started coming out of the loudspeakers, ghostly laughter, cackling, whooping; imitations of the Old Man. The Old Man was beside himself with rage now, rushing around the ship trying to find the culprit. He broadcast an instruction forbidding everyone except him and the senior officers to use the system. Almost immediately someone broadcast: "And me ..." followed by ghostly laughter. The Old Man was apoplectic. When he offered a reward for the unmasking of the phantom announcer over the loudspeakers, the spectral voice replied: "Whoooo-ooooo!"

It went on for days. Everyone looked serious and concerned when the Old Man was around. We all had our theories as to the culprit. I was convinced it was the second mate exacting his revenge. Others thought it was the third engineer. The Old Man implored the chief engineer to track down whoever was doing this, but the chief explained that the system had no such tracking capability. The Old Man stopped using the system. The spectral voice didn't; the whoo-ooing, cackling, whooping and rude impressions of the Old Man continued. The Old Man had the system disconnected.

☆   ☆   ☆

With the regularity of our passage, notwithstanding breakdowns, some people referred to it as a milk run voyage, same ports, same faces, week in week out. After a few months I felt I knew every headland and strait and rock and reef and light, the Jomard Passage, the China Strait, all the cuts between the islands. Our twenty-eight day voyage from the Islands to Australia crossed a lot of lines of latitude, from 2.5°S to 38°S, a difference of over 2,000 nautical miles. Kavieng was our most northerly call and Melbourne our southern limit. Most of our travelling was north–south, and the variance in longitude was small, from 143°E to 153°E.

In the southern winter, the coldest months are June, July and August. Our normal expectations were that Brisbane would be mild, Sydney cool, Melbourne cold. That year was particularly chilly, though, and we were in blues for the whole of the Australian coast. At its lowest point, the temperature in Melbourne went down to 23°F, and Sydney had its first flakes of snow since 1917.

In the Islands it was different. The temperature was in the low eighties Fahrenheit in most places, although there was a big contrast between the south and north coasts of New Guinea. Port Moresby was the only port we went to on the south coast; it was a hot, dry and dusty place, similar to northern Australia 150 miles to the south. Round on the north coast in Lae, the weather was tropical monsoon and it rained, rained, rained. It never seemed to stop.

Madang and Wewak, further up the coast, were wet but not to the extent of Lae. The outlying islands of New Britain and New Ireland were generally dry places, although Kavieng could surprise. The heavy rains would wash the salt water crocodiles out of the river estuaries. We saw several crocs around the mouth of the Sepik River near Wewak and a few around New Britain. The biggest concentration of crocodiles in Papua New Guinea was on the south coast by the Fly River delta but we never went that far west. The salt water crocodile, *Crocodylus porosus*, grows up to 17 feet in length and weighs over 2,000 pounds. It can live quite comfortably in salt water although mostly inhabits fresh-water mangrove swamps. 'Salties', the Australians call them. The saltie is a supreme predator and will take anything that comes within its range: fish, fowl, mammal. It is considered the most dangerous of crocodiles to humans. The Papuan crew would jeer and swear and shake their fists when they saw one.

I had my birthday in late July on the way back up to the Islands. Birthdays at sea are largely ignored, no one gets a card or a present; a lot of people don't even bother to make an announcement. We gathered in the late morning and I stood everyone a drink for which I received a toast in return. We discussed the event for fifteen seconds or so then the talk swiftly turned to the staple subjects: the ships we had sailed on, the people we had sailed with and the deeds we had done.

As was always the case, the older people banged on about the good old days and told stories in support, each one leapfrogging the previous in its scale. In truth, these were usually fairly mundane occurrences spun into ever more fantastic disguise, so they appeared as unbeatable and unrepeatable lifetime experiences that the younger ones could only envy. The younger ones metaphorically tossed their eyebrows to the deckhead and sometimes tried to recapture the conversation with talk of today and the future, but it was an unequal contest and the past always won.

Worryingly, I found myself wandering between the two groups. I fleetingly wondered where the turn in life was when someone started looking backwards more than they looked forwards.

As the drink flowed, the older set became maudlin and lamented on all that was lost or passing, the loosening of formality, the shrinking of deference, the emphasis on profit, the obsession with efficiency, the curtailment of the extended social life of a ship in port, the reduction in manning, the rise of competition from countries with no maritime heritage. The talk was of the collapse of civilisation as we knew it. The Old Man started to become metaphysical and began a long ramble about barbarians at the gates, declaring that something needed to be done to halt the slide. He raved about cheaply run flag of convenience ships being the ruin of us all, and said the way to solve the problem was draining the mangroves, not just shooting the crocs. I didn't really follow what he was talking about and I doubted that anyone else did either, although we nodded in sympathy and agreement, before going in for a late lunch.

And then it was done. In a snap, the days and weeks that had strolled by at a sedate pace were suddenly behind me. I was on the bridge that same evening, chatting to the Old Man as we cleared Jomard Passage and turned west for Port Moresby, when Sparks appeared suddenly and handed him a Marconigram.

The Old Man nodded, smiled and passed it to me. It read: *'Choff Hall to be relieved in Lae. Relief Choff to be confirmed.'* We were a week out of Lae. I wondered whether the personnel department in Hong Kong had timed the sending of the Marconigram to arrive on my birthday.

My paying off party was in Port Moresby. It was a warm clear night so we held it on the boat deck. All the officers were there, together with several Australians, the chief stevedore, the agent and a few I didn't recognise. The event went well. Everyone knew I was engaged to be married and I suffered the usual witticisms.

"Soon be back to see your good lady then, Simon," said someone.

"It's the point of no return," said someone else

"She'll be there waiting for you with the harness."

"You had better have a few beers while you can,"

"You'll be speaking in a higher voice next time we see you."

And so on. The night went on while we sipped cold lager and looked out into the dark. The Papuan full moon slowly rose over the silhouetted palm trees in a scene that could have given John Masefield his line: 'Dipping through the Tropics by the palm-green shores'. We toasted my good fortune.

I faced a fractured journey home: Lae to Port Moresby; Port Moresby to Singapore; Singapore to London, stopping in the Middle East. The flight from Lae was memorable. I got onto on a small propeller-driven plane crammed with locals and animals. I seemed to be the only one without a chicken. Hand baggage rules were ignored – people carried as many baskets and bags as they could manage. Rules on seat belts, sitting down and smoking were ignored. People stood in the walkway or perched on seats and jabbered at each other. A stewardess gamely tried a safety demonstration but everyone ignored her.

We eventually bumped off the ground and had a rough flight across the spinal mountain range to Port Moresby, 190 miles to the south. When we arrived I had several hours to wait before the London flight so I went to the agent's office where he arranged a call to England. When I was put through I arranged a date with Annie to meet under the big yellow arrivals sign in London airport.

7

In the Shadow of the Volcano

Three months later I was in the airport bar in Kai Tak airport, Hong Kong, drinking San Miguel beer and waiting for the flight south, back to New Guinea. in England, I now owned a house with Annie, a one-bedroom terraced place on the edge of east Bristol, which we had bought for £21,250. When I had arrived home from the *Coral Chief* it was still being built. so I stayed alternately at my mother's house in Oxfordshire and with Annie's parents in Bristol, uncomfortable in each, before finally moving in to our new place. Annie chose the furniture and furnishings, I chose a car and the dog we were going to buy once we were married, which was planned for the next time I was back in the country. I had finally been bested by maturity. All the wedding plans were made around me. I joined in where I could but didn't really know what was going on.

London to Kai Tak had been a long and uncomfortable flight, which I spent sandwiched between two grossly fat and malodorous men in the smoking section. I found it a tremendous relief when we stopped at Bombay for seven hours to remedy an undefined mechanical problem.

Having missed my connection in Hong Kong, I was put up by the company overnight in the Grand Hotel on Kowloon side, just off Nathan Road. The Grand had always been my favourite hotel in Hong Kong, an old grey-white colonial style building among the bustle. As I was checking in, an American standing next to me said they were knocking it down soon, which I found profoundly sad.

The London to Hong Kong flight had been uncomfortable but organised, even with the small crisis that had diverted us to Bombay. The Hong Kong to Lae flights were uncomfortable and shambolic. I changed at Singapore where the local agent met me to say the flight to Port Moresby was cancelled, then it wasn't, then it was, then it never had been cancelled and I was bundled on board at the last minute, praying that my luggage was with me. In Port Moresby

I took an internal flight to Lae, a bumpy repeat of the journey I had made several weeks beforehand, this time going the opposite way.

In Lae I was put on a local island hopper to Rabaul – cranky, juddering, propeller-driven, dangerous-looking, with an Australian captain who looked both mad and drunk. There were only half a dozen people on board among the dozen seats, each of us trying not to look terrified as the plane lurched about and finally thudded onto the runway outside Rabaul, sixty hours after I had left London.

The *Chengtu* was a similar ship to the *Coral Chief*, only her finish was not as smart. They were both Island size container vessels with a big gantry crane that travelled the length of the deck. She was sailing under the Singapore registry flag, which was significant for me as it was the first time I had ever signed on a ship that wasn't flying the red ensign.

The *Chengtu* had a distinctly budget feel about her. Not in the propulsion or the mechanical gear or navigational equipment, all of which was of a good standard, but in the cabins and fittings and the little luxuries that made our life sweeter. She was a Cortina rather than a Jag, a fish and chip supper rather than a restaurant meal, a cheap and tacky hotel the other side of the Costa del Sol highway in Torremolinos, not a ritzy place on the beach in Marbella. I had sailed on worse ships, but they were usually worse because they were ancient and nothing worked any more, although they still had a faded splendour, they still had class. The *Chengtu* had all the class of a penny arcade on the pier at Weston-super-Mare.

As a general rule, I was proud when we had guests on board because we lived in comfort and our standards were high, although on the *Chengtu* I couldn't help feeling a bit ashamed whenever the head stevedore or agent or one of the shippers visited; I felt they might view us as being of a poor grade. The bar was small and shoddy, and when there were ten of us in there it felt crowded. The gloomy dining saloon had one long coffin-shaped table and wasn't a place to linger. It reminded me of a small coastal ship I had sailed on out of Goole, where we all clustered in a dark ante-chamber off the galley to eat in collective grimness.

There were only two stewards on the *Chengtu*, which meant the standards were down. As chief officer, I had a decent size cabin with a dayroom, bedroom and bathroom, and an office next door. The ship wasn't that old, but the mattress on my bunk looked limp and exhausted and in the bathroom the toilet grizzled in a permanent leaky flush. I was better served than the junior and mid-ranking officers, though, who were stuffed into mean little boxes down the alleyway with communal showers and toilets a walk down the alleyway.

Our trading pattern was from the Islands to the Far East. The voyage turnaround time was thirty days: Manila, Hong Kong and Singapore in the Far East, Port Moresby, Lae, Madang, Rabaul, Kieta, Honiara and Wewak in the Islands. Occasionally we encountered the *Coral Chief* or one of her sister ships on the trade I had just left, the Islands to Australia.

The *Chengtu's* officers were mostly British, with a couple of Chinese and an Australian radio officer; the crew were all Hong Kong Chinese. The complement was lean: eleven officers and twenty-two crew.

We had our share of memorable characters although Ben, the second officer, stood out from them all. Ben was a gangly ginger-headed Geordie, a manic man in his late twenties who rattled out his sing-song accent with machine-gun quickness. I had lived in Newcastle for six months when I studying for my First Mate's Certificate and felt I had a pretty good ear for the dialect, but Ben would rush on by, three sentences ahead of my deciphering speed. He was hungry for life's events, and everything he had done or was going to do would be 'great' would be 'grand' would be 'fantastic'. He drank a lot of beer and became more and more exercised as he did so. His conversation would always be about how best to enjoy himself.

"Why-aye, Simon, how's it ganging, man?"

"Good, Ben. How about you?"

"Brilliant, man! Bloody brilliant! Tell me Simon, what's your favourite place for a run ashore – Singapore or Manila?"

"Singapore, probably. I like them both but Singapore more so. It's getting tidied up a bit now, but it's still the place for me."

"Nahh. Manila's the place. Wild and wide open. You can get anything you want in Manila. And those ladies, why-aye man. They're all so gorgeous, don't they just knock you dead?"

"Yeah, I like Manila, but, let's face it, Manila's a bit of a dump. You can't even get a decent meal there."

"Aye, you're right, the food's shite. But who wants a decent meal anyway? You can get a decent drink there in a decent bar with decent woman. What more do you want?"

"I take your point."

"Anyway, Singapore's becoming like a bloody boy scout toon. No long hair, no chewing gum in the street, the bars are closing doon. Bloody puritans."

"You won't be going out on the town in Singapore then?"

"Hold on, man! I didn't say that! Too bloody right I'll be ganging out on the toon. Ah'll be ganging doon Bugis Street wi' the Third."

"Careful you don't wake up next to a woman with bristles on her chin and a pair of conkers between her legs."

"Aghh, who bloody cares? It'll be summat to tell the lads back home."

"You've probably got worse down the Scotswood Road."

"Aye, that's true. Reet! Who wants another beer?"

I had known a lot of people like Ben over the years, completely over-the-top personalities who put their life and soul into every event, every conversation. When they were in a one-on-one situation, they often revealed themselves to be much more thoughtful and reflective, sometimes even quite sad. Not Ben.

When I arrived on the bridge to take over the watch at four in the afternoon he was usually capering around like a loon, screeching about what great weather it was, before launching into an amusing tale about a night out in Newcastle, which usually resulted in him ending up drunk and broke and sometimes beaten. At four in the morning he was equally loud and I could only listen in silence, leaning on the taffrail in the warm night, sipping my mug of coffee, while his voice clattered against my eardrums.

For the last few years I had worked with Chinese crews and I was used to their ways. More importantly, I had an understanding of the mannerisms and customs necessary to keep the whole project of shipboard management moving along. There were two aspects to it: the officer–crew relationship and the European–Chinese relationship. The officers who got things spectacularly wrong were those who transcribed both of these into some sort of master–servant relationship, which was to court disaster as sure as the sun rises.

Most crews – British, Chinese, Indian, Papuan, Filipino or other – accepted the fact that the officers were the executive and the crew the instrument. But some crewmen railed against the perceived difference in status, and of these it was most often the British, some of them constantly striving to demonstrate that they were 'as good as' the officers. Bad management apart, no one was claiming that the crews were in any way inferior; it was only occasional snobbery on the part of the officers, and feelings of insecurity and inadequacy on the part of the odd crew member that caused the problem.

With Chinese crews, this was less of an issue and the officer–crew relationship was accepted. It was the cultural differences that needed more careful attention; 100,000 words wouldn't even dent the subject of how the oriental interacts with the occidental. Suffice it to say – and this is a huge simplification – that the Chinese culture tends to give more deference to age than the British culture, which acknowledges class or position more.

The Chinese crew on the *Chengtu* were all pretty ancient compared to the officers. The Chinese were in their fifties for the most part, and were long-term company men, loyal and hard-working, if a bit patronising to a young chief officer like me.

The thing about people who spend their whole lives doing the same job, though, is that they have often difficulty in accepting that you don't necessarily get better by doing more of the same. If I spent six months splicing mooring ropes every day I would probably have reached my rope-splicing peak. Carrying on splicing for another forty years wouldn't make me that much better. This sort of 'I'm better because I do more of the same' attitude, together with the core cultural differences, tended to manifest itself with the *Chengtu* crew, particularly the bosun, as always knowing a better way to do things.

We were at anchor off Rabaul one day, waiting for a Bank Line ship to vacate the berth so we could go alongside. It was a balmy South Pacific day and we lay in a light breeze in the dark blue-green sea under a pale blue sky. The crew were working on deck, painting the ship's rails. The quartermaster had lowered a pilot ladder over the side as the agent's boat came out from the port. There was mail and a new box of films. The boatmen tied a line to the bottom of the ladder and the agent clambered on board with the bag of mail over his shoulder and went up to see the captain, leaving his man in the boat to deal with the exchange of film boxes.

We had our film contract with Walport, a company that had been supplying films to merchant ships for forty years. The films were mostly three-reelers, occasionally four. Each reel was fifteen inches in diameter and they were packed in large metal boxes, three films to each box. A large metal case with nine reels of film inside is heavy and awkward. After greeting the agent I stayed with the quartermaster, wanting to see the box of replacement films before we accepted it, because it wasn't unknown for us to get the same box back that we had dropped off last time.

The quartermaster lowered a rope, the boatman tied on the box and we heaved it aboard. I looked inside, pronounced myself satisfied, then took the rope from the quartermaster to tie on the box we were sending down. I could feel the bosun's eyes boring into my back as I tied my knot. I used a timber hitch, one of the best cargo handling hitches because it pulls tight against itself as the load comes on and falls away when the weight comes off. It only takes a few seconds to tie.

I had just finished when I heard the bosun huffing behind me. I turned round to see him shaking his head and waving his arms, a look of mild disgust on his face. I passed the rope to him so he could teach me a lesson. The bosun untied my hitch and then spent several minutes tying an elaborate rope cage arrangement which went round all four sides and culminated in a fancy knot in the middle. He stood back and look pleased.

The quartermaster picked up the box and started to lower it. Halfway down, the box lurched sideways and started to slip out between the sides of its cage. The quartermaster started lowering as fast as he could, the bosun screamed at him, the boatman screamed and dived for the back of the boat, the heavy metal box slipped out and smashed into the gunwale of the boat where it bounced off and disappeared into the depths of Rabaul Bay. I stared at the bosun, he screeched at the quartermaster. The crew working on deck tried not to laugh.

"You no tie good knot, bosun," I said accusingly.

"No! No! It good, it good!" Quartermaster stupid!" he said, desperately.

"Your knot no good. Deck boy knot."

"No! Quartermaster fault! Quartermaster fault!"

"We no have film now, all gone. Plenty money gone."

"Not my fault, not my fault. Stupid quartermaster."

"Stupid knot," said the quartermaster.

They started screeching at each other in Cantonese. I waited them out. The bosun kept looking at me out of the side of his eye, hoping I would go, but I wouldn't. It was an accident but I was going to milk the situation and reinforce my position as top dog in the pack. Eventually they stopped. The bosun turned to me, an embarrassed smile on his face.

"Stupid quartermaster," he said.

"You go get film box, bosun," I said.

"What? No can. Film in sea."

"You go in sea and get."

"What? No can! No can go in water and get box! Box at bottom of sea!"

"You no can tie knot? You no can swim? You bosun or deck boy?"

He was looking on the edge of panic. The quartermaster and crew were all smirking, but looking worried, too, in case I also ordered one of them in to swim down and get the box.

"Shark in water. Very dangerous."

"Dangerous for woman, not for proper bosun."

His face collapsed.

"Chief Officer. No can go in water, no can go in water." His voice took on a pleading note. I stared at him sternly for ten seconds, then smiled.

"OK. No go in water. Next time you tie proper sailor knot. I show you next time."

He nodded, bobbing his head and smiling eagerly. In his humiliation he probably hated me so much he wanted to kill me. I felt cruelly pleased, though, that I had gained the upper hand.

⋆　⋆　⋆

In port, the third and second mate split the cargo watches, sometimes one of them working the whole time in port, so the other could get ashore. It was pretty straightforward stuff, making sure the right containers were taken out and that those being loaded went into the right slots. I received the final load information shortly before we arrived and would make the necessary last-minute changes to the loading plan, then give a copy to each of the junior officers and one to the stevedore. As we took more weight on the upper tier we would pump more water into the double-bottom tanks to lower the centre of gravity, and as we rose or lowered in the water the gangway and mooring ropes would need adjusting. Apart from that there were no great challenges; occasionally the crane driver would be a bit reckless and would need to be brought to heel, and sometimes we had conventional deck cargo to load in the form of plant, machinery, lorries and other large items that couldn't fit into a container.

I patrolled the deck from time to time, making sure I was happy with what was going on, otherwise I worked in my office or sat in my cabin, except at lunchtime and in the evening that is, when I sat in the bar. I kept a walkie-talkie with me so that the duty officer, who had the other walkie-talkie, could alert me to any problems.

The third mate was a young Hong Kong Chinese who had adopted the English name Sampson. He was no Sampson-like figure, being quite small and weedy, although he clearly thought it was an appropriate handle. At that time it was the habit for Chinese people working within western businesses to take a European name. This was very much a case of self-selection, which I envied. I often wondered what I would call myself if I had the luxury of choice. I rather fancied Xanthier, which I thought conjured mystery and pedigree and was quite classy. For short, people could call me Zan. My standby name, in case another Xanthier hove into view, was Aurelian. I felt both of these were a long cut above Sampson. Among Chinese officers I had known a Roderick, a Benson, two Rockys and a strange man who called himself Blade. Occasionally the choice was unconsciously hilarious, like the engineer with family name Mo who called himself Arthur. He never understood why people cracked up with laughter when he introduced himself.

Sampson was a reliable officer, though, even if he was far too serious in his personality. His grasp of English was over-precise, as if he was constructing each sentence to maximum effect before he released it. He was a perfect antidote to Ben, and I found it cleared my mind in a therapeutic way to listen to a conversation between them.

"Why-aye man, Sampson, how yer ganging, man?"

"Perfectly well thank you Benjamin. How are you today?"

"Aye, bonny, bonny. Yous ganging for a few scoops after watch?"

"Scoops, Benjamin? What do you mean, scoops?"

"A few bevies man! A few beers!"

"Oh, I don't think so."

"You must be mad, what's wrong with ye?"

"Nothing, nothing at all. Why? Do I look ill?"

"No, you look OK. You just act bonkers, man."

"On another subject from bonkers, tell me Benjamin, I think I have a bit of perpendicular error on my sextant. How do you suggest I correct this?"

"Give it a good whack, man. That'll sort it out."

"Really. You think I should strike my sextant?"

"No, you daft booger, I was joking, it's a delicate instrument. Just correct it with the index screw, that's what it's for."

"The index screw?"

"Aye, the wee screw on the index glass."

"The index glass?"

"Oh for God's sake. I'll do it with you next time we change watch."

"Why thank you Benjamin. That is very decent of you"

"You need a few beers to lighten up, man."

"Would I then be as understandable as you, man?"

"Are yous making a joke, Sampson?"

"I might be … man."

Shippers' parties were fairly common in the Islands, particularly in Rabaul and Lae. The European community was quite thin on the ground in most places and there wasn't a lot for them to do apart from go to the yacht club, drink too much and flirt with each other's spouses. Typically, there would be three or four shippers' representatives, who could be the plantation managers or export controllers, together with a couple of senior staff from the stevedore firm, the pilot, the agent and several other entirely unrelated people who were living there. A lot came with their wives, ladies spoiled from the sun and spoilt by cosseted lives, many with wandering eyes. There was often an edge of desperation in their attempts to enjoy themselves. Altogether, though, the mix usually made for a decent bash.

Our cramped bar was too mean for an extensive party, so we either opened the door to the dining saloon opposite to let the crowd flow back and forth, or if it was a fine evening had the gathering up on the boat deck.

One evening in Rabaul we had an important event arranged for a number of new shippers with everything set up on deck, when the heavens opened and the rain came crashing down, herding us under cover. We moved the whole party to the bridge, which went down well. All the food was laid out on a trestle table at one end of the wheelhouse and the booze was placed on the chart table. The guests loved it. One became crashingly drunk and stood in front of the wheel pretending to steer the ship, howling "Hard-a-starboard, Cap'n" against the backdrop of our strained smiles.

Honiara was even more extreme. In Honiara the Old Man invited eight couples on board one Saturday night and they had such a good time and were so impressed they asked the officers to a beach party the following day. We still had cargo to take on board, which would be arriving sporadically throughout Sunday, and we were booked to sail at 22:00.

The next morning most of the officers headed for the beach while I stayed on board with Ben to deal with the loading. In the event the cargo was all finished by four, and we had the ship battened down and ready to sail by half past. Sampson came back from the beach, shaking his head and saying that it was all getting out of hand. He told us that everyone had been drinking beer and brandy in the sun and they were now starting to fall over. Ben and I collared a lift from the stevedore and went to see the spectacle and tell the Old Man and the agent we were ready to sail if the pilot could be brought forward.

The beach was a couple of miles west of town. Out of hand it was. Everyone was sprawled around the sand in various state of dress, some asleep. Cans and bottles littered the place. The Old Man sat in the shallows, one arm around the agent's bikini-clad wife, the other clutching a can of beer. The two of them were loud and raucous. The agent himself was affecting not to notice.

Ben and I helped ourselves to a beer and then told the agent we were ready to sail. He looked pleased. I told the Old Man. He looked annoyed, then became efficient, shouting at everyone that we were sailing. We crammed into the vehicles and set off. As we reached the road the fourth engineer fell out the back of the jeep and lay inert in the dusty road. For a minute we thought he was dead, but he was just dead drunk. We loaded him back on.

We sailed at 22:00 and the engines broke down 50 yards off the jetty. As the way came off the ship we started drifting back towards the beach. The Old Man was beside himself with rage and screamed down the phone at the chief engineer, who I could hear screaming back. The third mate was on the fo'c'sle head and was told to stand by to let go the anchor. The engineers got everything restarted in the nick of time and we headed out to deep water. The immediate crisis was averted.

Not the crisis with the chief engineer though, who was on his way up to give the Old Man a piece of his mind. The Old Man ordered me to come down with him to his cabin to discuss cargo matters, but this was cowardice, and poorly disguised too – he just didn't want to confront the raging chief engineer by himself. The chief arrived, barrelling into the cabin, black with fury at being shouted at as if he were some lowly deck boy. There was a bit more shouting, which ended with an apology from the Old Man and the chief accepting a drink to seal the peace.

Wewak was usually our last port before we went north along the western edge of the Pacific, transiting the San Bernadino Strait then threading our way through the Philippine Islands to Manila. Our voyage formed a 7,500 mile ellipse that we traipsed anti-clockwise, with Hong Kong at the northern point and the Solomon Islands in the far south. Our Far East ports were Manila, Hong Kong and Singapore, which made a 2,500-mile triangle. In calmer times it would have been nearer 2,000 miles, but we still avoided the western part of the South China Sea so as not to get too close to the coast of Vietnam and be confronted by boat people. As a problem this was now mostly over, and we were expecting an announcement at any time from our Hong Kong head office for all company ships to resume the western passage. In the meantime, however, we kept to the eastern side of the South China Sea, heading first towards the Philippine archipelago, then down the Palawan Passage to the bottom of Malaya.

From Singapore we steamed through the inner seas of the Indonesian Islands: the Java Sea, the Flores Sea and the Arafura Sea. These vast inner seas, along with the Celebes Sea and the Banda Sea, separate the 17,000 islands that make up the Indonesian archipelago, and comprise a larger body of water than the Mediterranean. The seas were well charted, traffic was generally light and I always found it a delight to travel the area. Makassar, the Celebes, Bali – places that tugged at history and evoked the great civilisations of the past 2,000 years. After clearing the Torres Strait we looped right, around New Guinea, calling into our ports as we did so, before turning north again for the Philippines.

We started receiving our cargo details on the way north, usually two or three days before we arrived in Manila Bay. Sunny, the Australian radio officer, would bring me a long coded telegram giving the provisional load details for the three Far East ports. To the casual observer it would be a jumble of letters and numbers, but it gave me all the detail I needed:

MA PM 16 × 15 Cop, 11 × 20 Cof translated into 16 containers of copra, 15 tonnes each, plus 11 containers of coffee, 20 tonnes each, from Manila to Port Moresby.

HK LE 28 × 15 cop, 32 × 10 tea was 28 containers of copra, 15 tonnes each, plus 32 containers of tea, 10 tonnes each, from Hong Kong to Lae.

Twice a day Sunny would bring me an update, which would show more and more cargo having been booked, and I would go to my office to check where everything was going to be slotted in.

It was complicated but not particularly taxing, a bit like constructing a jigsaw where the pieces kept changing. I had a primitive computer to calculate the stability, to make sure the ship didn't topple over if heavy boxes were to be loaded in the upper levels.

When we arrived in port I always had the cargo plan ready to hand to the chief stevedore, although I soon learned that the actual cargo waiting for us was unlikely to be the same as our latest update, and so there would always need to be some last-minute shuffling around.

Hong Kong was the busiest of all our calls, and the most exasperating. As it was our home port, people from head office would want to come and visit – a superintendent or perhaps someone from personnel. Running repairs would be carried out and spares delivered. I would occasionally be summoned ashore with the Old Man to attend some shipper's grim cocktail party, where everyone drank too much, made promises they would never be able to keep and told ever more fantastic lies to each other. These head office affairs were less relaxed than the shipboard parties we organised in the Islands, and they weren't an environment in which I was comfortable.

The crew would either disappear home to see their families – or, worse, their families would stay on board for the duration; either way the work was curtailed. Hong Kong was always a port with a frantic pace. Everyone shouted at each other and competed to go as fast as possible. All this, melded together, made our visits there exhausting.

I was sitting in my office one evening, recovering from a gruelling day and having finally balanced the loading calculations after several false starts, when the bosun knocked at the door and came in looking conspiratorial. He turned towards the open doorway so he had his back towards me, then stretched out one arm behind him, theatrically gesturing for me to take what he was holding. It was US$100. I took the money and looked at it, the bosun turned round, I looked at him inquiringly.

"This for old wire," he said.

"What old wire?"

"Old wire."

"What old wire?"

"Old wire."

"What old wire?"

"Old wire."

I could see this could go on for the rest of my life so I tried another tack.

"Old cargo wire?"

"Yes."

"Old gantry wire?"

"Only small piece."

"You sold the old gantry wire?"

"Only small piece."

"You sold some of the old gantry wire?"

"Old wire."

This was not uncommon. The crew would sell condemned wire and mooring ropes and other scrap. A blind eye was turned to this, as long as it was only old and useless scrap that was being sold. There was a pecking order for splitting the proceeds, which was generally the bosun and the senior deck crew. Some chief officers ran quite an aggressive disposal programme and netted several hundred dollars for themselves every round trip. There were rumours of this having escalated out of control on one of the company's ships a few years previously, with expensive new coils of wire being sold along with new mooring ropes and hundreds of litres of paint. Wholesale pillaging was taking place. From then it was only a short journey to start selling off parts of the cargo and so there were a handful of example sackings, designed to put the problem back in its box.

It wasn't in me to start selling off ship's gear, scrap or not. I wasn't sly enough, I was poor at bargaining, I didn't have an eye for business and the risk just didn't seem worth the gain.

I said: "How much they pay, altogether?"

He looked worried: "Small piece more."

"How much?"

"Small piece more."

"Bosun! How much pay for wire, altogether?"

"I give you more!"

He thrust another US$100 at me.

"How much?"

"You want more? I give you more! He delved into his pocket and came up with a $50 note."

He held it out to me with the second hundred. I put them on the desk together with the first hundred.

"Bosun, you tell me how much money for wire? $800? $1,000?"

He picked the low figure I had offered him. "$800. Chief mate take $250, bosun have $200, casab have $100, all other sailors have $250 for share. Good for chief mate."

He was presenting me as the main beneficiary, forgetting that he had tried to palm me off with $100 at first. I doubted very much that he had sold the wire for $800 anyway; it was probably more like $1,500.

I pushed all the money back at him

"You keep it, Bosun."

"You not want? Why not?"

"Not for me."

"Yes, for you."

"Not for me."

"Yes, for you."

I could feel the irritation rising in me and I did my best to resist. But East beats West hands down when it comes to patience and perseverance, and this was not a game I was going to win. I didn't really mind the bosun and his men selling off condemned ropes and wires and other scrap from time to time, but I didn't want to become a participant.

"Listen, Bosun. You sell old wire? OK. That's good, you keep money. No money for me. OK?"

He looked deflated.

"You keep some money, $200?"

"No."

"$150?"

"No."

"$100?"

"No."

"$50?"

He was desperate for me to have something, to become his co-conspirator. I relented.

"OK, I have $50."

His relief was palpable. "Good, good. Thank you, Chief Officer."

"Thank you, Bosun."

He went off clutching his dollars. I donated the $50 to the bar fund later in the evening.

Graft was pretty endemic in the East at that time. It wasn't viewed as dishonesty; it was the way to do business and an entitlement to a payment, depending upon where you stood in the chain. The bosun's wire selling was just an indication of a system that worked right through to the core. There was a lot of noise being made in the Hong Kong government about backhanders, and from time to time there was a clampdown, but it went on and on and there was no getting away from it.

When we were down in the Islands again, we received a telegram to say that Ben was being relieved in Manila. He had been on for over a year and didn't want to go. He was glum for about ten minutes then perked up and told us all how he was going to stay in Manila for a few days and paint the town red.

We planned to have a mighty party when we arrived in Manila, to celebrate Ben's paying off. Even though we were supposed to be a speedy turnaround container ship, the Manila port authority didn't take that sort of thing too seriously and we arrived to be told of transport delays, which meant we would discharge our cargo from the Islands and then sit alongside the wharf for a night and a day before loading.

Manila was a hotbed of crime, thieves swarmed over the docks and onto the ships, taking what they could. In recent years there had been greater efforts to control the problem by putting guards at the dock gates; they slowed the tide but didn't stem it. Most ships ordered a contingent of guards to stay on the ship while she was in port. We had about ten on board the *Chengtu*, whose job it was patrol the decks and the accommodation and keep bad people off. In truth, they mostly hung around the galley and the crew mess, scrounging food. The head guard, the only one who was armed, found a comfy spot early on and spent most of his time sleeping, punctuated by a stroll around at meal times, where the officers could observe him being diligent and where he was best placed to join in the eating. The head guard apart, the others were mostly young women armed with truncheons. A lot of them supplemented their income by selling themselves to the crew, who then felt doubly blessed: gratification plus a personal security guard.

The party was shaping up to be a bit tame, though, so the Old Man went and rounded up most of the security guards, leaving one on the gangway, and brought them in to produce party ambiance and dancing partners. They were a bit nervous and cautious about drinking at first. Then the head guard came in, ostensibly to make a protest, but of course he just wanted to be invited. Once he had downed his first drink the rest joined in with enthusiasm and the party took off.

We became a bit nervous about the head guard's weapons, though, thinking it a bad idea for everyone to be drinking away with a loaded Remington pump-action shotgun lying on the bar and with him wearing a Smith & Wesson 686 revolver. The guard was reluctant to hand them in, so he was told he could only stay if both weapons were unloaded and the ammunition put in the locker above the glasses; he could have the ammo back in the morning. It then transpired that the shotgun was empty anyway, and he only had two bullets for his pistol, which I put in my pocket. Ben's paying off party went on until the early hours and was judged a great success.

When we arrived back in Manila thirty days later, Ben was still there and had got himself married. He brought his new wife on board. She was a gorgeous Filipino named Angel who he had met in Ermita. We all said Hello, Angel, lovely to meet you. I thought she had predatory eyes.

There was no sign of Ben on the following voyage. We asked around some of the bars and the rumour was that he had gone back to England to show off his new wife to family and friends. Then on the next call, Ben came aboard looking chastened. His wife had left him, saying he was too mean to live with. Apparently he had put his foot down when her family all wanted to move in with them.

"There's bloody hundreds of them, Simon, man. It was bad enough that I had to buy them all presents, about twenty of the boogers. They should have been buying us newlyweds presents, but I was just expected to buy gifts for the whole tribe. That was only the start of it, though. Angel wanted me to give her mother an allowance, a monthly salary. Can you bloody believe it? In the end I gave her five hundred quid and told her that was it, although she still came on honeymoon with us. Great fun that was, as ye can imagine, my mother in law on my honeymoon. All the two of them did in Newcastle was gitter away to each other in Filipino or Tagalog or whatever it is they speak, moaning at me about how cold and wet it was in England and wanting to go home.

"So we come 'home', and straight away I'm under siege, dozens of her family coming round begging off me, bleeding me white. In the end I start throwing them out and the missus storms off saying I'm a mean man and she's too ashamed to stay.

"And then, few days later I was telling this to an Aussie bar owner, who told me that this was common and she had probably been married before. Some girls get married several times, with the sole purpose of fleecing their sucker husbands.

"I was pretty shocked at this so I got a lawyer to look into it – and yes, she was married before, to an Australian, and she still is bloody married. I'm now trying to get the marriage annulled and the lawyer's fees are costing me a fortune. Sometimes I think it would've been cheaper to carry on paying her family. I'm nearly broke. I told the lawyer that if he doesn't get it finalised soon I'm just going to say 'sod it' and I'll call my marriage annulled and bugger off back to England. I think that got the message across, although he's pacing himself to squeeze the maximum from me before finishing the job. I'm thinking about jumping on a plane without paying him. What a bloody nightmare. Why-aye man, your round!"

Later I heard he took a transfer to the company's offshore division to work in the Middle East, where he could earn a lot more working on oil-rig supply boats to repair his broken finances.

Despite my initial misgivings at the cheap appearance of the *Chengtu*, the trip took shape well. My down time was at the end of each leg. When we left our final port in the Islands, Wewak, we faced a five-day passage, the first three waiting for our cargo orders. After the last port in the East, Singapore, we had a seven-day trip to the Islands, again with three or four days before the cargo orders started arriving. These were the parts of the voyage where I awarded myself a few days of light duties. There was time for me to organise a programme to get the wires and ropes repaired or changed, and plan a good regimen of maintenance work for the crew. In warm calm days I had them hose-testing the hatches, stripping down the roller fairleads, greasing all the dogs and painting the ship to keep her looking smart.

After finishing the four to eight watch in the morning I had breakfast then an hour's walk around the deck, checking for any loose containers, making sure the gantry was secure, inspecting the crew working. That done, I went up to the monkey island to lie in the sun and read and bake myself a medium brown, enjoying the brief respite of only working nine-hour days.

If I was feeling sharp enough I would wade through my Herbert Spencer. I had carried both volumes for years and felt I was making headway drilling his 'synthetic philosophy' into me. It was hard going at times, particularly Volume II, but I found it rewarding. Religion had fled from me as a teenager although as a lapsed Catholic I found it never really lets you go, just allows you a longer leash, ready to start reeling you back in as mortality beckons. Spencer seemed to have reconciled deism with the scientific, which suited my long-leash status. When I wasn't up to tackling Herbert Spencer, it was John Creasy or Hammond Innes or whatever other easy read was lying around in the ship's library.

The ambiance of a ship comes down from the top. If the ship's captain is miserable, restrictive, punitive and mean the whole ship suffers, and she becomes a miserable, restrictive, punitive and mean place to inhabit. What made the *Chengtu* a good ship to be on that voyage – better than a lot of vessels that were far nobler in their appearance – was the quality of the masters I sailed under. The captain changed while I was there, but fortunately his relief was cut from the same cloth.

There was a strong focus on food, which resulted us being on the best fed ship in the fleet. If people are fed well then they are basically happy, or at least positioned to be happy. We had a poll to see what the preferred meal was for Christmas. Choice one was a traditional Christmas dinner, six courses: soup, seafood, fillet mignon, turkey, Christmas pudding, cheese and coffee, flushed down with several bottles of wine. Choice two was a Chinese banquet, nine courses: abalone and noodles, duck in soy sauce, sweet and sour pork, crispy beef, chow mein, king prawns, sea cucumber, chicken and mushrooms, rice, accompanied by Samsu rice wine and icy Tiger beer.

Every vote except the chief engineer was for the Chinese banquet. The chief sulked, he hated Chinese food, so the cook made him lamb chops and chips for his festive meal. The rest of us gorged. We were due to be in Manila on Christmas day so we had our feast two days early, before we reached the San Bernadino Passage. There were several speeches, several toasts, we wore hats, drank too much, ate two days' worth of food in a three-hour sitting. The meal finished at three-thirty and I went for a walk on deck to clear my head, first to the fo'c'sle to see the dolphin front runners riding our bow wave, then aft to the poop where I sat on the capstan and watched the flying fish stream away, skipping and skimming like flat stones thrown across a lake.

When we arrived in Manila on Christmas day, geared to start the cargo discharge, we went alongside to be told there was no work for two days. We drank champagne cocktails in the bar, followed by a light lunch, a sort of half Christmas meal, seafood followed by fillet mignon because no one wanted the full works. In the evening we went into Ermita and made fools of ourselves down Mabini Street and MH del Pilar until it was too late to go to bed. Boxing Day was muted. We moved slowly, talked little and had periods where we lay inert.

As January drifted into February, our voyages went on mostly unchanged, just enough variance to keep us from falling into a groove. I was due to be cycled home in late February. The second mate, a Yorkshireman called Geoff who had relieved Ben, was sailing with a Master's Certificate and he would be relieving me, which made for an easy handover. I would be leaving in Manila next call so I brought Geoff into all the cargo work from Port Moresby onwards.

It became apparent to me that after I left this ship and went home, my life would be irrevocably changed. I had a burst of acting outrageously, drinking too much, being too loud, first in last out, pushing for parties in the Islands. I unloaded my cargo duties onto Geoff, which he took loyally. I repaid his loyal behaviour by spending the afternoons in the yacht club in Honiara and Rabaul and Lae and wherever there was a yacht club, which was almost everywhere in the Islands.

In the bar one evening I boasted that I was so fit I could do a hundred press-ups without stopping. Everyone jeered and bet me I couldn't. I was given odds of six to one, all bets in Tiger beer. I told them to put their money where their mouths were. Everyone bet against me. I stood to win 240 cans of Tiger. At my odds of six to one I would pay out 40 cans if I lost. I lost spectacularly – fifty-two press-ups and my arms collapsed. Everyone cheered. I paid out my losses with good grace and then we drank it all between us. Others tried: the Old Man managed six, the chief engineer three. Sampson did forty-eight. I was planning to stand on his back if he got any closer to my fifty-two. The next morning I could barely lift my hands. I was supposed to be back in England six weeks before the wedding. I arrived thirty-three days before. Phew.

I married Annie on Grand National Day. The streets were obligingly quiet when the wedding convoy drove from the church to the hotel overlooking Avon Gorge, where we had the meal, the speeches, the cake cutting, the party. Her family was huge, as would be expected for one of eight children, my family was lost in the corners.

Most of my sea friends were at sea, I had lost touch with most others. A few came: Jimmy from cadet days, Frank from when I was on the New Zealand trade, Steve from my last bout at the School of Maritime Studies, Duncan from the *Funing*. I hardly had time to speak to them, which I regretted afterwards, but no one has ownership of their own time at their own wedding. I didn't have a stag night; I'd been a stag for the last twelve years. I wore my uniform, Annie wore a dress made by angels.

We honeymooned in Rhodes, drank retsina in the sun, ate squid, rode donkeys, swam in clear water, hired motorbikes, visited ruins and walked in the markets where every shop played 'Zorba the Greek'. My life at sea was a million miles away.

Back home again I spoke to my accountant. She said: "Get out of the country. You need ten more days out to keep your running total for 100 per cent tax deduction allowance." I only half-understood what she was talking about but it seemed sensible to heed her advice.

The author and his new wife, married on Grand National Day

We caught a ferry to St Malo and stayed for ten days in a tiny elegant apartment in an old house in the old town with a small ancient lift to take us up to our top floor flat; the lift moved as slowly as an insect. We walked the town, ate *fruits de mer*, drank Muscadet, visited museums depicting the English being thrashed by the French, built castles on the beach, took a bus into the countryside and got lost and bought cheap mementos, before we caught the ferry home. My life at sea was a thousand miles away.

The plan was for Annie to come with me on the next trip. Company policy was that the husband joined first and had to be on the ship for three weeks before his wife could arrive. There was a letter waiting for us. I was to fly in three weeks. I was being transferred to the offshore supply fleet; an oilfield supply boat, three months unaccompanied. I called the company and asked for a deep sea ship. They told me nothing was available. I told them I had just got married. They said, 'congratulations' then told me to go to the Indonesian embassy and get a visa. My life at sea was just around the corner.

We made the best of it, in our little house in Bristol. We weren't glum, just disappointed for a day. We practised married life; it seemed easy enough although Annie was better at it than me. We bought a second-hand BMW and went for long drives, went to the seaside, went to a ruined castle in Wales, ate in Italian restaurants, drank lager, met the neighbours, practised cooking. I learned to watch television. We visited her family, visited my family, talked about having a family. Two kids? Four kids? Six kids?

The confirmation telegram arrived. Join the supply vessel *Pacific Builder*. Fly Saturday 18 June British Airways London Heathrow to Singapore then fly Garuda Airlines from Singapore to Jakarta. The sea drew me back, like the pull of the tide, as if I had never left.

☆　☆　☆

I had been hoping for a stopover in Singapore, but no luck, just a six-hour wait in the transit lounge in the new Changi International Airport for the Jakarta flight. Changi had taken over from Paya Lebar Airport less than two years beforehand and it was the first time I had visited. The last time I was in Changi was when I lived in Singapore as a boy and was a fifteen-year-old student at Changi Grammar School, where I was expelled for bad behaviour, to the shame of my family. The Garuda flight was a ninety-minute hop on an A300 Airbus, stopping over at Jakarta on its way to Australia.

Kemajoran Airport in Jakarta, capital of Indonesia, was steamy and crowded, the old 1940s terminal building, built by the Dutch in the 1940s, no longer fit for purpose. The place was due to be closed down soon and replaced by a modern purpose-built affair west of the city.

Getting through immigration was painful. The official looked at my passport photograph, looked at me, looked at the photograph, looked at me. This went on for several minutes. Eventually he held out the passport although when I reached to take it he dropped it on the counter with a small smirk, staring at me unblinkingly all the time. I thought, This is a country to be careful in.

The agent was waiting for me in the arrivals lounge, standing there holding a board with my name written on it in large letters. We went out to his car. I had just brought a kitbag rather than my globetrotter suitcase. I wouldn't need my blues uniform, nor my whites in fact, and no sextant. Just a few clothes suitable for the tropics. I would get kitted out with some work clothes on the boat. He told me I would be staying overnight in the Hotel Borobudar, a top of the line place in central Jakarta, and would be picked up at 05:30 the next morning for the fifty-mile drive to Merak from where I would take a helicopter to an oil rig platform and then transfer to the *Pacific Builder*. It all sounded fine to me, but I was bone-tired after thirty hours without sleep, just a couple of catnaps, I was too tired to care and would have nodded at whatever he said. I ate a hurried meal in the rooftop restaurant then went to my room and fell into a black hole.

The sun broke over the Jakarta skyline the next morning as we cleared the suburbs and set out on the highway for Serang, then on to Merak. The roads were poor, and crowded with old cars, bicycles, motorbikes, huge lorries that lumbered along. The traffic was choked and whenever a sufficiently large gap arose to allow us to overtake we hurtled into it. My driver was morose, smoked constantly, drove as if he wanted to die. Every time he stamped down on the accelerator and swerved over the other side of the road to get past a lorry my eyes would lock onto the vehicle coming at us, watching the spectre of my approaching death.

Merak lay on the north-west tip of Java, at the top of the Sunda Strait, the body of water separating Java from Sumatra where the big deep sea ships coming up from the Cape of Good Hope enter the East. Right in the middle of the Sunda Strait is Krakatoa, probably the most famous volcano in the world.

When Krakatoa erupted on the morning of 26 August 1883 the sound of the four explosions was heard in Mauritius, 3,000 miles away. The governing Dutch authorities put the official death toll at over 36,000 from the thermal blast and shock and from the 120-foot-high wall of water that fell on the shorelines in the vicinity. Nearly 300 villages were destroyed or seriously damaged. It was the loudest sound recorded in history, and anyone within 10 miles was reportedly made deaf. That eruption was the one of the most powerful known. It was ten times more powerful than the nuclear bomb dropped on Hiroshima. The sky was blacked out for three days and there was so much debris hurled into the air that vivid sunsets were seen in Europe for several months afterwards. Volcanologists believe that an earlier eruption had caused a plug in the exit chamber, which had allowed pressure to build and build in the magma chamber until it finally blew with such catastrophic results. Krakatoa remains active; some experts predict another mighty eruption within the next hundred years.

I was dropped at the helicopter terminal at Merak, where I joined a group of people heading out for the rig. They all seemed to know what they were doing, so I followed them and followed their example. The helicopters were all flown by Americans, ex-Vietnam pilots reputedly, who had learned from necessity to fly too low and too fast. On our flight out to the rig we seemed to graze the water. I sat strapped in, in a line of others. The noise was infernal, the experience was fearful. We all sat stoically, posing as if it were a normal part of the day. I wondered what the others were thinking. I was thinking: 'Is this the last day of my life?'

On the rig we clambered out and I spoke to the man who was marshalling our arrival, telling him I was bound for the *Pacific Builder*. He had a conversation with his walkie-talkie then directed me to a crane which would lower me to the boat. They called up the *Pacific Builder* and she came backing in twenty minutes later, the Panama flag fluttering in the light breeze. The water was calm and my landing on the deck, along with my bag and some stores, was less harrowing than I had prepared myself for.

The *Pacific Builder* was a typical oil rig supply and anchor handling boat. Two hundred feet long with the accommodation at the forward end, and a long deck aft of that on which was sited the huge anchor-handling and towing winch. There was a complement of ten people, four officers and six crew, four of whom were deck crew, plus a cook and a steward. The officers were British, the deck crew Filipino, the cook and steward Chinese. There was no luxury; this was a pure working vessel. The officers shared a shower and toilet and we all did our own washing. There was no bar or smoke room, just a small rugged mess.

The oil rigs were anchored to the sea bed by huge anchors and heavy wires. The supply boats picked up each anchor and carried it to the position directed by the rig-master, where it was then heaved tight by the winch on the rig. The supply boat then returned for the next anchor. On this basis the rig was walked around the sea bed. Anchor handling is hard and dangerous work. If a wire breaks the released tension causes it to whip back and it can easily cut a man in half. If the anchor is lost the rig's divers will go down and find it and secure new wires so it can be heaved up on deck and the show can go on. Sometimes we would handle anchors non-stop for twenty-four hours. The rig-master was our ringmaster; we were at his beck and call at all times. He had no patience or sympathy.

If the sea was up and the boat was being flung around, that was no reason to stop or wait. We had to be in true peril to halt the work. From time to time all the anchors would be heaved up and we would tow the rig to a completely new area and everything would start again. On the second day we towed it fifty miles south, nearer to Krakatoa. We were also a general dogsbody, picking up supplies, fuel, water, drilling equipment, pipework, sometimes ferrying people. The normal routine was to spend twenty days in the oilfields then head to our base in Merak for a couple of days to resupply.

The captain taught me the fundamentals of supply boat handling over the first week so we could share the load. There was more to it than I'd thought, particularly backing into the rig in choppy seas, manipulating the twin engines to hold the boat steady against the thrashing of the ocean.

On duty in the oilfields we hung around a lot, either drifting or anchored ourselves, waiting for the tyrant rig-master to send work our way. The days were hot. We wore shorts and tee-shirts. On the deck I didn't wear a shirt, so my shoulders were burnt and I was grubby and greasy for a large part of the time. We usually ate on the bridge in the day, listening to the VHF radio for orders. In the evening we played cards and drank beer in the mess, although not to excess in case we were called, while one of the Filipino crew kept VHF watch.

When alone in my tiny cabin, tired and hot, I bemoaned my fate, my loss of seagoing comfort, the filthy labour, in thrall to a tyrant. Then I caught myself and was ashamed. I had cold lager to salve my body and was fed steak and roast lamb; I wasn't living in somewhere like the Gulf of Kutch, eating dog and living a lifetime in the dirt. I was born into a spoilt and nasty generation of educated westerners where white people saved for half a year to get a brown suntan, while at the same time they looked down in disdain on real brown people as being lesser creatures. We all deserved to be sent to the Gulf of Kutch; my discomforts in the shadow of Krakatoa were nothing.

Then one morning, a police launch came for me with an apologetic-looking agent on board. The captain woke me and told me to pack, quickly, and come to the bridge. It was 05:30.

I said: "What's going on?"

He said: "You're being transferred."

"Why?"

"No idea."

He looked worried.

"Is there a problem?"

"There seems to be, but I don't know what it is, some visa irregularity by the sound of it."

"Is there a replacement for me?"

"No, although someone is flying in for another boat tomorrow and he's being diverted here instead."

I got dressed and packed, which took me no time at all. The steward came in with a cup of tea, looking encouraging. I went up to the bridge with my tea and kitbag. The agent was waiting there. He smiled nervously.

"We must go," he said.

"Where am I going?"

"I get you flight to Singapore."

"Today?"

"I hope so."

"Why am I leaving this ship so soon?"

"I do not know."

"Where am I going when I get to Singapore?"

"I do not know. You go to company office in Singapore and they tell you."

"This is poor!" shouted the captain. "Don't you know anything? You can't just take one of my officers away without any explanation!"

"It's not me, Captain. The company tells me what to do."

"You're leaving me short-handed and I'm holding you responsible."

"It's not my fault, Captain."

I bade farewell to the others and climbed down into the launch. The two policeman watched me board with blank faces then turned away and started talking to each other.

Jakarta airport. There was no flight for me to Singapore that day; all the seats were taken on all the flights. The agent managed to get a place on the first plane out the following morning. We went back to the Hotel Borobudar for me to while away the day and night. After checking in I asked at the reception desk for a local map so I could go for a walk. The receptionist looked worried as he gave me one, and spent time impressing upon me how dangerous the city was, full of gangs and gangsters and muggers and murderers, all earning a living by preying on foolish westerners. He told me not to go anywhere near the docks to the north, and that to venture into south Jakarta was to ask for a quick death. He told me it was extremely dangerous to go east of the main railway line and even more dangerous to set foot west of the Ciliwung River. In other words, it would be best if I just stayed around the safe central district where the smart hotels and government buildings were.

I thanked the receptionist for his advice and walked north to the docks at Tanjong Priok to see what ships were in. The area was as universally grim as I remembered it. The last time I was there had been several years earlier and the occasion was memorable; I was in a bar when I was attacked by a Pole for no reason I could understand. The incident erupted into a massive inter-ship brawl, Britain versus Poland, bottles and chairs and people flying everywhere. I had lain dazed among the broken glass for most of it, wondering how badly hurt I was.

The roads around Tanjong Priok were still clogged and filthy, urchins and loafers watching me with sharp eyes, waiting to see if I would wander off into one of the smaller streets where I could be taken advantage of, girls hanging out the doorways of dangerous-looking bars giving me their siren call. There were no British ships in port, so after a while I walked back to the antiseptic safety of the central district.

At the airport the next morning I had to pay $100 departure tax and $40 airport tax before they stamped my passport. The agent stood next to me inspecting his feet and translating, rushing off as soon as I went through the barrier. I felt tainted as I left.

In Singapore there was no one to meet me so I took a taxi to the offices in the big Heong Leong Building in Raffles Quay where the agent took me to lunch and told me the story. The story was that there was a big clampdown on corruption taking place in Hong Kong, which was affecting all Hong Kong-based businesses and preventing them from carrying out their normal practice.

The shipping world in the East was run by a web of officials and bureaucrats in every country: customs officials, immigration officials, health officials, shipper's clerks, dock managers, warehouse managers, security firms, police, forwarding clerks, packers, stevedores, officials at each stage. They were generally poorly paid, and a few well-directed dollars would make the passage of business life so much sweeter.

In Indonesia, corruption was particularly rife at every level, and businesses had to pay to get anything done. People at the top were given highly paid jobs they couldn't do and didn't even turn up to. People in the middle were given payments to make sure the enterprise stayed in the system. People at the bottom were given a bonus just to sign the form or move the box. If you didn't pay, the wheels of commerce started to seize up.

The Hong Kong company I was working for had stopped paying and the wheels of commerce were seizing up. First came the delays, then came the obstructions, then came the petty revenges. I was caught up in all this, and selected as someone who was an undesirable alien without proper immigration clearance and was ordered to be flung out the country with little ceremony. It was a taste of what the company could expect if they didn't find ways to ease the system.

I had a nice lunch with the agent in the Four Seasons restaurant and he then drove me back to Changi Airport to catch a flight to Miri in Sarawak, the Malaysian-governed enclave on the island of Borneo, to join the *Pacific Protector*.

⋆   ⋆   ⋆

The *Pacific Protector* was an oilfield safety ship. She was much bigger than a typical supply boat and didn't do any towing or anchor handling. We had two main functions: the primary purpose was as a dive support vessel and the secondary was as a fire-fighting ship. We carried a group of forty divers who inspected the legs of rigs and carried out underwater maintenance and repairs. In the shallow areas they jumped off the back in their frogman's outfits, and in deeper water they went down in a diving bell. There was an on-board decompression chamber for them to sit in after coming back to the surface to avoid getting the 'bends', the agonising cramps caused by nitrogen in the blood precipitating into bubbles if they had surfaced too rapidly.

The *Protector* had massive pumps to send pressurised seawater through powerful water guns mounted on a high tower, should we need to tackle a major fire.

The divers kept themselves separate; they were insular people who existed in their own world in which they only seemed happy talking among themselves, like members of a sect. Most of them were American, a few Australians. I tried chatting to them on several occasions but it was an uphill task. The other officers thought divers were a bit dim, 'too much nitrogen in the blood', although it seemed to me that they just preferred their own company.

The ship's complement was bigger than that that of the *Pacific Builder*. There were six officers: a captain, two mates, a chief engineer, second engineer and electrical officer. The deck crew was Filipino, and there was a Chinese cook and a Chinese steward. My fellow officers were all long-term men, on their fourth or fifth trip. They drank a lot, and were universally lazy and permanently filthy, although they seemed to enjoy their time aboard.

The duties were dull; dive support meant hanging around for the divers to come back up again. The weekly testing of the water guns was exciting at first, although this soon paled. The accommodation was as mean and cramped as on the *Pacific Builder*.

I found my shipmates poor company and they no doubt felt the same about me. I obviously didn't fit in, and struggled to make the effort to do so. I had been at sea for nearly fourteen years by then, and I was used to order, structure, long hours and hard work, with reasonable comfort in off-duty hours. The *Protector* was more anarchic, the ship's company was too small to have much differential between the ranks, which meant there was there was hardly any structure and little formality. There were no uniforms, no blues or whites; everyone just dressed in work clothes, which were orange boiler suits, washed sporadically.

Everyone slept too much and drank a lot. I didn't mind the drinking, although I didn't enjoy sitting on the deck in a tiny cabin among unwashed bodies ingrained with oil and muck and sweat and body odour, listening to outlandishly exaggerated tales of some minor occurrence that had taken place on the last trip.

But it wasn't the company – it was the lack of work, the lack of things to do. People just got up, put on grubby work clothes and sat around for most of the time, which was what I hated. I needed to be busy. Coupled with this, my newly married state made me want to focus on more noble pursuits than watching the leci drink himself near insensible before trying to break his record of eating pickled eggs. My tour was twelve weeks, and I had only done three weeks on the *Pacific Builder*. I viewed the next nine with weary resignation.

Most of the divers were muscle men and they had built a gym on the upper deck. The equipment was largely free weights constructed of cement-filled paint cans. I started using the gym area daily, keeping off the weight I was in danger of gaining by spending most of my time sitting round eating and drinking. The food was excellent; high quality meals, properly cooked. The mess where we ate wasn't excellent, though, it was a squalid narrow Formica-clad box, the décor you might find in a cheap and nasty seaside café.

We would anchor for several days while the divers dived, then move somewhere else and anchor and so on. When there was diving activity, particularly when using the bell, it was crucial to keep the ship in the same position, so we either anchored by using our four mooring anchors, two on either side of the ship, or by using the engines to constantly trim the position. In addition to a conventional propeller there were side thrusters at the bow and stern. This 'Dynamic Positioning' system, DP as we called it, was computer aided and was challenging and satisfying to use, although the time at anchor was as dull as could be. A rumour began to circulate of us going to India when the current charter ended.

There was a video system on board in the mess although the quality was so bad the films were almost unwatchable. Most of them were either bad pornography or were about maniacs, neither of which were my cup of tea. We had curry on Sundays, steak on Wednesdays and barbecues on the deck from time to time.

People started to be replaced, and the new ones seemed better. The officers were mainly British but others were scattered around the world: Japan, Canada, New Zealand, Finland, the Solomon Islands. I socialised more as time went by, sitting on deck in the evenings under the tropical night, drinking cold beer and smoking and watching the night. To the east, the sky was lit by columns of flame from the oil flares and twinkling lights from the rigs, like a carnival. To the west it was black, black as cats, black as coal, black as a deep dark hole.

The insects were on the rise; cockroaches gathered in small armies, the big light brown ones, not the smaller blacks. A group lived in my cabin although they always scattered when I put the light on. Sometimes I would wake in the night and fling the sheet off as I felt one walk on my arm or my face and once I found a large brown splashing in my morning mug of tea. The ship was due to be fumigated in Singapore at the end of the charter.

The charter ended and we went alongside in Muara, the port in Brunei, where the charterers removed all their dive support equipment, including the diving bell. Welders swarmed over the ship cutting off anything believed to belong to the charterers, precise in claiming everything that was theirs. We pumped the excess fuel to another of their ships. There was a damage survey, followed by a squabble about what was charter damage and what was ordinary wear and tear. We took on bunkers and water and set off for Singapore.

☆   ☆   ☆

Our repair berth in Singapore. Workers surged on board, fitters, welders, labourers, cleaners, engineers. There was little for me to do; everything was being organised by the company superintendent. I hung around, read, loafed, carried out inventory work and occasional missions, making myself available in case I was needed. I spent a lot of time ashore.

Singapore was changing fast, becoming richer, the colour and the smells were fading, colonial history was being rewritten and expunged where deemed necessary by the government. When independence was granted in 1959, there had been an orderly handover by the British administration to the British-educated local elite, who had been operating as second-tier civil servants and who were now promoted. This process was now talked of as the 'liberation'. The years of discussion that had built up to it were referred to as the 'struggle for independence'. Singapore society was becoming increasingly less tolerant towards men with long hair, towards western rock groups, chewing gum and disobedience, towards the Barisan Sosialis Party and any other political party except the ruling PAP, the People's Action Party.

I went for a nostalgia tour of Katong where I had lived as a boy. Our house off East Coast Road was no longer by the sea, as several hundred yards of water had been reclaimed, leaving the house sitting inland in what was now just another outer city street. The neighbours had all moved on. In the nearby streets there were more cars, the Catholic Church seemed smaller, the monsoon drains were covered with concrete slabs.

In Joo Chiat Road, the textile shops, tailors, furniture makers and Chinese corner cafes, all of which I remembered as packed and noisy and disordered and colourful, were quiet and clinically clean. The street itself was now blocked with stationary traffic. The Katong Grange Hotel was gone, so was the Singapura Hotel. The Palace Cinema and the Roxy were now both showing Chinese films rather than English. All around me the ghosts were there – my father and mother and brothers and all my friends – but I felt like a visiting alien.

I walked all the way from Katong back to the waterfront, taking diversions as I went, Mountbatten Road, Geyang Road, Kallang Road, Victoria Street, North Bridge Road, the Thieves Market at Rochor Canal, Beach Road, then across the Singapore River past the Padang and down to the waterfront at Keppel. Everywhere was much cleaner, everywhere had changed so much.

When I went to live in Singapore as a thirteen-year-old there was resistance to the new laws that prevented the flinging of rubbish into the monsoon drains. Now there were laws prohibiting the dropping of cigarette ends onto the pavement. The Malay kampong villages were gone, the Anson Road bars were all closed down, Change Alley looked cheap and fake, the street markets were fewer and more organised, all the old Morris Oxford taxis had been replaced by sleek Japanese models, and the famous Bugis Street, notorious for its drinking, its fights, its seafood, its transsexuals and its wild late-night reverie atmosphere, was being closed down.

There were no hissing naphtha lamps and charcoal burners and mismatched stools for the late-night food stalls; the lights and cooking were now electric and the seating conformed to health and safety standards. Chinese street opera, gone. Firecrackers, banned. Connell house Seaman's Mission, closed. Raffles Hotel, full of Italians. Everyone walking the streets looked purposeful, looked studious, looked so serious. My feet ached. What fool me – I wasn't even chasing a dream, my thoughts were those of a schoolboy. Singapore was on the up and heading towards where it belonged. It was just no longer a place that drew me.

Pacific Protector

The rumours started to crystallise: India. The new charterer's representatives arrived for a ship inspection and to install replacement gear for everything that had just been taken off – a new diving bell, compression chamber, racks of dive equipment. The work went on. I hung about and sweated, crawled into tiny tank spaces to inspect them and came out covered in filth, wringing wet, sweated out, ending the day several pounds lighter. Icy cold Tiger beer tasted like the nectar of the gods. I inched towards the end of my stay.

We went into dry dock, I climbed down the ladders to the dock bottom and saw the revealed belly of the ship, green, dripping, slime-encrusted, studded with barnacles.

For the first two days in dock there was no water, no showers, no toilets. We sweated like hoofed animals, then queued and quarrelled at the end of the day in the dockyard wash-block. The dock work went on all night, crashing around me as I tried to sleep.

One night there was an almighty smash of metal, a hellish sound right next to me. I leapt from my bunk, thinking the whole ship was breaking up, only to discover they were end-for-ending the anchor chains in the chain locker, which was close to my cabin. Another night I woke because it was so quiet, silent as death. My light didn't work and it was pitch black. I stumbled out of my cabin, feeling my way in the inky dark until I arrived on deck. Shore power failure. We all stood around with torches until the power came back on and we could go back to bed again and sleep soundly in the noise.

The mornings were heat and sweat and filth as we inspected the deepest regions of the ship, the deepest tanks and void spaces. In the early afternoon I often found time to loaf in the sun and buff up my tan to impress the folks back home. On most days it rained in the mid–late afternoon. Sometimes it rained all day, Singapore showers, heavy blankets of water, the sort of rain that soaked me to my underpants in seconds. Sometimes the rain went on into the evening and we sat under the overhang and drank Tiger beer and ate cold chicken for our dinner and watched the rains come down, hypnotised by the constancy. The work was numbing, numbingly dull, with not a vestige of satisfaction. It drove most on board to drink more.

On a Saturday evening six of us went for a break-out to the Raffles Hotel, the famous colonial pile named after Sir Stamford Raffles, the man credited with the founding of modern Singapore in 1819. Raffles was a brilliant man; he split the local Malay aristocracy, charmed the local Rajah, thumbed his nose at the Dutch who controlled everything else in the vicinity and acquired the island for the British crown.

Raffles: warrior, author, linguist, founder of London Zoo, scourge of the slave trade, Raffles was the colonial adventurer-diplomat supreme, expanding the interests of the British Empire by his wits and his charm, by cunning, by gold, largesse, threat and brute force where necessary. He was a moral man by the standards of the day, and a devout Christian who supressed slavery, piracy, cockfighting and gambling in all the outposts he created or had a hand in running.

Raffles was born at sea off the West Indies and died shortly before his 45th birthday, found dead at the bottom of the stairs in his London home, victim of a brain haemorrhage. He'd had a stellar life and was acknowledged to be a great man, but the local parish church wouldn't allow him to be buried in the graveyard there because he had offended too many people with his anti-slavery activities. Cold revenge.

The Raffles Hotel in Beach Road is one of the world's great hotels, built in the 1880s, the heyday of the British Empire, an archetypal colonial building with its verandas and porticos and colonnades, its cane furniture and whooshing ceiling fans.

We took up residence in the bar, me, the captain, the chief and second engineers, the junior chief officer, the electrical officer, all of us dressed in our tropical best. The atmosphere was marred by the Alitalia monopoly which had crammed the place full of Italian tourists, but we overcame this and stayed for a couple of hours anyway, drinking Singapore Slings at exorbitant prices. When we were tipsy we switched to Anchor pilsner beer, and later still we went outside and whistled up three trishaws and had them race to Albert Street to eat steamed crab at Fatty Choys street restaurant, one of the few that was holding out against the change.

Time limped on. I wrote letters home daily, I received letters from home on most days. I missed Annie; she wrote of what she thought was trivia but I devoured every word. For several consecutive nights I dreamt of snakes. I was sure that dreaming of snakes would have some meaning to dream experts. Fear of something hidden? Fear of something forbidden? Fear of one's evil side catching up? I awoke beating at the sheets, fighting off my serpents.

We left dry dock at last and were given a place at the working dock. Now there were fewer on-board workers, and these were mainly technicians working on the DP system. The charter was to India was to start in two weeks. We carried out engine trials and DP trials, leaving our berth after breakfast and spending the day in the Johore Strait between Singapore and the Malay peninsula, where the technicians tuned the DP. A brigade of people squeezed onto the bridge, and we slid back to our berth in the Jurong shipyards after dark.

The second engineer and I made great play of testing the safety and maintenance boat, a Zodiac RIB powered by a massive Evinrude outboard motor. We raced around the harbour at high speed, the boat crashing against the waves, juddering our teeth and bones. One morning we went right through the Johore Strait, around Pulau Ubin Island where I used to camp as a boy, then cut the engine off the eastern point of the island, near Changi, south of Tekong Island, and drifted in the stream while we ate our lunch and drank cold beer, watching the ferry traffic and the local craft ply their ways. The sun grilled us and we swam in the chill waters off Tekong to cool down before pulling the big Evinrude into life and speeding back round the island to Jurong.

Towards the end, we abandoned the *Pacific Protector* while she was thoroughly fumigated, staying the night on another company ship to escape the poisonous gases. The second and I returned the next morning to set up blower fans to clear the air.

There was a screaming early one morning, a scream caused by metallic grating, and I got out of my bunk to find myself sliding down the deck. The ship was heeling over at an alarming angle. I went out to find the bulwarks had wedged under the dock as the tide was ebbing, and the ship was starting to hang. As the tide went out further she would either tear the dock down or pull off the bulwarks. Disaster was imminent one way or another. We were all gathered on the stern ready to leap into the water if she started to tip right over. Then a tug came charging to our rescue and yanked us free. The *Pacific Protector* snapped upright with a massive jolt.

And then my trip was done. The agent came out and told me that I was booked on the flight to London the next morning. The replacement chief officer would be arriving the next day although it wasn't necessary for me to stay and hand over because the ship was still on trials and he would be in on the final phase.

We had my paying off party that night, starting at the Red Lantern bar near the dock gates before going out to the famous Hillman Restaurant in Pasir Panjang Road, where local cuisine legend Wong Ling Onn himself was in residence, coming over to our table to see if everything was satisfactory. We gorged ourselves on shark's fin soup, pot turtle, sweet chilli crab, black pepper crab, happy beancurd, abalone, kai-lan in oyster sauce, sea cucumber, everything held together with rice. The meal was flushed down with the only worthy accompaniment for such a feast: ice cold Anchor pilsner in frosted glasses. In between the courses we smoked and had speeches and the best of wishes. The night ended back in the Red Lantern, all of us competitively drinking with the officers from the ship at the next berth and behaving badly.

The next morning I boarded the plane feeling subdued, I slumped for most of the flight to London. Annie met me at Heathrow airport. She said: "I'm pregnant."

8

Last Voyage to Wewak

Eight weeks' leave. Annie was three months pregnant. Life had set a new course and I was being ladled with responsibilities thick and fast to stop any backsliding into my immature ways. Marriage, children, mortgage, a dog. No going back now. Not that I was resentful, not in any way. My old life was dying. 'The moving finger writes and having writ moves on,' said Omar, and a new life was what I wanted. Time to plan.

It was mid-September, I would be back at sea in mid-November. At least if I was on supply boats I would only be away for three months, which meant that I would be back mid to late February. The baby was due in early March. The timing looked good. I became thankful I had been moved away from deep sea ships, where a trip would be between four and eight months. My eight weeks at home were full spent.

We bought a Rottweiler puppy who we christened Bruno. His job was to grow into a hulking brute to guard Annie while I was away. I was best man at Peter's wedding a couple of weeks after arriving home. It was a church affair followed by a casual reception at Peter and Alex's house in Colchester. I was a casual best man and when I look back I feel I should have done much better.

We were already crowding ourselves out of our small house, me, Annie and Bruno. We would have to move to a bigger place when the baby arrived. We shopped for baby items I didn't understand, we visited the different branches of Annie's huge family, and they pressed me for tales of the sea although I kept pretty mute in that area. In a shore setting with an audience who knew nothing of the sea, my stories had the ring of fiction and caused me embarrassment.

A telegram arrived at the beginning of November, I tore it open. "Fly London Heathrow to Hong Kong 16 November to join *Chengtu* as chief officer. Ticket and rail warrant follows. Obtain update inoculations cholera and TABT soonest." My heart sank. Back to the deep sea fleet. I would be away for the birth of my first child. I called the company and asked for a supply boat. They told me no. I pleaded my circumstances, they told me no.

So many officers had transferred to the supply fleet that they were getting short of deep sea personnel and they needed an experienced chief officer. I took a train to London to see the personnel officer in King William Street. He listened with sympathy, telling me he would see what he could do.

I toyed with the idea of resigning, but it was inopportune with a new wife, a new mortgage and a new baby. Jobs in the maritime world were now getting very thin on the ground. He wrote to me a couple of days later and said that in the circumstances they would try and relieve me after three months. It was as good as I could hope for. I volunteered to go a week early to give me a bit more margin, but was told that the arrangements were fixed. At least I knew the ship.

I flew out to Hong Kong and was billeted in the Mariner's Club Hotel, at the far end of Middle Road on Kowloon side. The agent's runner picked me up from Kai Tak following the usual harrowing descent. Kai Tak airport jutted into the harbour on reclaimed land, and the aerial approach was by banking through the mountains and then dropping sharply, rushing past skyscrapers so close that us passengers could see in the windows. The runner bagged a taxi and told me the *Chengtu* had been delayed in Manila and I would be kicking my heels in Hong Kong for three days. I trawled my old watering holes but there was no one in town I knew. Not that it mattered, I had always been a dab hand at making friends in bars, which I knew now was a poor talent to be proud of.

I occupied my time as a tourist, visiting the floating restaurants in Aberdeen, the Chinese border town of Sha Tau Kok, Mongkok market, the Peak Tram on Hong Kong Island. The Mariner's Club was a short walk from the Star Ferry terminal. Hong Kong was a constant roar, it never quietened. When I woke at four in the morning, as if ready for my watch at sea, the wall of traffic sound from nearby Nathan Road was undiminished.

One morning as I was returning from breakfast, there was an even bigger racket coming from the gardens. I went to see what was happening and found a survival exercise being conducted in the swimming pool; a twelve-man life raft was upside down with a group of people swimming round trying to bring it upright. I enjoyed the spectacle, remembering the first time I had been on a survival course. I was seventeen years old and a group of us had been emptied into the English Channel in February to swim 200 yards to a liferaft in water so cold I thought I was going to expire. We were then left to drift around, the raft half-full of freezing water and everyone vomiting into their laps. It was a brutal experience. The swimming pool event looked much more fun.

The *Chengtu* eventually arrived and I joined her for voyage number 29: Manila, Hong Kong, Singapore, Port Moresby, Honiara, Kieta, Rabaul, Lae, Madang, Wewak. My stamping ground. A thirty-day advertised schedule around ports I had called into, on and off, for most of the past six years.

The *Chengtu*. Well, well. Here I was, back again. She was still a heap, a cheap heap of a ship sailing under a Singapore flag. There had been no changes since I left nine months before. The same ancient Chinese crew were there, leaning over the rail and grinning at me like loons

Chengtu at Wewak

as I climbed the gangway. They were led by the same bosun who knew everything about everything, the one who had tried to bribe me into sharing his ill-gotten gains. I couldn't see how he could be pleased to have me back on board, although he put on a good show.

The familiarity of the ship made it seem less shoddy this time round. The tacky surroundings even seemed to hold a touch of class after the workaday bareness of the offshore supply boats. The chief officer was packed and straining to go. He was pleased that I had been on prior to his predecessor and therefore needed little handover. I walked the decks with him and went through the current state of the cargo before he left, feeling the ship was not in the good order she had been in when I'd left her in March. The officers had all changed, although I knew several from previous ships.

The chief engineer was an offensive man I had sailed with twice, an Australian evangelist, by which I mean he was an Englishman who had settled in Australia a few years ago and now spent a lot of his time crying the wonders of Australia and decrying the woes of England. A conversation with the chief entailed fending off his tales of barbecues on the beach and swimming in the sea on Christmas Day, and all that nonsense. I used to goad him by saying that the English are best suited to temperate climate with identifiable seasons and we were best eating pies not prawns. I told him he would end up moving back to England in his dotage, back to the old country to die, probably of the skin cancer he was picking up in Australia. This was always guaranteed to send him into a froth.

When I had first met him, several years previously, I'd thought of him as a bigoted man, someone who sneered at anyone who was different to him by virtue of colour, religion, class or financial standing. That was an under-judgement though. It wasn't just a case of sneering; he actually despised everyone outside of his own narrow range. If he had been alive in America after the Civil War, he would have been riding around dressed in a white sheet, wearing a pointed hat. If he had been a Berliner in the 1930s he would have been first to fling the books on the bonfire.

I had sailed with the third mate on two previous occasions. He was a South Pacific Islander, a good man although one blighted by an excessive appetite for alcohol, while being constitutionally saddled with a poor tolerance level for it. The fourth engineer was an old shipmate from the *Coral Chief* and a good hand. Sparks was a Pakistani, a devout Muslim who went by the name of Llewelyn; the second mate was a New Zealander who lived in London. The Old Man was an Old Man, quiet, unassuming, on the cusp of retirement, quiet company but a first rate shipmaster. There was also a cadet on board, which was always welcome.

I noticed that all the European officers apart from me had beards. I had never been a beard man myself, not even a moustache man. I had only ever grown a beard twice. The first time was when I was nineteen when I wanted to prove that I was capable of doing so. The second was to satisfy a bet between several of us that no one would shave or cut their hair for six months. I lost the bet, cutting mine off after a month because I couldn't stand it any longer. I didn't like the itching and the general feeling of being unclean.

In my experience, people grow beards for one of four reasons: practicality, vanity, hygiene or laziness.

There can be sound practical reasons, the most obvious being if someone is living in extreme cold where extra fuzz on the face is a common sense benefit. On the question of vanity, there are those who believe they look better with a beard; they may think they look more dignified and nobler or sexier. But when I've looked closer, they tend to be covering up a defect, a weak chin, hare lip, bad skin or some other unsightliness, perhaps warts or a birthmark. In terms of hygiene, I have met people who swore they were to allergic to shaving and it brought them out in a rash. But I've always thought the biggest reason for beard growing is sheer laziness; take a man with a beard and look at his shoes, scuffed, his dentistry, poor, his nails, dirty, his collar, grubby, his clothes, rumpled. A few beard wearers grow long rugs that harbour crumbs of food, with sprinkles of dandruff emerging from time to time.

The bearded officers on the *Chengtu* were a mix of the vain and the lazy. The Old Man felt that facial hair endowed him with the right sort of salty sea-dog appearance, and the fourth engineer had a rather over-manicured piece that went well with his personality. The rest had straggly messes and they all fell into my broad sweep of lazy people who couldn't be bothered to spend five minutes in the morning having a shave.

The Chinese officers were all beardless like me, although that was because they were generally less hirsute and only capable of growing thin and patchy whiskers, which look better off the face than on, by any measure.

I soon settled in. Company policy on steaming from Hong Kong to Singapore had changed recently, because the boat people sightings were now so occasional that it was appropriate to take the shorter western route again, down the coast of Vietnam, rather than going across to the eastern side of the South China Sea. I hadn't been down the Vietnam coast since I was a junior officer on a white oil tanker in the closing years of the US involvement in Vietnam, running jet fuel up the Saigon River to Nhà Bè refinery.

As we left Hong Kong and steamed south, the problem wasn't from the boat people. The problem was the two typhoons that were threatening to chop up the area. Typhoon Orchid was a big Category 4 typhoon that was howling towards the Philippines. The storm would either veer to the north where it would slow and peter out, or would roll right over the Philippines and into the South China Sea and come at us. A more immediate problem, though, was Typhoon Percy, which was already in the South China Sea, having formed in the Philippines and moved west-south-west. We were on a convergent course with Percy and were banking on it swinging to the north or running out of steam.

In the northern hemisphere, winds revolve anti-clockwise round a tropical storm, and our hope was that with Orchid to the east of the Philippines and Percy to the west the opposing wind patterns would diminish, if not extinguish, the power of the other. In the meantime we raced for the southern latitudes, hoping to reach the 10 degree parallel beyond which a formed typhoon rarely carries. There was no safe or certain way to act, because typhoons are unpredictable. Although their initial movement is from east to west, they will either continue west or veer to the north. Or sometimes they drop to the south. In any event, we knew we were better off at sea where we could batten the ship down and ride out the storm, rather than holding fast to a typhoon buoy in Hong Kong harbour and praying.

The rain was torrential and came down in sheets. Visibility was obscured, the radar was all but useless, just a screen of sea clutter as the scanner picked the high wave tops. And high they were: great green mountainous seas that smashed into our port quarter, pulling the ship over then releasing her into a violent roll. We had lashed down everything that could move and closed every watertight door, and it was now a case of holding on and making as much southward progress as we could, as quickly as we could manage. We went through the passage between the Paracel Islands and the Macclesfield Bank during as wild a night at sea as I had ever seen. An engine breakdown would be calamitous; we would be left drifting west into 800 square miles of reefs and rocks – we would be doomed.

As we made more to the south, the seas picked up further, rolling right over the rails, pitching us the other way as the water streamed off. Percy was coming straight for us, and we prayed it would swing north. I came back onto the bridge at four in the morning, after a fitful night, having pulled my mattress off the bunk and slept on the deck after twice being thrown out of bed by the heavy rolling. The sea was wickedly white, Typhoon Percy was flinging clouts of water at the wheelhouse windows with contempt. There were three of us on the bridge: me, the Old Man and the lookout. Occasionally there would be a visitor, someone who couldn't sleep and who wanted reassurance. We all clung on and hoped for the best. We didn't speak much, just held on and stared out at another of nature's lessons, hoping to spot any ships that came out of the rain. The radar was useless, blunted by sea clutter.

The Old Man had been up on the bridge all night. I persuaded him to have a lie-down in the chartroom for a while, which he did eventually, although he looked out every twenty minutes or so, especially after a particularly heavy thump of water. At eight in the morning the sea started to ease marginally, and by midday we were past the worst.

After lunch I went out on deck with the bosun and a couple of ABs, all of us wrapped in oilskins and harnessed by safety lines. The sea was down but still breaking over the rails and the Force 8 wind whipped the spray into our eyes. We made our way down the lee side, gripping onto the lifelines that ran down the side of the hatches, which we had rigged as we left Hong Kong. The ship was rolling heavily and we were wary of being too near the rails in case the deck dipped under the surface and the water suction pulled us through, shrieking, down into the green depths.

The cargo was secure and there were no breaches to the watertight doors or to any part of the integrity of the ship. We climbed onto the fo'c'sle head and made sure the anchors were still secure. There was minor damage here and there, paint stripped of the deck and halyards torn away. Under the fo'c'sle, the paint store was a shambles with several burst drums, and the chain locker had more water in it than usual. We looked in each of the hatches and they were dry. We didn't climb to the bottoms but we could see enough and there was no sound of sloshing water.

By late afternoon the sea was calming and we heard on the radio that the edges of the two typhoons had indeed begun to cancel each other out with opposing winds. We had a cheer for Typhoon Orchid for saving us from Typhoon Percy, then later we heard on the BBC World Service that Orchid had killed 167 people in the Philippines by sinking the Mindanao ferry. The thought of all those hands scrabbling at the hull as the ship was carried down, water blurring their vision, drenching their lungs, the panic, the panic, the horror, sent me to a cold and guilty gloom.

Singapore: only eight hours alongside, no sleep for any of the deck officers, then we were out again and crossing the equator towards the Java Sea. I felt I could relax for the first time since I had signed on. The chief engineer came on the bridge early one morning as we were passing Lombok while I was chatting with the Old Man, and gloomily reported a leak in the engine room, a seal apparently. He felt we were OK for the voyage, provided we didn't run into anything too extreme, although he wanted to book a repair gang for Hong Kong when we were back in the north.

We were gearing up for a fast race through the Islands, but then in Port Moresby, our first call, we came to a shuddering halt when we ran into a two-day dock strike. We reacted with late nights in the bar, celebrating our time off. I took more notice of the serious drinkers, the chief engineer and the third mate. In days past it would have been me. When we left Port Moresby, we picked up the pace. All the island destinations were short calls. Down and round to the southern tip of New Guinea, weaving through the islands of the Louisade archipelago and east across the Solomon Sea to Guadalcanal Island, to Honiara, capital of the Solomon Islands – in at daybreak, out at midnight. Then the beautiful run up the middle of the Solomon group, through New Georgia Sound, in sheltered green seas, Santa Isobel Island to the north, the New Georgia Islands to the south, outrigger canoes scattered far from shore, each occupied by a single man, arm raised in salute, flying fish skipping the surface, dolphins turning over in the wake, the warm sun on my arms and neck as I leant on the wind dodger.

After my evening watch I walked the decks on my rounds, the yellow pool of light from my torch dancing ahead of me. Everything was well, a rich and heavy tropical night, a gentle breeze, clear skies, rolling black sea looking as thick as gravy, stars casting their sharp lights into it like rows of stiletto knives. From the fo'c'sle head over the side, the night seemed as quiet as the grave, just the hiss of the water as we cleaved through it, and an occasional distant slap of water in the dark – a dolphin braving a leap into the night perhaps, or the broad flat tail of a baleen whale coming down. It was all so achingly beautiful. One night we passed the *Coral Chief* on her way to Australia, a black shape sliding past in the dark like a ghost, the two captains holding a conversation over the VHF, exchanging tales, each exaggerating and trying to outgun the other.

☆   ☆   ☆

To Kieta in Bougainville, in, out, to Rabaul in New Britain, in, out, then Lae, in for a three-day respite. Phew. Madang at daybreak, out at nightfall, and finally to Wewak, our last call in the Islands.

Wewak sits on the north coast of Papua New Guinea and is the capital of East Sepik province, lying about 100 miles west of the mouth of the Sepik River. It was a trading station used by the Germans and became more settled after the First World War. Wewak is the last port of any importance before the Indonesian border; there are just a couple of other small settlements further west.

In the Pacific War, the Japanese built a major airfield at Wewak, which earned it the sanction of being heavily bombed and flattened by the Americans and the Australians. There was a rough coast road that ran all the way across the Indonesian border to Jayapura, past quiet beaches with overhanging palms. Wewak had a flat and desolate feel and always felt like the last call it was. Our berth was at the end of a causeway road that stuck out into the bay, bleak and alone. I walked to town on one occasion, but there wasn't much there; the place had a frontier feel, a dusty street, a few stores, a yacht club, a Chinese restaurant. Wewak was wrapped in green, the dark green of the jungle to the south, the pale green of the Bismarck Sea to the north.

It was a forgotten place. We dropped off goods from the East together with some transhipments from further round the coast and took out a few containers of cocoa and coffee. There was never much either to deliver or to collect, but we always seemed to stay in Wewak longer than we did at most of the other ports. The pace was torpid. We spent hours waiting for the cargo to arrive and everything seemed to happen in slow motion. I watched the dock workers move at the pace of reptiles. They always seemed happy though, in their rags and cast-off clothes; they smiled and laughed and were enjoying life. There is a lot to be said for a place where people sleep in the sun, wash in the sea and plan no further ahead than the end of the day. If you have to be poor it's better to be poor in the sun I suppose. Wewak was the end of the line.

The third mate was drinking more and more. A couple of times he came onto the bridge reeking of alcohol; the smell of drink was a mantle that moved with him. He had started drinking with the chief engineer, the two of them sitting in the chief's cabin during the afternoon and evening, knocking back Tiger beer, growling at each other. I warned the third mate I wouldn't hand over the watch if he ever came up at eight o'clock too drunk to assume control. He told me of his drinking sessions with the chief, as if he was using a card of immunity. I told him I didn't care, I didn't care who he was drinking with, I wasn't handing over to a drunk, not in mid-ocean, certainly not around the Islands.

I couldn't escape the irony: me, who had drunk myself insensible on more occasions than I could ever remember, handing out lectures on the evils of alcohol. I didn't care. My drinking had always been in port or sometimes at anchor or when there was time to drum up a clear head before the next watch. I had never come up to the bridge incapable of taking the watch. Mildly drunk yes, hungover yes, ill sometimes, but always more sober than drunk.

I built myself up to reporting him to the Old Man and ending his career, but the need never arose. I was with the Old Man one evening at eight o'clock. He had come up to the bridge at quarter to and was hanging around, chatting. I knew he was waiting for the third mate. At five past eight there was a crash of the chart room door.

The third mate's voice: "Sorry, Choff. Sorry I'm late!" a slurred pair of sorrys.

The Old Man said to me quietly, "Don't speak to me," and he moved into the shadows.

The third mate emerged, like a mole, into the ink-black darkness of the wheelhouse. He didn't have his night vision yet and was unable to see.

"Whoo-oooo, ooooo-ooo … Where are you, Chief Officer?"

"Over here," I called. I was standing in front of the wheel.

He walked into the telegraph. "Arrggh! Oww! Shite! God! That hurt!" Then he chuckled.

"You've been on the sherbet, haven't you?" I asked.

"Juss a couple, Choff, juss a couple." He sniffed theatrically. "That bloody chief engineer. He forces drinks onto you. What can I do? I mean, what can I do? He's got four stripes, to my measly one stripe. How can I refuse?" He chuckled again.

"You're going to lose that one stripe, then you'll have none," I said.

"Whaddaya mean? Whaddaya mean?"

"You're too drunk to take the watch. Get below."

"I'm fine, I'm fine. I'll be OK. Cup of black coffee and I'll be fine." He snorted with laughter. "That bloody chief. Getting me into trouble."

"Get below, Third Mate. Get below now."

"Who's going to take the watch? You can't stay on."

"The cadet will take it."

"What will the Old Man say when he comes up? You know whad e's like, he's such an old woman. I'll get a right bollocking, I might get the sack."

"You're going to get the sack if you don't leave this bridge now!" I shouted at him.

"OK, OK, I'm goin', I'm goin'. No need to shout."

He wandered out to the bridge wing, tripping over the sliding door rail as he went. Then there was a clatter ending in a heavy thud as he fell down the ladder to the boat deck. I walked out onto the bridge wing.

"Are you all right?" I called down.

"Yes, Chief Officer. I'm fine, I'm fine," he replied in a muffled voice. "I'll have a shower and be back soon."

I went back inside the wheelhouse. The Old Man emerged out of the dark.

He said: "I'll have to sack him now."

"It's your call, Captain."

"What do you think?"

"Sack him if you want, but you'll have to promote the cadet to third mate. We can't go round the islands without a watch keeper for the eight to twelve, otherwise you would have to do it."

"Sod that," I heard him mutter under his breath.

"And did you hear what he called me? An old woman? Old woman indeed!" The Old Man sounded more concerned about the insult than the third mate's inebriated state.

I nodded in sympathy while thinking: 'I've called you worse.'

The problem was that it was the chief engineer who was the third mate's drinking partner. It gave the third mate a parachute; the chief should know better.

"I think you should have a word with the chief, Captain. He knows the third mate has a watch to keep and he shouldn't be encouraging him to drink all day long."

"He should be making him stop! The trouble is that the chief drinks like a bloody fish himself."

"He certainly does, Captain," I said, feeling some guilt, knowing full well my own habits over the years.

"And he's so prickly, flying off the handle at any perceived criticism."

It wasn't just the chief's character of course. It was the nature of the whole relationship between the captain and the chief engineer. They both wore four gold stripes, although the chief was in charge of the engine room while the captain was in charge of the ship, which included the engine room. This rankled with a lot of chief engineers and the Old Man always had to make sure he didn't step on the chief's dignity.

"You speak to him, Chief Officer," he said.

I'd thought that was coming. "I'll see what I can do, Captain," I said.

"I'll take the eight to twelve watch. Tell the third mate not to bother coming back to the bridge after his shower but to come and see me in my cabin tomorrow morning at 07:30." He trailed off with a mutter: "The little shit."

I left the bridge to deliver the message to the third mate, but he was on flat his back on his daybed, passed out and snoring, bleeding from a gash to his face which he had presumably picked up when he fell down the ladder after leaving the bridge. I rolled him over onto his side in case he vomited and choked himself, flung a blanket over him, then went down to the bar.

The place was deserted but I could hear a racket from along the alleyway so I followed the noise to the chief engineer's cabin. He was in there, sounding off at the second engineer, who was standing there in his grubby boiler suit, looking impatient. The chief was as drunk as a lord, waving a glass of gin and slopping it down his skinny chest. I paused outside the door, the curtain was drawn back and the chief waved me in.

"Hey, Simon. Party time! Come on in and have a beer."

"Thanks, Chief."

I helped myself from his fridge. The second engineer took the opportunity to scuttle away.

"So, whass happening?" asked the chief.

"Sun's down, moon's up, we missed the reef, the crew haven't mutinied and war hasn't broken out yet. All's well. Cheers."

"Cheers." He took a massive swig of gin.

"Problem on the bridge, though," I shook my head sadly.

"What's that?"

"The third mate's pissed. The Old Man has flung him off the bridge. There's going to be a lot of trouble over that."

The chief shifted uneasily on his seat. I could feel sobriety leeching into him.

"Err, what did he say?" he asked.

"Who? The third mate? Something like: I jess hada coupla liddle drings, thassall, honness." I contorted my face and slurred the words.

"No, the Old Man. What did *he* say? What's he going to do?"

"He's hauling the third mate up to his cabin first thing tomorrow morning to give him a monster bollocking. He might log him and sack him, depends upon the explanation he gives."

The chief looked intent. I could see his drunkenness being evicted by the fear of being held to blame for the third mate's condition.

I continued: "I expect the Old Man will send a telegram to Hong Kong and chuck him off the ship when we arrive at the next port. Good thing too, I've no time for drunks anyway. What do you think, Chief?"

The chief sat there looking worried, no doubt thinking how best to insulate his position and not end up being fingered as the man who had caused the third mate to become incapable of standing his watch.

"Hmm? Oh, yeah, I agree, can't have the ship manned by a load of piss-heads, can we? Poor show, poor show."

"Cheers."

"Cheers."

The next morning while I was on the four to eight watch, the Old Man came up at 06:30, and we were on the bridge wing leaning on the dodger and talking when the chief appeared.

"Ahh, got a minute, Captain?" he said.

I walked into the wheelhouse and left the two of them in conference. The upshot was the chief explained to the Old Man that the third mate had been depressed recently and the chief had been trying to snap him out of it. Unfortunately, during one of these heart-to-heart discussions the third mate had drunk too much. It was an unusual circumstance but the third mate had problems at home and the Old Man shouldn't be too hard on him. It was a complete pack of lies, of course, but the Old Man nodded wisely and told the chief he would think about it. The chief came across to me and started to chat in a friendly way, trying to build allies presumably. I kept a non-committal look on my face, and he went away looking glum.

The Old Man gave the third mate a roasting at 07:30 and told him not to show his face in the bar or order any cabin beer for a week. Any repetition would result in his immediate dismissal.

The Old Man came and saw me afterwards and told me it was the right result in the circumstances. The third mate took over at eight o'clock, apologised for his behaviour, told me about his carpeting by the Old Man and said that the outcome was the best result in the circumstances. The chief engineer caught me after breakfast to tell me the Old Man wasn't taking the matter any further and it was the right thing to do in the circumstances. It probably was the right thing to do in the circumstances, although if I had been the Old Man I would have sacked the third mate on the spot.

A Sunday was always a special day at sea and was no less so on the *Chengtu*. As a cadet on day-work at sea it was a rare day off, and I remember cherishing the luxury of being able to lie in bed until gone eight o'clock then wash and dress at leisure before having a whole day in clean uniform. We didn't exactly have the whole day off because there was a morning inspection and in the afternoon we were expected to study, but it was as close to a day off as we ever came.

Sunday was inspection day. Now the inspection party was the captain, me, the chief engineer and the chief steward. Inspection started at ten o'clock and went through the whole ship, every cabin, to make sure they were clean and there was no damage. The cadet was always given a theatrical and completely unnecessary bollocking, just for being there, although otherwise the chief steward had to explain if any of the officer's cabins were below par. The crew cabins were expected to be in a state of respectability and everyone was supposed to be out of their bunks.

We went round the store rooms and the galley, smoke room, dining saloon and crew mess, and walked all the alleyways. The Old Man was a bit of a martinet. We were all in full uniform, and he and the chief wore their caps complete with gold leaf splattered on the brim. My hat was too shamefully battered and flattened to wear, so I just carried a clipboard and pen to note down any miscreants. Uniform caps were rarely worn at sea, inspections and burials being the exceptions. Sometimes, one of the crew would use the occasion to raise a complaint about some nonsense. We pretended to listen and I made notes although it was all for show; more often than not the complainant was just making a scene to impress his friends.

The inspection round was timed to conclude at 11:00, at which time we would repair to the Old Man's cabin for drinks. The second engineer joined us then. Occasionally he would come along with the inspection team, but usually just appeared at the end for drinks. The chief steward left, not being part of the senior team. Although I was a beer man, the post-inspection tradition was a large gin in a long glass, which I would enjoy as long as there was a lot of ice and the tonic was cold. When the ship's whistle sounded at noon we were three double gins heavier, and we all went down to the bar in a pack to have two more.

Sunday lunch was curry. The cook wasn't a great curry cook, although he thought he was and always hung around the serving hatch fishing for compliments. Chicken, lamb, beef or pork in a medium hot blend with far too many potatoes thrown in. The lamb curry was generally the best, although he used the scrag end and it wasn't unusual to get a mouthful of stringy fat. The others liked curry meals more than me; I would have preferred a decent Chinese meal. Cold Tiger beer was the accompanying drink.

We tended to have a film showing in the evening on a Sunday. The best of these were when they were shown out on the boat deck when we had the wind astern, blowing just hard enough to neutralise the air movement caused by the speed of the ship. This then meant that the sheet we tacked up didn't flap about and move too much, and didn't distort the image. We all loafed in cane chairs or just sat on the wooden deck under the tropical night. The film quality was generally poor, further accentuated by our duff equipment, and the films themselves were never blockbusters. But they were good nights.

I turned my mind to other things. I still loved the sea, but my life there wasn't going to work any longer. I was a married man with a child on the way, and everything had changed so much. If the ships and the trades and the way of life had remained the same then perhaps I could have made some sort of compromise but it was all now so different from the way it had been when I'd left school. Turnaround in port was becoming so quick there was no shore time to speak of, crews were smaller, standards were down, and there was massive job insecurity. My ship flew a Singapore flag. The previous two had had Panama flags. It was no longer what I really wanted to do.

I wrote letters to places where I thought there might be an appetite for my talents, such as they were. The Department of Fisheries and Agriculture, the National Environmental Research Council, all the major ports in Britain, then the minor ones. I wrote to dredging companies, ferry operators, coastal companies, companies selling marine equipment. Some replied, some didn't bother. Those that did didn't offer much encouragement. I resolved to continue and to carry the search for another form of employment when I went on leave.

Christmas was approaching, Annie was six months pregnant and I was the other side of the world, carrying coffee and copra around small South Pacific islands. Her letters stirred my soul but her news made me feel excluded from the real world. Bruno the Rottweiler was turning vicious, my younger brother Anthony was engaged to be married.

I polarised my prospects. Option 1: stay at sea, make captain in about ten years, see my wife and family every four to six months, become a complete drunk, hopefully retire before I die. Option 2: leave the sea and do something else. Option 2 seemed the better route. I could build a life ashore, have children, commute to work, cultivate a circle of friends, take holidays and celebrate the passing of the years. I would be there for the weddings, the christenings, the funerals.

Apart from my own, I had only ever been to a few weddings: my brother Peter, my cousin Jacquetta, my cousin Paul, Uncle Jim's second time around the park. There had been others, but I was always away. I got drunk and made a fool of myself at all of them. I had only ever been to one funeral: that of my father, a grim day that felt colder than the death we were celebrating. I had never been to a christening. I needed more events of all type, I needed to build a life and fully shed my mantle of self-indulgence.

Life rumbled on, incidents bizarre and commonplace. At half past four one afternoon there was a terrible screaming from the main deck, the full-throated screaming of pain rather than the shrillness of terror. I sent the quartermaster down to investigate. He came back to tell me the cadet had managed to hammer a three-inch nail through his foot. The second mate operated on him and later came onto the bridge to tell me what had happened.

"Apparently the cadet was working with casab, building a wooden frame for that hull scrubber we took on board on Hong Kong. He was sitting on the deck hammering two-by-four timber together and the silly bugger was bracing the timber with his foot. He whacked a nail through the first piece, missed the second and drove it through the heel of his foot."

"Ouch!"

The hull scrubber was a machine the company had bought and were keen for us to test out around the Islands. It consisted of four round steel brushes, each one the size of a dartboard, which were held in a steel frame. When connected to the compressed air line, the brushes spun round furiously, the idea being that it was lowered over the side of the ship below the waterline and it would scrub off the accumulated weed. It looked hopeless to my eye, a real Heath Robinson affair, although we would give it a go and see what happened. The bosun and the casab had decided however that the frame was too short to properly manoeuvre the machine and it would do better with a larger wooden outer frame bolted on. I let them get on with it. This was what had caused the cadet's accident.

"Ouch is right," continued the second mate. "The casab came rushing into my cabin to tell me what had happened so I told him to bring the cadet to the dispensary. But the old casab was ranting, 'No can do! No can do! You come quick! You come quick!' So I went down to the deck to see what was going on. The poor old cadet was firmly nailed to a length of timber. It was a 6-foot length that was joined to another 6-foot length, so he couldn't walk or even crawl. He was squealing like a stuck pig. Looked bloody funny actually, I wish I'd had a camera."

"Sounds a right hoot," I said.

"Anyway, I told the casab to get his saw and cut the timber either side of the foot, so the cadet would then only be nailed to a small block of wood. We could then carry him up to the dispensary and get the nail out somehow."

"I suppose when you got him to the deck store, you could lay him on the work-top and put the block of wood in the vice."

"Yeah, maybe. But things got worse. The casab started sawing but the cadet started screaming even louder. The vibration and juddering close to his foot was causing him even more pain. I don't think the casab's saw was that sharp either, which made it worse. The Old Man came down to see what all the fuss was about, so did the leci, then the chief engineer and half the crew. Soon there was a huge crowd gathered round, all giving advice. The casab started sawing again and it was all too much for the cadet. He ripped his foot out, blood everywhere, howling like a banshee, hopping round the deck. Every now and again he'd step on his heel and scream even more. The he skidded on the blood and went down and belted his head on the deck with a right whack."

"I bet everyone found that good entertainment."

"Too right. They thought it was hilarious. I kept telling them all to shut up because the poor lad was in real pain, but it didn't stop them laughing. They could see it wasn't life-threatening and so felt they had a licence to laugh. Mind you, the chief engineer didn't help. Guess what he said to the cadet when we were carrying him up to the dispensary?"

"What was that?"

"You shouldn't be knocking nails into your foot, Sonny; it isn't Easter yet."

In the South China Sea we had an incident with seagulls. The Chinese crew would find a way to eat most things and from time to time they would catch a seagull. It's not very good eating, I tried a bit once and found the flesh too strong and salty for my palate. Anyway, they liked to have a seagull on occasions and the way they caught them was to start flinging bread over the stern to bring in the gulls, which would swoop down and catch the bread in the air. When they had a good group they would take some fish-hooks on strong fishing line, load them up with bread and throw them in the air. The gulls would swoop, swallow the bread and they were caught.

That was the easy bit. Bringing the seagull on board was more challenging. As they dragged it on board the gull was in a frenzy, flapping and clawing and flashing its big beak at anyone who got near. They were strong birds, particularly when in a blind panic. The man reeling them in would wear a welder's mask and thick gauntlets to protect him from attack.

As soon as the bird was over the rails a mob of sailors would rush at it with sticks and clubs and beat the poor creature to death. Once the bird had been battered into submission, someone would step on the neck and then bend down and cut off the head, after which they would bear the corpse down to the galley for the cook to make seagull delicacies. I witnessed this grisly spectacle once as a cadet and a more gruesome sight would be hard to imagine. Most captains banned catching seagulls by fishing for them with hooks, it was thought too cruel.

The Old Man came onto the bridge early one morning, looking vexed.

"The bloody crew are catching seagulls down on the poop!" he exclaimed. "Cruel bastards! They're inhuman! Go down there and put a stop to it!"

I handed over the watch to him and walked down to the poop. I didn't share the Old Man's thinking that the crew were inhuman; the Chinese just had different thought processes towards animals than Europeans, particularly when they were intending to eat them. Less hypocrisy as well.

Whatever the rights and wrongs, I went down to end the fishing expedition. When I arrived it was apparent they had got wind that I was on my way, because everyone was standing around in innocent groups, looking out to sea, smoking. There was blood on the deck and I could see the bodies of two large gulls badly hidden under a tarpaulin behind the capstan. I called the bosun over.

"Bosun, you catch birds?"

"Wha?"

"You catch birds?"

"Wha?"

"Whyfor you catch birds? No good to catch birds, no good!"

"What bird?"

"This bird," I said, pointing to the ones behind the capstan. I walked over and picked one up by the leg, its headless corpse hung down.

"Ahh. Steward catch bird for chow," he said, aping eating motions, sweeping imaginary food into his mouth.

"Captain say, no catch sea-bird. You know already."

He hung his head, smiling. I flung the bird over the rails, then picked up the other and threw that over too. The crew looked outraged. I spotted the cook in the shuffling crowd, glowering at me. There was a rising murmur and a lot of muttering. I walked off and back up to the bridge, feeling their eyes lasering into my back.

"Well?" the Old Man demanded. "Did you stop them?"

"I did captain and I threw the birds back into the sea."

"Well done. That'll teach them."

"I thought they were going to throw me over for a second."

"Well done, Chief Officer. They won't do that again."

Of course they will, I thought. They just won't get caught next time.

We occasionally had small boat trouble as we went through the Indonesian islands. These little canoes travel miles from land with just one occupant who spends the night fishing by hand. They have oil lamps or naphtha lights, although they only turn them on if a ship comes too close. I had found myself within a group of canoes at night on many occasions, the sea suddenly coming to life with a blanket of close flickering lights, as if we were approaching a swarm of fireflies.

It was usually possible to nudge round them at the last minute, although occasionally it caused a close quarters situation. We sometimes brushed them aside with the bow, which caused them to rock and bang down the side of the ship. When the sea ahead was an unbroken line of lights I sometimes had to wait until one disappeared below the line of the fo'c'sle head as seen from the bridge, at which time I would swing the heading 10 degrees one way or the other to avoid running the boat under.

A number of watch keepers did run them down, saying that it was their own fault and they ought to make some effort to keep out of the way. I sailed with one second mate who said that he would feel worse running over a dog with his car than he would running over a fisherman who was clogging up the sea lanes with his canoe. Although I shared his frustration I didn't regard the fishermen as sub-dog and always made sure I avoided ploughing them into the sea, even though I must have swamped a few when we passed them close by.

The really big groups tended to be in the northern part of the Indonesian archipelago, between Sumatra and Borneo and also further up in the Philippines, particularly outside Manila Bay. Down in lower Indonesia, in the Java Sea and the Banda Sea, the small boats and canoes were in groups of three or four. Sometimes there was just a solitary fisherman.

For a fortnight we had a safety officer on board, a trapper. His job was to unearth all our dangerous practices and make us more diligent. He was a seconded chief officer, which vested him with enough authority to do what was a very unpopular job. The *Chengtu* was a busy ship on a busy run and although we had our rest times, we had a schedule to keep and were often starved of sleep and pushed to the limits of our endurance. The last thing we wanted was someone telling us to wind the lifeboats up in a different manner.

The safety officer was with the engineers for the first few days, which suited me as I was able to get a feel for his expectations by speaking to the second engineer. The second was soon gnashing with rage at having to make his men clean any oil off the floor plating at the end of each watch, hang pointless warning notices and ensuring no one rolled up the sleeves of their boiler suits.

"The man's a bloody half-wit," he fumed. "He's not even an engineer, what does he know?"

"I expect he's been on an engineer's safety course," I said, goading him.

"An engineer's course! Aye, that'll be right! I spent four years as a cadet, a year as junior, a year as fourth, three years as third and I've been second for three years. I've got a chief's ticket in steam and motor and he's telling me the way to run the engine room! It's bloody lunacy!"

"Oh come on," I said, "we all need to be told to pick up our game sometimes and stop killing off the crew."

The second looked at me sharply, then realised I was mocking him.

"You wait, Simon," he said. "He'll be with you next week."

He was. It was dreadful. The man clung to me like a rash. He wore a buttoned-up boiler suit, notebook at the ready, offering wisdom at every turn. Everything from a stuck dog to an errant smear of grease went into the book. A ship should never be mistaken for a safe environment; people have to know what they're doing and keep their wits about them, so everyone accepted that we needed to be trained in new equipment and we had to implement safe working codes. But the drive to record our activity went down very badly. The second engineer gloated at my pained expression at the end of the day.

A full fire and boat drill was called and was going to be a two-hour affair. We all groaned, although it was made less painful following the Old Man's brainwave of putting the safety officer in charge of the whole thing. This allowed us all to stand and look at him with smirking expectancy, awaiting his direction.

When things went wrong, which was inevitable, we put our common sense on hold and turned to the safety officer and waited to be told his safe method of putting matters right. The lifeboat stuck while being lowered, which happened from time to time. When it did we would put the brake on then wind it up half a turn and release the brake again, the procedure taking less than a minute. This time though, the crew effected gormlessness and did nothing, causing a painful fifteen-minute delay.

Both hose parties and the breathing apparatus party crowded the safety officer, hemming him in, spraying him with water, making him lose his temper, which was better than any of us had been hoping for. To give him his due, though, he bullied the boat and fire drill to conclusion, although looking almost beaten by the finish.

He wrote a massive report towards the end of his stay and gave me a copy. I skim-read it and pinned it to the noticeboard in my office, where it would stay until he departed. I found myself cruelly praying for rough weather so he could show us how to dodge the breaking seas in a safe manner.

The last night we were talking alone in the bar and he confided to me that his job was awful and he hated it. He was pleased that this was his fifth and final tour before going back to serve as chief officer again. He said the company would be on the lookout for a replacement and asked if I would be interested. I said that I was a seaman not a seagoing office-wallah and would need to be under the whip before I would ever do a job like that. We sat up late and talked about ships we had served on in the past. He turned out to be a decent enough man, stuck in a bad job.

☆   ☆   ☆

The whole of the south-west Pacific sits in an unstable area of seismic activity. Honiara, the capital of the Solomon Islands, lies right on a fault line which runs up the New Georgia Sound and across to New Ireland and New Britain. Earthquakes have been common in the Islands for hundreds of years, the only difference in recent times being that they are better predicted and more accurately measured. There had been a couple of big quakes in the surrounding hills the day before we arrived in Honiara and a few people killed, and there was now a concern there might be another big movement that evening. We were hurried off our berth not long after we arrived so as not to be caught. The port authority made a request we couldn't refuse, which was to sit out in the sound to act as a rescue ship and medical centre if there was a major disaster. We drifted a few miles off the coast for the night, waiting for something to happen. Nothing did, so in the morning we exchanged views with the authorities who thanked us for standing by, then took us back alongside to finish discharging our cargo.

The dock workers arrived late and too drunk to work. The bus they had been travelling on had run over and killed two people outside the town, and they all agreed it was best to go to the nearest bar and have a few drinks in respect and commiseration. We ended with an overnight stay in Honiara and went to the yacht club for the evening, where we traded conversation with expats in blazers and ties. Although they were lifted from another era, it all seemed strangely normal.

As we left Honiara the bosun took badly ill, whey-faced, wringing wet, coughing blood, as weak as a small child. We carried him ashore in Rabaul and the agent took him up to the hospital in the back of his jeep, later coming back to say that the bosun was in a very bad way and wouldn't be rejoining the ship.

I had a discussion with the Old Man as to which of the senior deck hands we should promote to bosun. There were only two contenders, both quartermasters: Wong Lam and Cheung Li. They both had their flaws, Wong being an inveterate gambler who was unpopular with a lot of the crew for winning large sums off them at mahjongg. They felt he won too much and too conveniently. He had also blotted his copy book recently by going AWOL for a day in Port Moresby and then being flung into gaol for fighting with one of the locals. Cheung, on the other hand, had a taste for rice wine and was a bit of a drunk, which was fairly rare among Chinese crews. When Cheung had been drinking he always managed to put on a good impersonation of sobriety, but he was an unreliable man. We were discussing which of our two flawed contenders would be given the role, the drunk or the fighting gambler, and were leaning towards Wong as the less of the two evils, when a delegation of sailors arrived and knocked at the captain's door. The front man was Jimmy Ho, another quartermaster.

"We no want Wong for bosun," he announced without preamble.

There was a rumble of assent from the crowd behind him

"Why not Wong?" asked the captain.

"We no like him."

"Wong good sailor."

"Wong bad man."

"Only for short time, Jimmy," said the captain. "New bosun join in Hong Kong next time."

"We no want Wong. We want Cheung Li."

"Wong is a number 1 sailor, Jimmy."

"Wong is bad man."

"OK. I hear you. Me and chief officer talk, then tell you by-and-by."

"You choose Wong, sailors not work."

"That bad talk, Jimmy," the Old Man warned.

"Wong stupid man. Too stupid to make sailors work. We try, but Wong too stupid. You choose Wong, ship not happy, work not get done."

"OK, Jimmy, we get the message," I said. "I come see you by-and-by."

"We no want Wong," he said as he left, to underline the point.

Jimmy Ho left. The captain and I looked at each other.

"No point in inviting grief, Captain," I said. "If you install Wong Lam as bosun, the rest of the crew will slouch about doing little or nothing until we get to Hong Kong. I didn't realise they hated him that much."

"Me neither. Cheung Li the boozer for bosun, then."

"Good old Cheung. Shall I invite him up for a drink to celebrate?"

We both had a good chuckle at the thought.

I called Cheung Li up to my office to give him the news. He looked both pleased and smug, although at least he was sober. No doubt he would be lording it over Wong Lam in the crew's mess later.

I told him to get the crew painting the forward part of the accommodation while the weather was so good. I could see he didn't really like the thought of that, probably because it was as baking hot, and he suggested he set them to do repairs to the mooring lines on the poop. I overruled that idea, though, as I could see that he was angling for a job in the shade. He started to argue the case, which annoyed me having just promoted him, so while we talked I picked up a red pen and started tapping it on the desk in front of me. Cheung eventually focused on what was on the desk and saw that I had the monthly overtime sheets laid out. Cheung went silent. He didn't want to get off on a bad footing with me taking the red pen to the crew's overtime claim as this would be a severe loss of face to his new authority. He decided it would be better politics to just get on with things as directed, and left to round up the crew for painting in the sun. I put the red pen back in the drawer, pleased with my cunning.

Christmas loomed. The weather deteriorated as we headed across the north-west Pacific from Wewak to Hong Kong. The last typhoons of the season gave us a lashing as they raged towards the Philippines. We dodged them as best we could, the wind howling through the stays and blowing sheets of water across the decks as we pitched and lurched our way along. I called the crew out at five in the morning and we made a working party to lash everything down, close everything up, check that anything moveable was secured. We put double wire lashings on the lifeboats and secured every door and hatch. We returned after an hour, refreshed by our drenching, bruised by the falls we had all taken as the ship flung herself around.

This would be my last Christmas at sea. Llewelyn the Pakistani radio officer made a cardboard Christmas tree, which was good of him as he wasn't even a Christian. We tied the tree in an almost upright position next to the chart room table.

Christmas Day arrived as we were steaming down the Vietnam coast. Presents were diverse. The bosun gave me a bottle of scotch, which I didn't drink, so I re-wrapped it and gave it to the Old Man, who gave me a bottle of gin in return. I wrapped up a paint brush and gave it to the cadet for his Boxing Day job of painting the monkey island, which he took with good grace.

For his present, the third mate got the sack from the Old Man at last, after he had turned up to his evening watch on Christmas Eve barely able to walk. I was called to act as witness. He wasn't actually sacked on the spot, otherwise we would have been a man down, but his behaviour was recorded in the log book and the Old Man sent a telegram to Hong Kong asking for an immediate replacement. He was effectively passing the sacking to Hong Kong, which I thought was a bit weak.

We prepared to gorge. Drinks in the captain's cabin at eleven o'clock, followed by a ten-course meal so mighty it would have been impossible for anyone to finish, no matter how long they sat there and how greedy they were. The day passed in good spirit. The chief engineer corrupted the day worker officers and the cadet, all of them becoming flush then sick with alcohol. The third mate kept a low profile, even though it was now too late to undo the damage.

Christmas dinner finished at three in the afternoon, I was on watch at four so walked a few circuits of the ship, breathing in the fresh salt air until I felt the overfed drum of my stomach start to relax. I passed a ragged group of sailors sitting on the poop deck, and I stopped to talk with them for a while as we wished each other a Happy Christmas. We smoked a cigarette together and watched the wake peel away, exchanging emphatics in broken English.

We had picked up an infestation of weevils and cockroaches in Singapore and they broke cover in a meaningful way as the hygiene slackened in the galley and food stores. The weevil is a small beetle; it's harmless to eat and I must have eaten scores of them over the years. Shipboard weevils get into the stores and find their way into biscuits and flour and other dried foodstuff. On the *Chengtu* the weevils were in the sugar, in the cornflakes, in the flour, small black and wriggling. Those in the flour would be cooked and we wouldn't know any more about them although it was never welcome to be served fresh weevil in the saloon in sugar and cereals.

Like most people on board, I took care to separate out my weevils and push them to the side of the bowl or plate although some people, particularly if they wanted to horrify a first tripper or a newly arrived wife, would wolf them down, smacking their lips and saying: "Yum, fresh meat. It's the only time you'll find it on this ship," causing the newcomer to go grey with revulsion.

We had two kinds of cockroach on board: the big brown oriental and the smaller European version. The European was known as the German cockroach for some reason, *Blattella germanica*, and was half the size of the oriental *Blattella asahinai*. Ours were mostly the oriental version, great hefty creatures, colloquially known as Bombay six-wheelers. They were tough, and if you failed to stamp on one heavily enough it might survive. The orientals gathered around the food areas, the galley, the pantries, crew's mess and officers' dining saloon. There were some Germans in the food areas, but they generally preferred the cooler climate of the chilled food stores.

Cockroaches liked the dark. If I went into the pantry in the evening and switched on the light to see if there was anything I could rustle up to eat, there would be a heaving carpet of them covering the surfaces, all scuttling for cover as I came in. Cockroaches weren't just in the food areas but were all over the accommodation and would be found in most cabins. When I turned my cabin light on at night I would usually see a few disappearing into cracks or running down the side of the mattress. Most people at sea became used to cockroaches and tolerated them although there were some who never got over the horror.

Occasionally we would catch a few and have a cockroach derby but they were poor performers and rarely ran in a straight line. A few cruder people would try and put on cockroach fights, pitting three Germans against an Oriental, but these were unsuccessful bouts with the different *blattellae* not displaying much aggression among themselves. Ours on the *Chengtu* were probably too well fed.

There was talk of a cruel sport where people starved several German cockroaches in a jar for a few days and then put them in a bowl or sink, or some such suitable arena, with an Oriental that was smeared with jam. The cockroach fighting apparently then became very savage. That sort of thing didn't appeal to me. Anyway, these were second-hand tales that had probably grown in the re-telling.

Every six months we had a rat survey in order to obtain our Deratting Certificate, which was an important requirement, demanded by most of the larger ports. The second mate and the third mate both told me they had seen rats in the hold, although I hadn't seen any myself and was sceptical. Rat infestation meant clearing the ship, which was then given a fumigation with hydrogen cyanide, and I suspected the two junior mates might have been angling for a night in a hotel in Hong Kong while the fumigation went on.

Our survey was cursory. The surveyor asked me if there had been any sightings of rats. I said no, making the obligatory joke about head office personnel excepted, at which he politely snickered. The shipping world was becoming ever more precious about rats, and more and more ports were demanding valid Deratting Certificates. We always rigged rat-guards on the mooring lines. These were metal shields to prevent rats trotting up the line and hopping on board. The bottom of the gangway was painted white, because a rat dare not pass over white paint, apparently.

Despite our best efforts, rats still found their way on board from time to time. On general cargo ships they sometimes came as part of the cargo, especially in containers. But then, in fact, it was irrelevant to the ship, as a rat would come aboard in a container, stay there for the voyage, eat whatever it found in there and then depart in the container. On a ship like the *Chengtu*, the entry points for rats were with the food stores, past a poorly secured rat-guard or perhaps up the anchor chain.

Every wharf area in every port in the world has rats, some shy and rarely sighted, some brazen and fearless creatures that ignore man. The brown rat, *rattus norvegicus*, can grow to the size of a small cat and take on an horrific appearance when it emerges from foul dock waters, dripping and slime-encrusted, beady-eyed and sharp of tooth.

Rats carry a wide range of diseases including typhus, leptospirosis and bubonic plague. Most of the rats found on ships are of the brown rat variety, the biggest type.

The author's last Christmas at sea

The slightly smaller black rat, *rattus rattus*, is less common, but will still get aboard if given half a chance. The rat may be the world's most successful mammal but they are as unwelcome on board ship as anywhere else.

Although the Christmas meal had been fine, the quality of food had been declining throughout December. Immediately after Christmas, it became dire, as if the cook had finally given up. Trouble started to brew when he was suspected of abandoning cooking as such and was just boiling the meat and fish, before then shoving it in a hot oven to quickly brown, irrespective of whatever the meal as supposed to be. He denied this and survived a couple of snap inspections but everyone was convinced that his ruined meals were a consequence of him being a meat boiler.

The chief engineer made a spectacle of himself one lunchtime between Christmas and New Year, picking up his piece of fish by the tail, shouting: "Look at this! Look at this! It's boiled, it's bloody boiled! It's like a piece of rubber."

"No. Is fish," said the steward helpfully.

"It's rubber!" shrieked the chief. "Bloody boiled rubber!"

He waved it in the steward's face before flinging it on the deck and storming out. The captain kept chewing his rubbery fish stoically, ignoring the chief's outburst. The rest of us looked on. I ate my fish with plenty of soy sauce, thinking it was quite good actually.

After lunch I had a chat with the Old Man, telling him there was a lot of dissatisfaction with the food and he ought to have a word with the chief steward and get the cook to start making more effort. It was a waste of time, though; I could see my words bouncing off his skull. It was a repeat of the bad food patch I had experienced on the *Coral Chief*.

New Year approached. We were due a Chinese banquet for New Year's Eve. Opinion was polarised; some thought the cook would either excel, being Chinese, others predicted a meal of such vileness that the pressure to have him replaced would become overwhelming. The cook excelled and the meal was marvellous, as if he had been stockpiling his talents and released them all at once.

It started it with the classic challenge to the westerner: 100-year-old eggs. These were eggs preserved in various potions for 100 days actually, the yolk turning dark green, the white a dark brown. The pungent flavour either levered open the taste buds or sent them into shutdown. Several officers wouldn't touch them, declaring the dish toxic, poisonous. I forced one down, as did several others, accompanying mine with several mouthfuls of Tiger beer. The steward and cook looked on approvingly. It was a hard swallow, but I felt I would have lost face if I didn't get it past my gullet. Its piquancy certainly sharpened the appetite.

Afterwards the banquet proceeded in earnest with shark's fin soup, steamed bream in ginger, beef and oysters, several ducks, chicken in lemon and a procession of other dishes. There were several speeches fuelled by alcohol, none particularly good, mine included. At midnight the cadet went forward to ring in the New Year on the ship's bell, the only time sixteen bells was ever struck: eight bells for the old year and eight bells for the new. We all shook hands and toasted the arrival of 1984.

I didn't eat on New Year's Day, being too bloated. The cook resumed normal service on 2 January when the roast chicken we were served had a distinctly boiled appearance. It sat there on my plate not looking like food. It looked like a small white boulder, a boiled boulder.

My letters brought me the flavours of home. Annie remained a prolific writer, writing one letter a day every day, written in conversational style, not as news, nor were they intended to be, just as conversation and observation and an expression of her thoughts. She was getting bigger, our child was kicking her. Bruno was turning into a monster, Cerberus himself, slinking around, growling. We wondered at the wisdom of getting such a hell-hound with a baby on the way. Our second house was still being built and should be ready in time for the birth.

There was a long wave radio in the bar, and through the BBC World Service we kept in touch with the happenings in the world, out there on our long tether. Gales in England; riots in Hong Kong; Brunei gains independence although Britain keeps a battalion of gurkhas there to guard the Sultan; Ronald Reagan makes overtures to the Soviet Union about constructive dialogue on disarmament; disaster in Bulgaria as an airliner crashes; Manchester United are knocked out of the FA Cup by Third Division side Bournemouth; average cost of a pint of beer hits 60 pence; average house prices approach £30,000; George Orwell's *Nineteen Eighty-Four* outsells every other book. Music news was told to us by excitable World Service DJs. We all like 'Marguerita Time' by Status Quo, and my favourite was 'Islands in the Stream' by Kenny Rogers. Everyone hated the irritating ditty from Roland Rat.

And I could feel the end approaching. I didn't travel towards it. I just waited as it slid towards me, a silent certainty.

Now that I had decided to leave the sea, I started to feel fear, a rising dread of what would happen next. The sea had been my home since I was sixteen years old. I had matured among seaman and formed my views of what was right and wrong, I had taken my stand in life, and the facets of my thinking and personality had been shaped and formed as a result of living my life at sea.

I had had spells ashore of course, frequent ones, but to me these were interludes between the main acts. The sea was my refuge. It was my home and my companion. Leaving the sea was like breaking with a group of friends that had been irritating you more and more over the years until you could stand it no longer. But they were still your friends and it was difficult and painful to let go.

I soon found myself only remembering all the good times, and I hid from the bad. I counted the days. Soon it was less than a month. Thirty days, thirty days and it would all be over. Then twenty. Whispers of disquiet sung into my ear: 'What will you do? How will you live? How will you cope? This is your life and you're throwing it all away after all it's done for you.'

Panic scratched at me. Mine was a life of open water, big skies, the wide world, adventures in strange countries with strange people, not a cramped carriage to a cramped office to work in a stunted environment.

I started to hate the thought of my world coming to a close; the change to come started to frighten me more. I stayed up later, I existed on four hours sleep a day, eking out my time, elongating it as much as I could. All the things I disliked became endearing, all those whose company I shunned became good shipmates. As I felt myself slipping towards a new world I clutched my memories close and tight, as if they were my lovers. The days slipped past.

On the way up to Wewak, steaming along the north-east coast of Papua New Guinea, we passed Manam Island at four in the morning. Manam sits at the edge of the Bismarck Sea, separated from the mainland by the Stephan Strait. It's a highly active volcano and at night the fiery insides cast a red glow up into the sky. Several officers had asked to be called when we were due to pass the island, and we stood together in a group on the bridge wing under the star-studded, flat calm tropical night with our mugs of coffee, gazing across the water at Manam. Gazing at the boiling liquid rock inside the mountain, which was projected up and onto the dark sky to form a swirling red blanket over the peak. The red glow in the sky was then in turn reflected back down into the inky black sea, ringing the island as if it were surrounded by a moat of blood.

There are moments of majesty that quieten life's chatter. The Northern Lights off the high Norwegian coast, radiating bands of brilliance across the heavens, as if by sorcery. The dolphin nurseries in the southern Indian Ocean, fleets of young miniatures leaping and turning, flanked by adult minders. The yellow sky in the morning over the South China Sea, flinging its colour down onto shattered yellow waters. On my last voyage to Wewak, Manam Island was a moment of such majesty, one of those times in my life when I knew I had a soul and it was singing inside me. No one spoke as we glided past. What more fitting end?

9

The Indigestible Anchor

To swallow the anchor: 'to retire from the sea and settle down ashore,' is the definition given by the *Oxford Companion to Ships and the Sea*. Swallowing the anchor was a mighty meal and one that I never really finished. I retired physically from the sea but it swam in my blood like a worm, and the sea never retired from me. The tide just went out.

Whenever I see the sea, every single time I see the sea, my breath shortens.

Whenever I pass old docklands, sold off, marred with blank-faced apartments each with a soppy Juliet balcony and a view of the water, I feel a heaving in my chest. Whenever I see old wharfs that served hundreds of thousands of ships for hundreds of years and took in all their cargoes from all every corner of the world, all the spices and the teak, the tea and the palm oil, all the goods from all over the globe. Whenever I think of all that used to be, now so irredeemably, irrecoverably lost: the Union Castle liners to South Africa, the British India fleet, all the Palm Line ships for West Africa and the Ben Line ships for the Far East and many, many more. And before them, the schooners and the sloops, the clippers and the Down Easters.

Whenever I see these wharfs now as pleasure marinas with boats that never even go to sea, with coffee shops and grills. And whenever I think of all the people who used to sail on all the ships over the centuries: the jolly-jacks and the pigtailed Chinamen, the Americans off the Down Easters, the Finns on their square riggers, and in my lifetime the salt-of-the-earth British sailors, the West Coast Scots and the men of the Clyde, the scousers, the London crews, the wild men from Tiger Bay, the Hong Kong Chinese and the crews from Goa, the Dutch and the French and the Germans and Norwegians, all the men of the sea, all roving the docks and the pubs and the places where sailors go.

And now? When I see the soft and smirking peoples with naval clothes and sunglasses on string and city jobs, sitting by the dock-fronts sipping latte and haw-hawing, it is so painful for me that I feel my soul is bruised and bleeding and I want to weep.

I can't see a ship without wondering where it's been and what it's carrying. Whenever I land at an airport near the water and the plane banks and turns on its descent I strain to catch the vista of ships lying in the glittering roads, waiting their turn.

I could take the anchor and chop it into small pieces, I could mince it, season it, cook it slowly in oils and spices until tender, then eat it slowly accompanied by a fine wine. But I would still have difficulty in the swallowing.

I was of a generation before travel was the norm, before a thousand satellite TV channels and a thousand million internet pages opened the belly of the world for everyone to inspect, inviting them all to come and see. I was of a generation before cheap flights made it convenient to go to the other side of the world for a long weekend.

Mine was the end of a generation where wandering the world came with steamers and liners and the dark arts of navigation, where countries were strange and insular and their peoples stranger still, with habits and food so alien they might as well have been aliens.

And I was then so young and fresh and now I am so old. Sometimes I wish I was a bird, because birds never seem to get old. They never look old. Can you imagine an old albatross? Birds just fly, then they die.

At sea we had no anthem for ourselves and we didn't engage in self-congratulation. The way of life was easy to explain to a shore-sider, but not easy to convey. In the same way as an Englishman might explain cricket to a Russian, who could never really understand, or a Russian might explain the rituals of a vodka toast to an Amish. What is clear to me, though, is that the parts of me I hand down to the next generation, my legacies good and bad, were fired by my experiences at sea.

I went to sea when I was sixteen years old, fresh from school, although it was a continuation of school actually, just a school with harder knocks. I was so hopelessly naïve and unprepared that when I look back I wonder how I coped. Sometimes I'm surprised that I am still alive.

I left the sea when I was thirty years old, not long after I married. There were many married men at sea, but to me the way of life wasn't compatible for me, not with children arriving anyway.

I was a Master Mariner, still am a Master Mariner, although my Certificate of Competency is long out of date and I couldn't use it to sign on a British ship these days. The ancillary certificates and updates that are now required are legion and I don't have any of them. My certificate sits in a drawer in its black gold-embossed cover, and I catch sight of it every now and again.

Do I miss the sea? Yes. But I wouldn't go back now; it's all so different and I wouldn't fit in. I am jealous of those who still ply their trade on the deep sea routes but I'm not envious; I always told myself that envy is the weak man's cruelty and I'm neither weak nor cruel.

I wouldn't go back now? No, that's not right. I *would* go back if I could, but only under impossible terms whereby I was transformed into a younger man who could slip through time and dimension to steam the South China Seas again under the yellow morning light and then return to my happy married life without anyone knowing I had left.

Leaving the sea was the right thing to do and if I had my time again I would do the same again. Since leaving, my life has been full and I have been blessed with a happy marriage, four children, good health and no shortage of wealth. I have no regrets and I am thankful for everything. I am a lucky man.

My fourteen years at sea have left me with two residues, one positive and one negative. On the positive side, I know the value of hard work and of not letting others down. A ten-hour day is not a struggle to me, and I would work twelve or more rather than not fulfil what was expected of me. On the negative, I am restless and prone to rush to the next event before savouring what I have just completed, which means I miss out of some of life's joys. I have to accept this, though, as an indelible part of my character.

I used to wonder where all the dragons were that I was going to slay. I wanted life's challenges, I wanted to do noble deeds, rescue unfortunates, overcome the menacing. And I wanted fame, not celebrity fame, just fame within the narrow band of my peers. I wanted to go to war, I wanted to steam up silent muddy rivers, hemmed in by jungle, and see strange peoples, I wanted to savour the heightened senses that danger in perilous places brings. I wanted to see the wicked side of nature, her temper so mighty she smashed everything around her, I wanted to be in storms so fierce they took the breath from me. I wanted to go to the far ends of the earth and see what was there, to see if was as I imagined it to be. Then I found towards the end that all the dragons were in my head and they were not to be slain, but instead just to be visited, just to be fed. And I visited them all.

In the days I was at sea, the days on the ocean itself, I spent a lot of my time longing to be in port so I could indulge myself and my fantasies. I searched for my soul in low bars in the waterfronts of big ports of the East, on the beachfront harbours of Australasia, the African coast, the Caribbean, up rivers to small wharf stops, rivers with names to conjure dreams, the Rajang River, Pearl River, Hooghly River, Bonny River, Rio Catatumbo, Nhà Bè River. But when I look back, the things I want to remember are not of the shore but are of the sea and my times at sea.

I remember all the colours of the oceans. The washed-out green of the inner seas of the Indonesian Archipelago: the Java Sea, the Banda Sea, the Flores Sea, the Sulu Sea, the Celebes Sea, the Arafura Sea and the Makassar Strait. Washed-out greens flecked with foam, studded with driftwood sent out from the 17,000 islands that make up the archipelago. The wide, wide reach of the Pacific Ocean, such a deep, deep blue, a cerulean blue, the blue of blue eyes from a level gaze of a calm person on a calm evening. The dark greens of the Indian Ocean, from cyan green by the Arabian Sea to the viridescent green of the Bay of Bengal, to the aquamarine of the Persian Gulf, then down to the sinister dark forest green of the Southern Ocean. And in the Atlantic, brutal grey in the north, brilliant azure in the Caribbean, darker blue by the African coast, muddied to brown around the vast river deltas.

I remember the calm days of no wind, not a gust, not a flicker, not a zephyr of air, the sea so flat, like melted glass, folding back from the bow as we cut our way through, laying open the ocean's underbelly, rolling the water back. At night with a full moon the water so black as it rolled away and fell from the hull like molten toffee. At night with no moon and no clouds, just the spangled heavens with stars so bright they were caught in the water, mirrored, as if the sea had trapped the gods at last.

I remember the wild days with the wind howling through the stays and the seas ripping across the main deck like a run of artillery fire, the ship canting under the edge of the ocean then shaking and levering herself upright, water cascading out through the scuppers and rails, with us, wild-eyed in the wheelhouse, braced against the forward bulkhead, awaiting our fate, helpless against a show of nature's fickle anger that could take us down among the fishes before we could cry 'Noo-ooooo …'.

I remember the warm days in the tropics, leaning against the teak rail of the bridge wing, the sun hot on my arms as I waited for the sun to reach its zenith, my sextant sitting easily in my hand as I bounced the sun's image off the horizon at its highest point to record the day's latitude. Down below on the decks the sailors worked, their chatter drifting up to me on the bridge as they painted or spliced or holy-stoned the wooden boat decks or greased dogs or carried out one or many of the myriad of other tasks that keep a ship in seagoing order.

I remember the life of the sea. The wandering albatross in the southern oceans, lying on the air with its ten-foot wingspan, the largest of any bird on earth, never flapping its wings, just wheeling and gliding. The colossal blue whale, spouting then sounding, allowing us just a glimpse of its mighty frame. The rugged humpback whale, leaping and crashing, then diving into the depths with its great tail fin slapping the surface with a cannon crack. The dolphins in their dozens, leaping in formation, charging towards the ship then breaking right and wheeling round the stern, or riding the bow wave, in turns, sleekly rolling as they barrelled along like torpedoes, playing the best fairground ride in town. The flying fish skipping across the water surface, fleeing from their predators. The sinister bull shark circling driftwood in the Bismarck Sea.

And I remember the hour before sunrise, alone on the bridge in the early morning in the South China Sea as the sky lightened and the colour flooded in; ambers and reds and yellows, colours shocking the sky, painting the sea. Red sky red sea, yellow sky yellow sea, a shattered sea in colour so vivid and striking it took my breath and raced my heart and made me feel as if I were the smallest life in all of the world.

All my memories, my memories of the sea, all my kaleidoscope of thought, turning and re-forming, similar but never the same.

It's all too easy to say how much better things were all those years ago. Older people said that to me for years on end when I was younger: it was better in the old days, it was better in the War, it was better before the War, it was better still before the First World War, and so on. I started to think that I had missed the boat, no pun intended. But it wasn't better. Life at sea during the so-called 'golden age', from the mid-1940s to the mid-1980s, wasn't better than life at sea today. It was just different, in the same way as it was different in the 1930s and the 1890s.

I was lucky, though, in that I had gone to sea at the tail end of the golden age of British shipping. A time when we would steam into port, leaning on the rails in the early morning light, and there was always a cargo ship flying the red ensign. Sometimes the wharfs would be lined with them, all the great British shipping names on show: Port Line, Ben Line, Bank Line, Bibby Line, Palm Line, the Pacific Steam Navigation Company. New Zealand Shipping, Clan Line, British India, P&O, Geest Line, Blue Funnel, Blue Star, Union Castle Line and so many more. Some are still trading today although most of the names are now consigned to the pages of history and to the volumes of Lloyd's Register and reflective memoirs such as mine.

In my early years at sea there was such a shortage of officers and men that jobs were to be had on a single telephone call. When I passed my first professional examination, the Second Mate's Certificate of Competency, I went for a walk around the shipping offices in the City of London and the personnel officers were almost begging me to join, they were so desperate. A freshly minted deck officer with a shiny new certificate was like gold dust to these people. One told me: "Someone like you coming in here and asking for a job is as rare as rocking-horse shit. We all want you, of course we do." If the shanghaiing of sailors had still been a recruiting practice I would have been whacked on the head and bundled aboard a ship in the East India docks before the day was out.

In my latter years, though, it was so different. By the mid-1980s the British fleet had shrunk to a shadow of its former self, companies that had traded for a hundred years had vanished, redundancies were *en-masse*, companies were flagging out to Liberia, Panama and Singapore, British crews were on the beach, officers were scrambling to get a job on any ship under any flag. It was no longer a career as a way of life, it was a job of work if you could get it. Officers returning from study leave were reporting that half the people in the class had no job to go to when they finished. The training system started to fall apart, companies stopped taking on cadets; the next generation of ships would be manned by old men from the old shipping nations and young men from the emerging world. In all of this I never suffered a day out of work. I just saw a slow attrition of the life.

I changed too, though; I wasn't immune. I left behind my early life of carousing and I adopted a more serious outlook. I learned how to worry about things, my hair started to thin, I no longer looked young, I made more use of a counterfeit smile. When I came ashore, life continued to excite me but I harnessed my energies and channelled them into areas that I believed were more meaningful and productive. I climbed the ladder successfully and strived to do my best in my new world. I acquired the showy things that impressed people, which I pretend to like but deep down I don't really give a fig about such objects; they are just trifles.

I wonder about the myth that we only use 10 per cent of our brain, and I wonder what the other 90 per cent of mine is doing. Is it just sitting there as a lump of unused tissue, or is it the vault of all my hopes and memories, where every sense and scent and sight and sound of my days at sea is deposited, waiting there for me, revealed only in the craziness of dreams that grip me for ninety seconds after I wake, before they evaporate? Or is that 90 per cent the area we call God?

I could never understand the difference between my mind and my soul anyway; one works the others, but I'm not sure which does which. Whatever the answers, I used my 10 per cent well and life has been kind to me as my shore-side years have gone by. The times when I wanted to run for the Islands were brief and rare, and now they are no more. Those days are long over.

Last was the camaraderie, which I still miss now. Young men living together in extreme conditions develop a commonality and bond that is difficult to replicate within the confines of modern society. I meet old comrades still, perhaps once a year, old shipmates, old students from the School of Maritime Studies, and things become briefly as they were all those years ago. Sometimes it feels as if we are picking up unfinished conversations without even bothering to give them a dusting off. In those reunions, it doesn't feel like we are looking back, it feels like … being back.

The point of it all, though, is that it's not the period; it doesn't matter whether it's 1870 or 1970, and it won't matter in the year 2070. Here's the reality: in any century, in any country, in any walk of life, if you put a group of young men together in a disciplined environment and at the same time grant them freedom and access to sights and experiences that few people will ever encounter, what happens? They will have the time of their life, that's what happens. They will have the time of their life.

Epilogue

After I paid off the *Chengtu* in early 1984 and came back to England, it was all change. My arrival home was just a few days before the birth of our first child; Annie hadn't even packed a bag, determined not to give birth until I was there. The country was crawling out of recession with pockets of simmering resentment, occasionally exploding onto the streets, over the harsh measures imposed by the government to curb the unions; unemployment was the highest for decades. I was without connections, and getting a new job and a new life wasn't going to be easy. Bruno the rottweiler had turned truly vicious and would have to go. Having scaled to near the top of my profession, I began my new life back down at the bottom, looking up the ladder at the backsides of those above me, my gold stripes and adventurous times immaterial to the twenty-three-year-olds who began to order me about.

I never returned to the sea, not as a professional seaman anyway. As a family, we once went on a yachting holiday around the Greek islands, which a few years earlier would have been unimaginable for me, as someone who viewed yachties with such derision. No merchant ships tried to run us down, thank goodness. And later, I went on a short voyage on a passenger liner, a corporate beano, a boozy affair down to the Channel Islands. I tried to strike up an empathetic conversation with the ship's officers, but they viewed me with the polite disdain that I used to reserve for the few passengers we carried from time to time.

After I'd got back home I'd put my head down and worked harder than most, made money in the business world, big deal, had three more children; that *was* a big deal. And I watched from the stands as the British shipping industry completed its decline, shipping lines falling away like ten green bottles: and then there were none. Almost none.

Next will be a more relaxed life, with family and friends; I'll visit obscure places where few others go, and take time to stop and stare and do the things I wish I'd done when I was younger. And I'll lie in a hammock and read books and drink wine, and sometimes let the book slip from my grasp while I drift off and think of those early mornings under the yellow sky of the South China Sea, and I'll think of my privileged younger life, which I've been so lucky to lead.

By the same author – *read the whole trilogy*

Under a Yellow Sky

A tale of the sea and coming of age

Simon J. Hall

£16.99   978-184995-094-7

 'Simon Hall's new book … stands out from the crowd – being not only very well written, but also thoughtful and reflective. … His fine writing style draws the reader in and captures the magic and chaos of foreign ports … [a] finely observed and well written book...' *Nautilus Telegraph*

www.whittlespublishing.com

'**Book of the month**... Hall is a gifted  writer and for those of us who sailed on similar ships, it will awaken many memories of how life at sea was then. This book is a must buy! Highly recommended'. *Sea Breezes*

'...superior seafaring memoir...his compelling narrative… vividly and entertainingly evokes the people, places and vessels he encountered, creating an accomplished work which deserves a wide audience'. *Nautilus Telegraph*

Chasing Conrad

A tale of the sea and a glimpse into the abyss

Simon J Hall

£16.99   978-184995-155-5

also available as eBooks – see our website